Social Studies & EXCEPTIONAL LEARNERS

DARREN MINARIK & TIMOTHY LINTNER

NCSS
Bulletin 115

National Council for the Social Studies

8555 Sixteenth Street • Suite 500 • Silver Spring, Maryland 20910

NCSS BOARD OF DIRECTORS, 2015-2016

ISBN: 978-0-87986-110-0

© Copyright 2016 National Council for the Social Studies. All rights reserved.

Printed in the United States of America • First printing, May 2016

5 4 3 2 1

TABLE OF **CONTENTS**

PART I LEARNING ABOUT SPECIAL EDUCATION

PART II EDUCATING STUDENTS WITH EXCEPTIONALITIES

PART III RESOURCES & GLOSSARY

PART I
LEARNING ABOUT SPECIAL EDUCATION

Introduction

How can I teach the same content to students with differing academic needs?

Can my exceptional learners pass state mandated standardized exams?

Are my exceptional learners able to think and reason historically and participate in more engaging inquiry-based practices?

How will the other students react to a student with significant cognitive, emotional, behavioral, or physical challenges in my classroom?

Are the accommodations that exceptional learners receive "fair" to the other students in my classroom?

How do I successfully collaborate with special educators to support the students in my classroom?

What do I need to do to ensure that exceptional learners are successful in my classroom?

Across the nation, an increasing number of teachers ask these questions as exceptional learners are more fully included in general education settings. Although there is significant information available to help teachers answer some of these questions, there is limited attention devoted to research addressing specific social studies content or the role of social studies teachers in the education of exceptional learners.[1]

Despite the limited research considerations given to teaching social studies to exceptional learners, social studies educators must still figure out how to work with this population in inclusive settings. The National Council for the Social Studies (NCSS) civic mission "demands the inclusion of all students—addressing . . . learning diversity that includes similarities and differences based on . . . exceptional learning needs, and other educationally and personally significant characteristics of learners."[2] The NCSS civic mission reflects classroom trends as more than 90 percent of exceptional learners receive their social studies instruction in a general education setting.[3] However, having a seat in a classroom with non-disabled peers does not necessarily equate to an inclusive setting if teachers lack the knowledge, skills, or dispositions to support the academic and social needs of students with exceptionalities. Social studies educators need to begin asking if their classrooms are truly inclusive settings or if they are just practicing a form of reluctant inclusion.[4] A good starting point to this reflective process is to consider what our youth with exceptionalities expect from educators.

Do not label me. Do accept me for who I am.

Do not think that you know about people with disabilities. Do educate yourself about all disabilities.

Do not presume that you know what is normal. Do presume that nobody is normal.

Do not see me through my disability. Do see me as an individual.

Do not call me by my label. Do call me by my name.

Do not tell me what I can do. Do let me show you what I can do.

Do not patronize me. Do be understanding and helpful when I ask for assistance.

Do not assume I am stupid. Do let me show you that I am smart.

Do not call me inferior. Do call me intellectual.[5]

The young people who made these statements represent a wide spectrum of intellectual, physical, emotional and behavioral disability labels. Their goal was to express the views of youth with exceptionalities and position themselves as advocates for a life they envision for themselves and others identified as disabled. Their words were in part a product of experiences in the classroom and reflect a belief that inclusion is more than simply a seat in a classroom. Schools represent a space where all students learn and model the principles of effective citizenship. Exceptional learners represent a diverse group within our schools that expect the same opportunities as their peers without exceptionalities.[6]

WHY WRITE ABOUT DISABILITY AND SOCIAL STUDIES?

The driving force behind this publication was the limited number of empirical investigations and teacher practitioner articles currently available for social studies educators who want to address the needs of exceptional learners in their classrooms. Prior to this publication, there was only one book dedicated to compiling the latest research to support K-12 social studies teachers in inclusive classrooms.[7] An examination of the literature since the passage of Public Law 94-142 (Education of All Handicapped Children Act) in 1975 revealed limited intersections between disability studies, special education, and social studies, even with a significant increase in publications over the last decade. None of the major social studies handbooks provided studies or discussions pertaining to social studies and special education other than a single literature review completed in 1991.[8] There are numerous studies examining best practices in teaching exceptional learners, but few of these investigations specifically address social studies even though it is an essential content area for all students.[9] It is our hope that this book will serve as a primer for social studies educators, bringing together the latest research in special education and social studies education to form an easy-to-use guide for those at the elementary, middle, or secondary level. This book may also serve as a guide for preservice teachers

as they learn the skills necessary to navigate the needs of diverse learners they will encounter as professional social studies educators.

STRUCTURE OF THE BOOK

We divided the book into three parts designed to allow the reader to form a knowledge base of central issues about disability and special education and then learn ways to apply this knowledge in the classroom. Part I, "Learning about Disability and Special Education," examines the social and medical construction of disability in our society and addresses the most common disability categories evidenced within general education settings. We then turn to the laws driving disability services in our schools, addressing best practice for the involvement of general educators in working with exceptional learners. Finally, we tackle the importance of collaboration in schools and how teams and, specifically, co-teaching, can support more inclusive classroom settings for exceptional learners.

Part II, "Educating Students with Exceptionalities," begins with an examination of how exceptional learners can exercise their rights and responsibilities as citizens through modeling self-determination skills and the ability to self-advocate. We use the theme "citizenship for exceptional learners" to kick-start how teachers can support positive social and academic outcomes for exceptional learners. Second, we focus on organizing instruction by addressing effective pedagogical practices to support exceptional learners in the classroom, including Understanding by Design (UbD), the Universal Design for Learning (UDL), the C3 Framework, and differentiated instruction. Third, we identify classroom strategies intended to engage students, increase content knowledge, and challenge students to think critically. These strategies provide varying ways to differentiate instruction to meet diverse learning needs. Next, we address the role of assessment in promoting successful academic and social outcomes for exceptional learners. We then examine how technology assists exceptional learners. Finally, we address classroom management and provide positive supports to address unique social and behavioral needs in the general education setting.

The second half of Part II focuses on the Inclusive Classroom. It is an activity-centered section providing detailed examples of lessons, activities, and other practices for elementary, middle, and secondary social studies classrooms. The intention here is to apply the topics addressed in the earlier chapters through examples designed for specific grade levels and subject matter. We wrote these activities so that a teacher could immediately use them in the classroom, with or without a co-teacher or other support personnel. A lesson plan format is provided that teachers are encouraged to consider for their own planning practices. The format integrates the use of differentiated instruction, Universal Design for Learning (UDL), and the C3 Framework, and considers optional collaborative roles for teachers and support personnel.

Part III is a brief section providing connections to resources and organizations that support teachers who work with exceptional learners. Recognizing the exponential growth of information online, we selected Web links that are informative, timely, and will hopefully serve as a teacher resource for years to come. A bibliography lists relevant articles and books in the field that support effective social studies instruction for exceptional learners. We also provide a glossary of terms to unravel the common words, phrases, and acronyms used when talking about exceptional learners in an inclusive educational setting.

Together, each section of this book provides a roadmap for K-12 educators at the preservice and inservice level to become informed about disability, special education, and how teachers can create accessible social studies content in an inclusive setting. The inclusion of exceptional learners in the general education classroom is no longer a philosophy for how to best serve such students. It is a reality, driven in part by federal and state law and by the fundamental belief that "separate but equal" is not always the least restrictive learning

environment for exceptional learners. People with disabilities expect access to the same fundamental rights, freedoms, and opportunities afforded to any citizen in our society. In order to prepare exceptional learners to become active and participatory citizens, we must provide access to the same educational programs and settings as are provided for students without identified disabilities. The social studies classroom represents a natural place to encourage this access. Now is the time to consider what practices best support exceptional learners in our classrooms as they develop into informed and participatory citizens. 🖼

NOTES

1. Emily Bouck, Carrie Anna Courtad, Anne Heutsche, Cynthia Okolo, and Carol Sue Englert, "The Virtual History Museum," *Teaching Exceptional Children* 42, no. 2 (2009): 14-20; Ralph Ferretti and Cynthia Okolo, "Authenticity in Learning: Multimedia Design Projects in the Social Studies for Students with Disabilities," *Journal of Learning Disabilities* 29, no. 5 (1996): 450-460.

2. National Council for the Social Studies (NCSS), *National Curriculum Standards for Social Studies: Introduction* (Silver Spring, MD: NCSS, 2010), http://www.socialstudies.org/standards/introduction, accessed June 1, 2015.

3. Windy Schweder, "Knowing Your Students," in *Practical Strategies for Teaching K-12 Social Studies in Inclusive Classrooms*, edited by Timothy Lintner and Windy Schweder (Charlotte, NC: Information Age Publishing, 2011): 9-18.

4. Roger Slee, "Driven to the Margins: Disabled Students, Inclusive Schooling and the Politics of Possibility," *Cambridge Journal of Education* 31, no. 3 (2002): 385-97.

5. These quotations are taken from the "Youth Credo" video accessed July 1, 2012. http://www.imdetermined.org/youth/.

6. Walter Parker, "Democracy and Difference," *Theory and Research in Social Education* 25, no. 2 (1997): 220-34.

7. Timothy Lintner and Windy Schweder, ed. *Practical Strategies for Teaching K-12 Social Studies in Inclusive Classrooms.* (Charlotte, NC: Information Age Publishing, 2011).

8. Janis A. Bulgren, Patricia Sampson Graner, and Donald D. Deschler, "Literacy Challenges and Opportunities for Students with Learning Disabilities in Social Studies and History," *Learning Disabilities Research & Practice* 28, no. 1 (2013): 17-27; Charles Curtis, "Social Studies for Students At-Risk and with Disabilities," in *Handbook of Research on Social Studies Teaching and Learning*, edited by James Shaver (New York: Macmillan Publishing Company, 1991): 157-74; Susan De La Paz, Petra Morales, and Philip M. Winston, "Source Interpretation: Teaching Students with and Without Learning Disabilities to Read and Write Historically," *Journal of Learning Disabilities* 40, no. 2 (2007): 134-144; Judith L. Fontana, Thomas E. Scruggs, and Margo A. Mastropieri, "Mnemonic Strategy Instruction in Inclusive Secondary Social

Studies Classes," *Remedial and Special Education* 28, no. 6 (2007): 345-355; Marie Tejero Hughes and Michelle Parker Katz, "Integrating Comprehension Strategies into Social Studies Instruction," *Social Studies* 104, no. 3 (2013): 93-104; Thomas E. Scruggs, Margo A. Mastropieri, and Cynthia M. Okolo, "Science and Social Studies for Students with Disabilities," *Focus on Exceptional Children* 41, no. 2 (2008): 1-23.

9. Bouck, et al., "The Virtual History Museum," *op. cit.*

CHAPTER ONE

Learning About Disability and Special Education

Before addressing how to educate exceptional learners, let's learn about the conceptual underpinnings of disability and special education in addition to the evolving language of discussion about disability. First, it is important to acknowledge the difficulty in defining "disability" because there is no unanimity in the literature and it is frequently described as abstract and generalized.[1] There are a number of conceptual frameworks addressing disability. Two, in particular, shape how exceptional learners are taught in school: the social and the medical models of disability. The framework frequently espoused by disability rights advocates is the social model of disability, whereby disability is defined as a construction created by societal interactions and norms. This model recognizes people with disabilities as vital contributors to society, not as burdens or challenges.[2] The linguistic representation of the word "disability" is seen as negatively positioning the ability of an individual and only presents someone from a limitations perspective, demonstrating how society marginalizes people not considered to be able-bodied.[3]

Those who support the social model propose that people without disabilities are defining and judging normality and framing much of what is assumed about disability through their own eyes without considering the lens of people who actually experience disability.[4] The social model challenges these "able-bodied" assumptions, encouraging recognition of those who have been excluded in the past.[5] It brings into question how normality is defined and focuses on how people with exceptionalities enrich and contribute to society, instead of highlighting the potential challenges they face.

In contrast to the social model of disability, the medical model addresses the biology of the disability. This way of viewing disability is also sometimes referred to as the deficit model, functional limitations model, or rehabilitation model of disability.[6] Because of a focus on medical prevention, cure, or rehabilitation, the medical model places little or no emphasis on the complex social issues affecting people with disabilities.[7] Federal laws that define disability based on the result of one's pathology reinforce the medical model. For example, the 1990 Americans with Disabilities Act (ADA) defined disability as an impairment affecting daily life, painting the picture of disability as a deficit in need of special services or supports. In the field of special education, teacher understanding of disability is often connected more to the medical model because special education services are driven by the 13 disability categories defined under federal law as impairments affecting the daily life of a child. Classroom instruction in special education is often framed in terms of interventions and targeted strategies to improve below-average student academic performance and address social and behavioral issues that do not fit the norms of school. With the advent of high stakes testing, the focus is frequently on what students are failing to do as opposed to what they are doing well.

Although we present the social and medical models as a dichotomy, we are suggesting that an understanding of both models serves as a way to better inform our teaching practice. Table 1.1 summarizes how both models address important aspects of disability and how we approach education and inclusion within society.

Table 1.1 Medical Model versus Social Model

THE MEDICAL MODEL OF DISABILITY	THE SOCIAL MODEL OF DISABILITY
The child has a medically diagnosed disability that is pre-ventable, curable, or improved with rehabilitation.	The child's disability is a complex condition affected by context and significantly influenced by prejudice and marginalization.
Focus on diagnosis, labeling, and the impairment first.	Focus on the person first with an emphasis on strengths, needs, and ways to address challenges.
Emphasis on educational environments that improve the impairment, which may mean alternative services and settings instead of inclusive settings.	Emphasis on inclusive educational environments first with consideration of alternative settings only after exhausting inclusive options.
Society sees disability as abnormal and views people with disabilities as needing to adapt and fit in.	Society evolves to question the definition of normal and how society can change to better include people with disabilities.

It is important to note that the advent of inclusive schooling for exceptional learners encourages educators to recognize issues raised through the social construction of disability. It is possible that the environment we create in our classroom potentially "disables" a student. Consider how a student who has challenges with short-term memory might struggle with a classroom teacher who only gives oral directions for activities. If the child also had access to written directions or other visual queues for reference, struggles with short-term memory no longer create a challenge to learning. The classroom enables rather than disables learning.

Since more than three out of four students with specific learning disabilities, attention deficit hyperactivity disorder, emotional and behavioral disorders, and mild intellectual disabilities are educated in general education classrooms, we need to take time to consider both of these models when addressing the needs of exceptional learners.[8] Aligning ourselves with solely one or the other model limits our overall understanding of disability. Focusing solely on the social model is problematic as this would suggest that a physical, cognitive, or other impairment has no medical basis.[9] Likewise, reliance on the medical model limits a larger understanding of the experiences people with exceptionalities face on a daily basis.

As an alternative to the medical and social models, disability scholars proposed a minority group model for disability. This model theorizes a similarity between the challenges that people with exceptionalities face and the challenges faced by people that are premised on their race, ethnicity, gender, sexuality, or age.[10] This model was highlighted with Blatt and Kaplan's (1966) *Christmas in Purgatory: A Photographic Essay on Mental Retardation*, which underscored the horrific conditions of institutions in this country and how people with intellectual disabilities were treated as non-citizens.[11] Likewise, Ed Roberts and others who led the disability rights movement in the U.S. used aspects of this model to organize and gain support for passage of the Americans with Disabilities Act.

Regardless of where you may see yourself in this discussion, these models raise important questions when examining how researchers write about special education and disability in social studies literature. The models also raise questions about the discourse used in social studies standards and classroom curriculums when discussing the advancement of civic competence and citizenship development. These theoretical models framing disability and special education provide foundational knowledge of scholarly discussions and help support social studies educators as they encounter exceptional learners in their classrooms.

Disability advocacy associated with the social model is beginning to focus attention on the curriculum taught in social studies classrooms and how disability is rarely addressed. It is safe to say that disability history is not currently embedded within the social studies curriculum, a phenomenon that has not gone unnoticed by historians.[12] There may be a historical or contemporary figure identified with a disability or a specific event related to disability, but one must dig deep to find these references.[13] Fortunately, disability history is gaining some traction as states begin to adopt awareness weeks and months bringing attention to disability. Since 2006, over half the states across the U.S. have adopted disability history and awareness weeks or months (primarily in October) to educate citizens about the history of individuals with exceptionalities. Young people with exceptionalities in Virginia are lobbying at the national level to introduce legislation to create a national disability history and awareness month.[14] State and national disability history movements represent an opportunity for social studies educators to integrate disability topics into the curriculum and to address stigmas and negative stereotypes found within the social studies curriculum and in daily interactions. They also highlight involvement by youth with exceptionalities in actions associated with participatory citizenship.[15]

Another outcome of the discussion regarding the medical and social models is the evolution of disability language. Debates about how language defines people as individuals abound. One example involves people who are identified as deaf or hearing impaired who align themselves in a "Deaf culture" community.[16] The word "Deaf" is capitalized to identify this cultural alignment. Deafness becomes part of a larger shared historical

context, a shared form of communication through American Sign Language, and a general way of life, as opposed to a term describing perceived challenges defined by the hearing community. People who describe themselves as big "D" Deaf are proud of their cultural heritage and understand being deaf as just another part of their lives, not a disability. This form of "identity-first" language is also evident with people identified on the autism spectrum. Organizations like the Autism Self Advocacy Network argue that autism is part of an individual's identity and should be embraced.[17]

Another movement in contrast to "identity-first" is the use of person-first language. Many disability advocacy groups support the use of emphasizing the person over the disability in written correspondence and oral communication. The argument framing person-first language is that the disability descriptor aligns with the medical diagnosis, and people generally do not define themselves or others by medical diagnoses in conversation. It is not a matter of political correctness; it is simply respecting human dignity. People with exceptionalities are not that different from people without exceptionalities, so why emphasize that which is different? Likewise, writing style manuals are also encouraging person-first language as a way to prevent research study participants from being described more like objects, hence losing their individuality.[18] Table 1.2 provides a short list of suggested ways to change how we address disability in our conversations and writing.

Not only has disability language evolved in daily writing and communication, change has also been seen in federal and state law. Early in the 20TH century, children with exceptionalities were described as defective, backward, or subnormal. Children with physical disabilities were "crippled" and those with intellectual disabilities were "retarded." Many of these terms were regularly used in early legislation. Recently, "mental retardation" changed to "intellectual disability" as a more respectful way to refer to a person with cognitive challenges, thanks in part to Rosa's Law signed in 2010.[19]

Table 1.2 Examples of People First Language

SAY:	INSTEAD OF:
People with disabilities.	The handicapped or disabled people.
He has an intellectual disability or is a person with an intellectual disability.	He is mentally retarded or a mentally retarded person.
He has Down's Syndrome.	He's Down's; a mongoloid.
She has a learning disability.	She's learning disabled.
She's of short stature/she's a little person.	She's a dwarf/midget.
He uses a wheelchair/mobility chair.	He's confined to or is wheelchair bound.
She receives special education services.	She's in special education.
My students with IEPs.	My IEP students.
Children without disabilities.	Normal, healthy, or typical kids.
He has a brain injury.	He's brain damaged.
Accessible parking or hotel room.	Handicapped parking or hotel room.

Adapted from Kathie Snow, "People First Language Chart," *Disability is Natural.* 2009, https://www.disabilityisnatural.com/pfl-articles.html

The way we understand and communicate about disability and special education impacts how we teach exceptional learners. As social studies educators, we appreciate the historical impact of language, labeling, prejudice, and perception on marginalized groups in society. In addition to clear challenges associated with learning, exceptional learners must also negotiate the prejudices and perceptions that underlie the school environment. To create an inclusive environment in our schools for all students, we must continue to address the academic, social, behavioral, and physical challenges that impact learning. We must also consider how our schools include or exclude exceptional learners through the labels we attach, the language we use, and the perceptions we hold. Understanding the conceptual foundations of disability and special education is a positive first step in creating an environment that enables positive academic and social experiences for exceptional learners. 🖼

NOTES

1. Catherine J. Kudlick, "Disability History: Why We Need Another Other," *The American Historical Review* 108, no. 3 (2003): 763-93.

2. Linda Ware, "Many Possible Futures, Many Possible Directions," in *Disability Studies in Education: Readings in Theory and Method*, edited by Susan L. Gabel (New York: Peter Lang Publishing, 2005): 103-24.

3. Dimitris Anastasiou and James Kauffman, "A Social Constructionist Approach to Disability: Implications for Special Education," *Exceptional Children* 77, no. 3 (2011): 367-84.

4. Michel Foucault, *Discipline and Punish: The Birth of the Prison* (New York: Pantheon, 1977).

5. Gregor Wolbring, "The Politics of Ableism," *Development* 51 (2008): 252-58.

6. Susan Burch and Ian Sutherland, "Who's Not Yet Here? American Disability History," *Radical History Review*, no. 94 (Win 2006): 127-47.

7. Tom Shakespeare, "The Social Model of Disability," in *The Disability Studies Reader*, edited by Lennard J. Davis (New York: Routledge, 2006): 197-204.

8. United States Department of Education, *Individuals with Disabilities Education Act (IDEA) data (Table 1.3)*, (Washington, DC: Author, 2011).

9. Shakespeare, *The Social Media of Disability, op. cit.*

10. Susan R. Jones, "Toward Inclusive Theory: Disability as Social Construction," *NASPA Journal* 33, no. 4 (Sum 1996): 347-53.

11. Burton Blatt and Fred Kaplan, *Christmas in Purgatory: A Photographic Essay on Mental Retardation* (Boston: Allyn & Bacon, 1966).

12. Douglas Baynton, "Disability and the Justification of Inequality in American History," in *The New Disability History*, edited by Paul Longmore and Lauri Umansky (New York: University Press, 2001): 33-57.

13. Burch & Sutherland, *"Who's Not Yet Here?" op. cit.*

14. Matthew Shapiro, personal communication, August 8, 2011.

15. See "Establishing Disability History Awareness Initiatives – A Roadmap for States and Territories," at the website of the Department of Labor, http://www.dol.gov/odep/alliances/roadmap.pdf

16. Carol A. Padden and Tom L. Humphries, *Inside Deaf Culture* (Cambridge, MA: Harvard University Press, 2005).

17. Lydia Brown, "Identity-first Language," *Autism Self Advocacy Network*. 2013. http://autisticadvocacy.org/identity-first-language/

18. Publication Manual of the American Psychological Association.

19. "President Signs Rosa's Law!" Accessed December 18, 2012, http://cecblog.typepad.com/policy/2010/10/president-signs-rosas-law.html

CHAPTER TWO

Exceptional Learners: Whom Will I Teach?

Today's students come from diverse cultural backgrounds, possess varying ability levels, and bring into the classroom a myriad of exceptionalities. In addition, with the push towards inclusion, a growing number of exceptional learners are participating in general educational settings where they are expected to learn the same content as their non-disabled peers.[1] It is therefore incumbent that teachers learn more about the students they may—or will—have in their classrooms.

Table 2.1 provides a general definition of the 13 categories of exceptionalities identified in the Individuals with Disabilities Education Improvement Act (IDEIA 2004). For a student to receive special education and related services he or she must fall within one of the 13 disability categories. An eligibility team determines if the disability affects the student's educational performance in such a way that special supports are needed.

According to the U.S. Department of Education (2013), the most common disabilities evident in the general education classroom are learning disabilities (LD), speech and language impairments (SLI), intellectual disabilities (ID), and emotional and/or behavioral disorders (EBD). Of all students receiving special services, over three fourths of students ages 6-21 were included in one of these four categories. Other health impairments (e.g. Attention Deficit Hyperactivity Disorder, Epilepsy) comprised the fifth largest group of students receiving special services.[2] One of the fastest growing disability categories is Autism, which comprises nearly six percent of students who receive special education services.[3]

These categories serve as a starting point for social studies educators who want to learn more about the exceptional learners in their classroom. Yet there are additional steps to follow when learning about how to educate such students in the general education setting. The best way to gather information about an individual student is through communication with the special education teacher who wrote the student's Individualized Education Program (IEP). Although it may not be necessary for you to read the entire IEP, special educators often provide general educators with short "at-a-glance" descriptions that include background information about student strengths, challenges, and needs. These informational sheets often list academic, social and behavioral goals, required accommodations, modifications, and general tips for teachers.

If the IEP is available to read, the Present Level of Academic Achievement and Functional Performance is the best place to start. The "present levels statement" or PLOP serves as an overview of the IEP, describing the impact a student's disability has on academic performance in the general education setting as well as how the student performs in daily living situations. If the student is turning 16 years old (14 in many states), the present levels will also address transition and the future plans of the student following completion of high school. Reading the PLOP is an excellent way to gain summary information about a student in your classroom without reading through an entire IEP.

TABLE 2.1 Thirteen Categories of Exceptionality

FEDERAL TERM	DEFINITION
Autism	A developmental disability affecting communication and social interaction and generally evident before age three.
Deaf-blindness	A combination of hearing and visual impairments causing communication and developmental delays so severe that there is a need for services other than those offered to students with blindness or deafness.
Developmental Delay	A category reserved for children ages birth to nine who exhibit delays in one or more of the following development areas: physical, cognitive, communication, social, or emotional.
Emotional disturbance	Behavioral or emotional responses significantly different from those of all norms and referent groups. The term includes schizophrenia but does not apply to children who are socially maladjusted unless it is determined that they have an emotional disturbance.
Deafness and hearing loss	A permanent or fluctuating loss in hearing.
Intellectual disability	A significantly sub-average general intellectual functioning (65 or below IQ) that exists concurrently with deficits in adaptive behavior (e.g. daily living and socialization skills) and is manifested during the developmental period (before age 18).
Multiple disabilities	A combination of impairments that causes such severe educational needs that the student cannot be accommodated in a special education program provided for one of the other 12 IDEIA disability categories. This category does not include individuals with deaf-blindness.
Orthopedic impairment	A term referring to students with physical disabilities or physical impairments.
Other health impairment	A chronic or acute health problem causing a student to have limited strength, vitality, or alertness in the educational environment.
Specific learning disability	A disorder in one or more of the basic psychological processes involved in understanding or using language (spoken or written) that may manifest itself in an imperfect ability to listen, think, speak, read, write, spell, or to do mathematical calculations.
Speech or language impairment	A communication disorder resulting in impaired articulation (e.g. stuttering, substitution, omission) or language impairment (difficulty comprehending or producing language).
Traumatic brain injury	An acquired injury to the brain resulting from an external physical force that causes a functional disability and/or psychosocial impairment. This term does not include brain injuries that are congenital or degenerative, or brain injuries induced by birth trauma.
Blindness and vision loss	An impairment in vision that, even with correction, adversely affects a child's educational performance.

Source: Windy Schweder, "Knowing your Students" in *Practical Strategies for Teaching K-12 Social Studies in Inclusive Classrooms*, edited by Timothy Lintner and Windy Schweder (Charlotte, NC: Information Age Publishing, 2011): 9-18.

If you still have an interest in learning more about the disability, there are many resources available on the Internet. Part III provides an annotated list of Web resources that teachers would find useful. One such site is the Center for Parent Information and Resources. This site provides information about the disability categories, pertinent laws, and evidence-based research. Regardless of how you choose to collect information about the students you teach, remember that the best way to educate exceptional learners is to educate yourself about disability categories and the associated strengths, challenges, and needs that students possess. ▧

NOTES

1. Margo A. Mastropieri and Thomas E. Scruggs, *The Inclusive Classroom: Strategies for Effective Differentiated Instruction*, 4TH edition (Upper Saddle River, NJ: Merrill, 2010).

2. United States Department of Education, *Thirtieth Annual Report to Congress on the Implementation of the Individuals with Disabilities Education Act* (Washington, DC: Author, 2008).

3. United States Department of Education, *Individuals with Disabilities Education Act (IDEA) data (Table 1.3)*, (Washington, DC: Author, 2013).

CHAPTER THREE

Disability and the Law: The Role of the Teacher

Contemporary special education law has its roots in the civil right movement of the 1950s. In 1954, the courts ruled in *Brown v. Board of Education* that segregated schools were, in fact, not equal and thus mandated the integration of both schools and students. Some began questioning if providing separate educational services for exceptional learners was appropriate. During the next decade or so researchers examined not just the educational rights of exceptional learners, but the discriminatory "stigma" attached to such students. What became clear was that special education was not just a means of assisting exceptional learners; it was also a means of combating overt or covert discrimination. Parents began to question why the same principles of equal access did not apply to their children with disabilities. In *Pennsylvania Association for Retarded Children (PARC) v. Commonwealth of Pennsylvania* (1972), a class action lawsuit challenged a state law preventing students with intellectual disabilities from attending public school premised on the assumption that they could not be educated. This landmark decision established the precedent that a free appropriate public education (FAPE) is the right of all children with disabilities. This decision would influence the writing of Public Law 94-142.[1] Table 3.1 provides an abridged overview of landmark laws affecting children and adults with disabilities. Though each is important in its own right, we specifically focus on two laws that provide the legal foundation for current policy and practice regarding educating exceptional learners.

INDIVIDUALS WITH DISABILITIES EDUCATION IMPROVEMENT ACT (IDEIA 2004)

The Individuals with Disabilities Education Improvement Act (IDEIA 2004), the most recent iteration of the Education for All Handicapped Children Act of 1975, is arguably the most significant piece of legislation addressing the educational welfare of exceptional learners.[2] Simply, IDEIA 2004 and its accompanying amendments are designed to ensure that exceptional learners have access to all benefits provided via a public school system. The premise of IDEIA 2004 is that all students, irrespective of physical and/or learning needs, are entitled to a free and appropriate public education (FAPE). The term "appropriate" may entail students receiving educational benefits in both general education and special education settings. A range of related services (e.g. physical or occupational therapy) are also provided to assure students are accessing a FAPE. To document that a student is receiving a FAPE, schools are required to create an Individualized Education Program (IEP). The IEP outlines the ways services and supports will be provided specifically addressing the needs of a given student. The IEP is frequently reevaluated and amended to monitor compliance and assess student progress in meeting the stated goals of the IEP. In addition, IDEIA 2004 promotes that learning take place in the least restrictive environment (LRE). Individual schools comply by specifically addressing the individual needs of the student.

To be eligible for services provided under IDEIA 2004, students must satisfy certain criteria. The law requires that school-based personnel identify and evaluate students whom they suspect may have a disability. Children identified as having a qualifying condition (as specified in the text of the law) may receive services. A multidisciplinary team who are familiar with the student must conduct evaluations. This evaluative team might consist of a school psychologist, school social worker, school nurse, speech and language pathologist, reading specialist, special education teacher, or coordinator of special education services. Parental consent is required. The goal of the evaluation is to ensure

Table 3.1 Landmark Laws Affecting Children and Adults with Disabilities

NUMBER OF LAW OR SECTION	DATE	NAME OF LAW	PROVISIONS
Section 504	1973	Rehabilitation Act of 1973, Section 504	Guarantees basic civil rights to all people with disabilities. Requires provision of accommodations.
PL 94-142	1975	Education for All Handicapped Children Act (EHA)	Guarantees FAPE in the Least Restrictive Environment (LRE). Requires students to have an IEP.
PL 101-476	1990	Individuals with Disabilities Education Act (IDEA)	Adds transition plans. Adds autism as a special education category. Adds traumatic brain injury as a category.
PL 105-17	1997	IDEA '97 (reauthorized)	Adds ADHD to "other health impairment" category. Adds functional behavioral assessments and behavioral intervention plans.
PL 107-110	2001	NCLB (reauthorization of The Elementary and Secondary Education Act)	Implemented high-stakes accountability system based on student achievement. Requires evidence-based practices and instruction. Insists on highly-qualified teachers.
PL 108-446	2004	Individuals with Disabilities Education Improvement Act IDEIA '04 (reauthorized)	Requires SPED teachers to be highly qualified. Requires all students with disabilities to participate in state and/or district annual testing with accommodations or in alternate assessments. Changes identification procedures for learning disabilities. Allows students to be placed in an alternate educational setting for weapons, drugs, or violence.
PL 114-95	2015	Every Student Succeeds Act (ESSA)	The reauthorization of NCLB transfers authority for accountability, teacher evaluations, and school improvement from federal to state governments and local districts. For exceptional learners, an emphasis is placed on access to the general curriculum through Universal Design for Learning, providing adequate accommodations for assessments, and evidence-based interventions to improve academic and behavioral outcomes.

Source: Adapted from Deborah Deutsch Smith and Naomi Chowdhuri Tyler, *Introduction to Special Education: Making a Difference*, 7th edition (Upper Saddle River, NJ, 2010).

that the student is educated in the least restrictive environment and is integrated—both academically and socially—with his or her peers to the greatest extent possible.[3] Table 3.2 provides a brief overview of the seminal components of IDEIA 2004 most applicable to classroom teachers.

Table 3.2 Key Components of IDEIA 2004

FEDERAL TERM	DEFINITION
Free Appropriate Public Education (FAPE)	Following the principle of zero-reject, children, regardless of the severity of their disability, can learn and cannot be excluded from a free appropriate public education. Special education services noted in the IEP are provided at public expense.
Nondiscriminatory Evaluation	All testing and evaluation used to identify and assess students with disabilities are free of racial and/or cultural discrimination. Evaluations requiring tests are to be in the student's native language and must be validated and administered by a trained professional.
Least Restrictive Environment (LRE)	The preferred placement for students with disabilities is in the general education classroom. When success in the general education classroom cannot be achieved, alternative placements are to be considered.
Individualized Education Program (IEP)	Within the principle of FAPE, an IEP must be developed for each student with a disability and include (1) current levels of performance; (2) annual goals; (3) extent of participation in the general education classroom; (4) dates and duration of services; and (5) evaluation methods. Participants in IEP planning must include at least one special and one general educator, a district-level representative, an evaluation specialist, any related-services specialists, and parents. Best practice also includes students in the planning process.
Parent Participation	Written permission by parents is needed for all testing, evaluation, and subsequent changes in services. Parents actively participate in the IEP development and review process.
Procedural Safeguards	Adequate notice is provided for all meetings. Disagreements can be settled through mediation or due process hearings.

Source: Adapted from Michael S. Rosenberg, David L. Westling, and James McLeskey, *Special Education for Today's Teachers: An Introduction*, 2ND edition (Upper Saddle River, NJ: Pearson, 2011).

SECTION 504 OF THE REHABILITATION ACT (1973)

This act was the first civil rights legislation specifically intended to safeguard individuals with disabilities. The law broadly defines *disability* as impairments that limit one or more life activities, including walking, seeing, hearing, speaking, and learning.[4] At its core, Section 504 prevents programs that receive federal assistance from discriminating against persons with disabilities. Public schools clearly fall under the purview of Section 504 and, similarly mandated in IDEA, are required to provide a FAPE to every student regardless of abilities. Unlike IDEA, which lists specific qualifying conditions, any student under Section 504 is eligible to receive school-based accommodations even if their impairment (e.g. a student with asthma or Type I diabetes) does not qualify them for special education services.

The evaluation process outlined in Section 504 is in many ways similar to that found under IDEA. The student is evaluated by a team of specialists and is ultimately placed in the LRE whereby the student has maximum access to his or her peers. Students are periodically reevaluated. Though mandated under IDEA, Section 504 does not require an IEP.

THE IEP PROCESS

A major provision in special education law is the requirement that every student who receives special education and ancillary services must have an individualized education program (IEP). The IEP provides opportunities for teachers, parents, school administrators and related service providers to collaborate on specific ways to improve the learning opportunities and outcomes of exceptional learners. Though general education teachers perceive the IEP to be useful in providing exceptional learners appropriate goals and support the instructional plans inherent in them, they often feel marginalized from the IEP team.[5]

The IEP follows a sequence of interrelated stages, each meeting the legislative mandates of IDEIA 2004. Figure 3.1 illustrates the stages in the IEP process.

Figure 3.1 The IEP Process

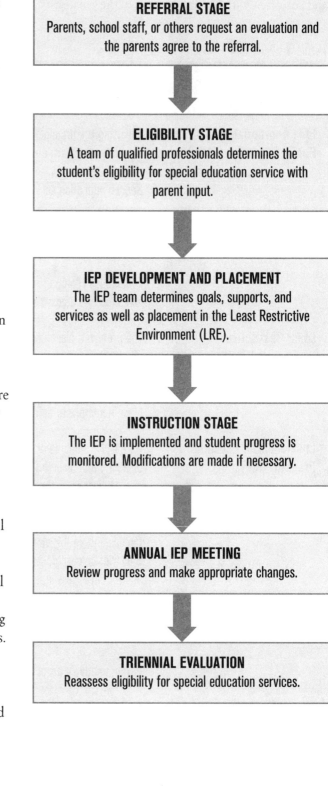

REFERRAL STAGE
Parents, school staff, or others request an evaluation and the parents agree to the referral.

ELIGIBILITY STAGE
A team of qualified professionals determines the student's eligibility for special education service with parent input.

IEP DEVELOPMENT AND PLACEMENT
The IEP team determines goals, supports, and services as well as placement in the Least Restrictive Environment (LRE).

INSTRUCTION STAGE
The IEP is implemented and student progress is monitored. Modifications are made if necessary.

ANNUAL IEP MEETING
Review progress and make appropriate changes.

TRIENNIAL EVALUATION
Reassess eligibility for special education services.

Referral Stage. If the general education teacher notices a student encountering difficulties, he/she typically consults an instructional support team comprised of peer-group colleagues who, in consultation with the special education teacher, design interventions to assist the student. If these interventions are successful, the student is not referred for an evaluation. If the interventions are not successful, the student can then be referred for an evaluation. The initial referral of a student for special education evaluation can come from the general education teacher, the parent, other specialists familiar with the student and, on occasion, the student.

Eligibility Stage. During this stage, academic and/or behavioral information is gathered and analyzed by an interdisciplinary team of specialists (i.e. school psychologist, speech and language therapist, school social worker). The eligibility team must include at least one teacher and one specialist in the area of the student's suspected disability. Once the information is evaluated, the parents are informed of the eligibility decision. If the child is found not eligible for services, the process stops unless the parent disagrees with the eligibility decision. If the child is found eligible for services, the IEP team meets to plan the first IEP.

According to IDEIA 2004, participants on the IEP planning team must include the following:

- The parents or legal guardians.

- At least one general education teacher of the student.

- At least one special education teacher.

- A representative of the local school district who is qualified to provide or supervise the designation of services, is knowledgeable of the general education curriculum and/or is knowledgeable of available district-level support services.

- At the discretion of the parent, other non school-based experts who are familiar with the student or the student's particular disability.

- When appropriate, the student with the disability.[6]

The IEP document must contain the following provisions:

- A statement of the child's current levels of academic achievement and functional performance.

- A statement of measurable annual goals.

- A description of how such goals are to be measured and when reports on student progress towards meeting such goals are to be provided.

- A statement of the special education services required.

- A statement of the degree to which the student will not be participating in the general education classroom.

- A statement of appropriate accommodations to be provided.

- The duration of services provided.[7]

When a child reaches the age of 16 (14 in many states), the IEP must include a transition component that provides a coordinated set of activities to support successful movement from secondary to postsecondary activities in education, training, employment, and independent living.[8]

Instruction Stage: The instruction stage involves the teaching and monitoring of student progress pertinent to the parameters of the IEP. This stage involves the implementation of the IEP through classroom instruction and revisiting the IEP on an annual basis. Student progress is reviewed and the IEP is reevaluated or amended accordingly. The IEP must delineate how the reevaluation will be conducted, who will administer it, and what assessment procedures will be followed. Parents are informed about their child's progress as frequently as parents of students without disabilities. Every three years, a review is required. New assessment data is collected and the IEP team determines if the student is still eligible for special education services. If the student is still eligible, the IEP team uses the newly collected data to update goals, supports, and services.

As previously mentioned, an increasing number of exceptional learners are accessing social studies content in a general education setting.[9] Over and above the instructional implications, there are legal implications as well, particularly in the design, delivery, and evaluation of the IEP. Given this, what is the role of the social studies educator in this process? First, the teacher must be attentive to the learning preferences and resultant outcomes of each student. The first domino in the IEP process is the teacher recognizing student difficulty. Second, the teacher needs to be an integral—and valued—part of the IEP team. Collaborating with school-based personnel, specialists, and parents, the teacher offers his/her insights into how best to design instruction to meet a student's established learning goals. Lastly, the general education teacher is charged with implementing the IEP through support of pertinent annual goals, providing any required accommodations and modifications, and delivering instruction in a manner that affords access to the curriculum. Monitoring student progress and suggesting possible revisions to the IEP are both essential roles general education teachers play in the IEP process. General education teachers also serve as excellent advocates for exceptional learners, emphasizing their strengths and encouraging student involvement in the IEP process. ▨

NOTES

1. "Pennsylvania Association for Retarded Citizens (PARC) v. Commonwealth of Pennsylvania," Public Interest Law Center of Philadelphia, accessed December 18, 2012, http://pilcop.org/pennsylvania-association-for-retarded-citizens-parc-v-commonwealth-of-pennsylvania/

2. Michael S. Rosenberg, David L. Westling, and James McLeskey, *Special Education for Today's Teachers: An Introduction*, 2ND edition (Upper Saddle River, NJ: Pearson, 2011).

3. Kelley R. Taylor, "Inclusion and the Law: Two Laws—IDEA and Section 504—Support Inclusion in Schools," *Principal Leadership* 76, no. 9 (October, 2010): 8-9.

4. Marilyn Friend, *Special Education: Contemporary Perspectives for School Professionals*, 3RD edition (Boston, MA: Pearson, 2011); Kelley, "Inclusion and the Law" *op. cit.*

5. Jerome J. Ammer, "Discrepancy Between Ideal and Reality: An Overview of Regular Educators' Perceptions of Their Role in the Special Education Decision Making Process," paper presented at the annual conference of the Confederated Organizations for Teacher Education, Syracuse, New York, April 1982; Gina Dildine, "General Education Teachers' Perceptions of their Role in Developing Individual Education Programs and Their Use of IEPs to Develop Instructional Plans for Students with Disabilities," Ed.D. Dissertation, Tennessee State University (2010).

6. Janet W. Lerner and Beverley Johns, *Learning Disabilities and Related Mild Disabilities*, 12TH edition (Belmont, CA: Wadsworth Cengage, 2011).

7. Lerner and Johns, *Learning Disabilities and Related Mild Disabilities, op. cit.*

8. Paul Wehman and Katherine M. Wittig, *Transition IEPs: A Curriculum Guide for Teachers and Transition Practitioners*, 3rd edition (Austin, Texas: PRO-ED, 2009).

9. Windy Schweder, "Knowing your Students" in *Practical Strategies for Teaching K-12 Social Studies in Inclusive Classrooms*, edited by Timothy Lintner and Windy Schweder (Charlotte, NC: Information Age Publishing, 2011): 9-18.

CHAPTER FOUR

Collaborating with Special Education

Collaboration—the pooling of instructional and related service assets to benefit the learning needs of all students—is a cornerstone of sound educational policy and practice. As a result of federal legislation such as No Child Left Behind (NCLB) and the Individuals with Disabilities Education Improvement Act (IDEIA 2004), which require the general education classroom to be the preferred place of instruction for exceptional learners, collaboration and co-teaching have become increasingly integral to the success of exceptional learners in the inclusive classroom. The primary goals of collaboration and co-teaching are to increase access to a diverse range of instructional opportunities, increase participation, and enhance the academic and behavioral outcomes of exceptional learners.[1] So, what are collaboration and co-teaching all about?

The old adage "two heads are better than one" certainly applies within the field of education. Though teaching can be an isolating and lonely endeavor, the creation of collaborative partnerships that share similar purposes can greatly impact both classroom practices and student outcomes.

Collaboration is essential, particularly in addressing the needs of exceptional learners. Schools rely more on collaborative team structures in which the individual team members contribute their expertise and knowledge base to support teacher instruction and positive student outcomes. According to Friend, such collaborative models can be *multidisciplinary, interdisciplinary*, or *transdisciplinary*.[2] A team of educators and specialists represents the *multidisciplinary* model. They participate in the decision-making process yet assume distinctly separate roles and responsibilities. In the *interdisciplinary* model of collaboration, communications among team members are more

frequent and focused, yet each professional still delivers services separately. Lastly, with the *transdisciplinary* model, information is readily shared, skill-sets amongst members are coordinated and classroom practice is based on collaborative ideas generated from the team. Transdisciplinary teams are the most collaborative, yet are also the most difficult to create and sustain.

CO-TEACHING

The push for inclusion resulted in the need for alternate service delivery options that allow exceptional learners to access the general education classroom while receiving the support services they need. A result of collaboration between special and general education teachers who work in inclusive settings is the model of co-teaching. Co-teaching is defined as "an educational approach in which general and special educators work in a co-active and coordinated fashion to jointly teach academically and behaviorally heterogeneous groups of students in educationally integrated settings (i.e., general education classrooms.)"[3] Simply, co-teaching is structured and sustained collaboration between a general education teacher and a special education teacher. Both are charged with co-planning, co-instructing, and co-assessing.[4] The premise is that teachers, working together in the same classroom, can provide greater expertise and supports to all students.[5]

There are several options to consider when designing a co-teaching partnership. Table 4.1 provides a brief overview of select models.

Co-teaching has been found to be an effective model for meeting the needs of all students, particularly those with disabilities.[6] Students in co-taught classes get the attention (and expertise) of two teachers. The curriculum in co-taught classrooms

Table 4.1 Select Co-teaching Models

MODEL	DESCRIPTION AND APPLICATION
One Teach, One Observe	One teacher leads instruction while the other gathers data on a single student, a group, or a whole class of students. While either general or special education teachers can collect data (through quantitative observation or qualitatively), this task is often prescribed to the special educator.
Parallel Teaching	In this model, the class is divided heterogeneously in half with the general education and special education teachers assuming equal responsibility for "their" half. Each half is simultaneously provided the same instruction. Such partitioning may lead to an increase in student participation and facilitate a more immediate response to student questions. Issues of noise and resulting distraction may be evident.
Station Teaching	Here, the teachers divide instruction into two, three, or more components or stations spread throughout the room. Each student participates (receives instruction) in each station. For example, one station may work with the special education teacher on organizational schemas, a second station analyzes primary source documents with the general education teacher, while the third station works independently on a persuasive advertisement.
Alternative Teaching	Alternative teaching enables either teacher to pull a small group of students to the side for instruction. Though remediation may take place here, this model also provides opportunities for preteaching and enrichment.
Teaming	This is the most cohesive and seamless model of co-teaching as both teachers equally share in all aspects of instructional design, delivery, and assessment. For example, one teacher may contextualize the notion of nationalism while the other teacher provides examples. One teacher may move through a presentation on longitude and latitude while the other interjects questions.
One Teach, One Assist	In this model, one teacher leads instruction while the other typically circulates through the classroom offering needed assistance. Some issues with this model include the dominant/subordinate structure, and student perception of one teacher as "the teacher" and the other teacher as "the helper."

Source: Adapted from Marilyn Friend, *Special Education: Contemporary Perspectives for School Professionals*, 3RD edition (Boston, MA: Pearson, 2011).

is more enriched, layered, and responsive than in a typical classroom. Both the general education and special education teachers report a high level of achievement for exceptional learners in their classrooms.[7] Lastly, the co-teaching model has the potential to create a new cadre of young educators familiar with collaborative practices and responsive to the learning needs of all students.[8]

Though the potential and promise of co-teaching is evident, there are a handful of concerns that warrant attention. Kohler-Evans believes that in the scramble to meet federal and state mandates, districts have often jumped on the co-teaching bandwagon by throwing "two teachers in the same room at the same time" and calling it co-teaching.[9] By doing so, the integrity of the co-teaching enterprise has been reduced to compliance rather than best practice.

Another potential concern with co-teaching is the use of support personnel such as paraprofessionals in the collaborative relationship. It is important to recognize that planning and teaching in a co-teaching partnership is led by licensed educators, not support personnel. Paraprofessionals provide important assistance to students and their services should be included within lessons. They also provide valuable input about student strengths and challenges that co-teachers can use to differentiate instruction and support positive academic and social outcomes.

Having two teachers in the same classroom can lead to resentment, fatigue, and the emergence of a distinct power differential. Cook warns, "co-teaching is not simply having two teachers in a classroom with one acting as a glorified paraprofessional or an in-class tutor for one or two students."[10] Yet such role differentials routinely occur within co-taught classrooms.[11] Roles are ill-defined or not defined at all. Tasks are not equitably shared. The general education teacher often lacks the knowledge and skills to adequately address the learning needs of exceptional students; the special education teacher is often not a content expert. When the model gets mired in logistics and power-plays, the students suffer. One way to address roles is to map out responsibilities during a lesson. Table 4.2 provides a list of suggested tasks that licensed teachers and support personnel can fill during a lesson.

Though there are steps to address within the co-teaching model, we nevertheless encourage you to create purposeful and sustained collaborative opportunities in your classroom and throughout your school. There are several strategies to consider when starting a co-teaching partnership.[12] We provide a few below to assist you in designing an equitable and respectful co-teaching relationship that facilitates rich and engaging social studies learning for all students.

- *Walk down the hall.* The first step is the step taken outside of your classroom. Find a partner whose personality is compatible with yours and who shares the same vision of educational excellence for all students.

- *Seek out administrative support.* Although you can create your own co-teaching relationship, an administrator who supports this type of collaboration is essential if change is to take place at the school level. If an administrator supports one successful co-teaching team, the structures put in place by that team provide a catalyst for school-wide expansion of the model. An administrator who does not support co-teaching as a collaborative model can end the partnership before it ever has a chance to get off the ground.

- *Make time to plan.* Carve out regular opportunities to plan for instruction. A great deal of planning energy needs to be expended well before the co-teaching actually begins. Although a common planning time is ideal, this is not always possible with complex school schedules. Planning time may require utilizing technology to communicate or finding time before or after school or during lunch to meet. Finding at least an hour a week is a good rule of thumb.

- *Practice respect.* As previously stated, poorly paired and poorly organized co-teaching practices often devolve into role differentials. Establish the prescribed roles and responsibilities of each teacher up front. Each member possesses different skill sets, yet it is in such differences that the potential benefits of co-teaching exist. Share your strengths, challenges, and pet peeves with each other and agree to keep an open line of communication. Understand too that the special education teacher may be co-teaching in multiple content areas and has a caseload of students to monitor. Both teachers may be in charge of extra-curricular activities such as sports or clubs. Be understanding of these other school-based obligations when establishing roles and responsibilities for your co-teacher.

- *Share responsibility and accountability.* Co-teachers talk about "our students," not "your students" or "my students." Student behavioral and academic outcomes are the responsibility of both licensed teachers. Co-teachers need to communicate expectations for classroom management and academic success and then consistently implement these expectations.

Table 4.2 Suggested Tasks for Licensed Teachers and Support Personnel

IF ONE TEACHER IS:	THE OTHER TEACHER IS:	THE SUPPORT PROFESSIONAL IS:
Lecturing	Modeling note-taking and providing breaks to review and process information	Monitoring on-task behavior and/or collecting data on individual students
Taking attendance	Reviewing last night's homework; introducing a social or study skill; leading a bell ringer activity	Collecting homework and making sure all of the students have materials out and are prepared for the lesson
Passing out an assignment and providing directions	Reviewing directions or modeling the first task on the assignment	Monitoring that all students are following the modeled task
Giving instructions orally to the whole class	Writing down instructions on the board; repeating or clarifying any difficult content	Writing down and repeating instructions for individual students
Checking for understanding with a large heterogeneous group of students	Checking for understanding with a small heterogeneous group of students	Circulating, checking understanding of specific individuals
Prepping half the class for one side of a debate	Prepping the other side of the class for the opposing side of the debate	Providing individual preparation for the debate
Facilitating a silent activity	Circulating, checking for comprehension	Offering individual support for the activity
Facilitating a writing activity to analyze a topic	Providing small group support to organize student analysis in a visual organizer	Working with an individual student on an alternate way to demonstrate analysis
Providing large group instruction	Circulating, using proximity control for behavior management and academic support	Monitoring on-task behavior

- *Debrief daily.* Successful co-teaching partners talk at the end of the day, often at the end of each lesson. Open, honest, constructive communication is essential.

- *Modify and adjust.* Assess your student needs. If your co-teaching instruction is not meeting the needs of all students, change course. There is great flexibility in co-teaching design and delivery.

- *Have fun.* If it is not enjoyable it will not work. Enthusiasm is contagious. Let your students see how enjoyable teaching and learning can be.

More exceptional learners are entering general education classrooms—social studies classrooms—than ever before. Over and above the legal mandates, responsive teaching requires providing all students with appropriate and engaging learning. One way to do so is by establishing collaborative teams and developing co-teaching partnerships.

IF ONE TEACHER IS:	THE OTHER TEACHER IS:	THE SUPPORT PROFESSIONAL IS:
Running last minute copies or errands in the building	Reviewing homework, previewing a study skill or test-taking strategy; bell ringer	Monitoring on-task behavior
Re-teaching or pre-teaching with a small group to catch them up with the large group	Monitoring the large group as they work independently	Offering individualized support to help a student complete the work
Facilitating sustained silent reading	Reading aloud quietly with a small group; previewing upcoming information	Reading aloud with an individual student or monitoring sustained silent reading
Reading a test aloud to a group of students	Proctoring a test silently with a group of students	Providing test accommodations/modifications to an individual student
Creating basic lesson plans for standards, objectives, and content curriculum	Providing suggestions for modifications, accommodations, and activities for diverse learners	Providing suggestions for supports within the lesson for individual students
Facilitating or leading instruction in stations or groups	Facilitating or leading instruction in stations or groups	Monitoring stations or groups to support completion of the tasks
Explaining a new concept	Conducting a roleplay or modeling the concept, asking clarifying questions	Monitoring on-task behavior or supporting an individual student
Providing modification needs	Providing enrichment needs	Providing accommodation needs

Source: Adapted from Wendy Murawski and Lisa Dieker, "Tips and Strategies for Co-Teaching at the Secondary Level," *Teaching Exceptional Children* 36, no. 5, (Mar-Apr 2004): 52-58.

Though we encourage fostering collaborative partnerships that ideally lead to co-teaching opportunities, the stark reality is that, for the vast majority of social studies general education teachers, co-teaching is elusive at best. The disproportionate number of general educators to special educators, coupled with the emphasis on improving academic outcomes in English and mathematics, means that there are simply not enough special educators to co-teach in social studies settings. Likewise, some social studies classrooms are fortunate to have paraprofessionals or instructional aides. Such aides,

though well intentioned and enthusiastic, are not licensed teachers and may lack specific training in how to reach and teach exceptional learners. Though we support the co-teaching model and believe that, if structured and sustained with fidelity, it has the potential to meet the learning needs of all students, we readily acknowledge the present gap between theory and practice. The lesson plans we developed for Part III include roles and responsibilities for a co-teacher and paraprofessional. All of these lessons have been successfully implemented in the classroom with and without an additional teacher or support personnel. They are designed to model how lessons can be easily adapted to include other professionals within the classroom setting.

Though co-teaching as a specific delivery model for instruction may not be common practice, we believe that collaboration can and should be encouraged. Based on the simple and applicable suggestions listed above, general educators can benefit from the pedagogical expertise of their special education colleagues. While special educators may not be physically present in the general education classroom, the insights and suggestions provided during the collaborative process can be invaluable for the general educator committed to supporting the learning needs of all learners. 🔲

NOTES

1. Naomi Zigmond and Kathleen Magiera, "Current Practice Alerts: A Focus on Co-Teaching: Use with Caution," *Alerts* 6 (2001): 1-4.

2. Marilyn M. Friend, *Special Education: Contemporary Perspectives for School Professionals*, 3RD edition (Boston, MA: Pearson, 2011).

3. Jeanne Bauwens, Jack J. Hourcade, and Marilyn M. Friend, "Cooperative Teaching: A Model for General and Special Education Integration," *Remedial and Special Education* 10, no. 2 (Mar-Apr 1989): 17-22.

4. Wendy W. Murawski and Lisa Dieker, "50 Ways to Keep your Co-Teacher: Strategies for Before, During, and After Co-Teaching," *TEACHING Exceptional Children* 40, no. 4 (Mar-Apr 2008): 40-48; Joe Nichols, Alana Dowdy, and Cindy Nichols, "Co-Teaching: An Educational Promise for Children with Disabilities or a Quick Fix to Meet the Mandates of No Child Left Behind?" *Education* 130, no. 4 (Sum 2010): 647-51.

5. Thomas E. Scruggs, Margo A. Mastropieri, and Kimberly McDuffie, "Co-Teaching in Inclusive Classrooms: A Metasynthesis of Qualitative Research," *Exceptional Children* 73, no. 4 (Sum 2007): 392-416.

6. Kathleen Magiera, Cynthia Smith, Naomi Zigmond, and Kelli Gebauer, "Benefits of Co-Teaching in Secondary Mathematics Classes," *TEACHING Exceptional Children* 37, no. 3 (Jan-Feb 2005): 20-24; Wendy W. Murawski, "Student Outcomes in Co-Taught Secondary English Classes: How Can We Improve?" Reading and Writing Quarterly 22, no. 3 (Jul-Sep 2006): 227-47.

7. Elizabeth Keefe and Veronica Moore, "The Challenge of Co-Teaching in Inclusive Classrooms at the High School Level and What the Teachers Told Us," *American Secondary Education* 32, no. 3 (Sum 2004): 77-88.

8. Jacqueline Sack, "Divide Over Co-Teaching Widens in Florida," *Education Week* 25 (2005): 26-28.

9. Patty Kohler-Evans, "Co-Teaching: How to Make this Marriage Work in Front of the Kids," *Education* 127, no. 2 (Win 2006): 260-64.

10. Steven A. Spenser, "An Interview with Dr. Lynne Cook and June Downing: The Practicalities of Collaboration in Special Education Service Delivery," *Intervention in School and Clinic* 40, no. 5 (May 2005): 297.

11. Margaret Weiss and John Wills Lloyd, "Congruence Between Roles and Actions of Secondary Special Educators in Co-Taught and Special Education Settings," *The Journal of Special Education* 36, no. 2 (Sum 2002): 58-68.

12. See Murawski and Dieker, "50 Ways to Keep your Co-Teacher."

PART II
EDUCATING STUDENTS WITH EXCEPTIONALITIES

CHAPTER FIVE

Self-Determination, Social Skills Development, and Citizenship Preparation

Early in the book we introduced the voices of youth advocating for how they wanted to be seen and treated in daily life. These young people view people with disabilities as active and equal citizens who are contributors, not burdens to society. Their strong self-determination, self-advocacy, effective social skills, and understanding of their rights and responsibilities as citizens sustain this vision for equality.

Democracy is a life experience and citizenship is a series of opportunities in life that teach people how to live and interact with societal diversity. Our schools serve as the space to model and learn the principles of effective citizenship within democracy.[1] Citizenship education has the opportunity to function as a way to educate youth and prepare them for full membership and participation in society.[2] Full membership and participation describe the essence of inclusion. In special education, the inclusive school is a community where the least restrictive environment (LRE) is seen as full membership and participation in the general education classroom to the greatest extent possible.[3] There is a positive tension and sense of belonging in an inclusive school community. This tension anchors exceptional learners in the general education classroom, only pulling them away for more intensive interventions that teachers are unable to effectively provide within the general education setting.

Moving toward full membership and participation for youth with disabilities requires school support for self-determination, self-advocacy, and social skill development. These concepts provide a direct connection to the purpose for teaching social studies, namely citizenship practices. Self-determination has many definitions, but in principle, it describes an individual who exercises the right to lead his or her own life.[4] Many of the skills identified in self-determined behavior, such as choice-making, decision-making, problem solving, goal setting, leadership, and advocacy, mirror citizenship skills taught in social studies.[5] Table 5.1 identifies some traditional skills listed in social studies standards and some commonly acknowledged self-determined behaviors.

The self-determined individual has the ability to self-advocate and exhibits strong social skills. The self-advocate is a person who demonstrates the ability to promote one's own interests. Self-advocates use skills such as public speaking, leadership, teamwork, active listening, decision-making, communication, negotiation, and compromise.

Table 5.1 Self-Determined Behaviors and Citizenship Skills

SELF-DETERMINED BEHAVIORS	CITIZENSHIP SKILLS
• Choice-making • Decision-making • Goal setting and attainment • Leadership • Problem-solving • Self-advocacy • Self-awareness • Self-efficacy • Self-knowledge • Self-regulation and self-management	• Acquiring and using information (informed) • Assessing involvement • Communicating • Cooperating • Decision-making • Making judgments • Problem solving • Promoting interests • Responsibility • Respect (for laws, for others)

They also may have some understanding of legal and citizenship rights and responsibilities.[6] Social skills are the specific, identifiable, and discrete actions and responses that students need to navigate and negotiate social conventions both inside and outside of the classroom. Effective social skills are characterized by the ability to establish and maintain positive relationships, while managing an array of challenging social situations using ethical and constructive approaches.[7] Self-determination, self-advocacy and social skill development all support the opportunity for full inclusion in society, provide relevant instructional connections to the social studies classroom, and are evidence-based predictors of successful postsecondary education and employment outcomes.[8] Let us now look at how teachers can support and incorporate these concepts into the social studies curriculum.

ENCOURAGING SELF-DETERMINATION

Teaching and encouraging self-determination involves an instructional shift to a more student-centered approach. Begin by having all of your students set goals for learning and incorporate a way for them to track progress of these goals. From a planning standpoint, a curriculum planned with the principles of Universal Design for Learning (UDL) is a good starting point. A UDL classroom creates multiple means of representation, expression and engagement in learning.[9] Students frequently have greater choice in how they learn. UDL is explained in more detail in Chapter 6 as it offers an excellent way to make a social studies classroom fully accessible to exceptional learners.

Within this idea of UDL, one option is to create a classroom where students have more choice about class assignments, providing multiple ways for them to express their knowledge. This, in turn, facilitates student engagement. Teachers who support more self-determined behavior provide opportunities for students to choose what activities to complete, how to complete them, with whom to complete the activities, and the timeframe for completion. These choices initially come with scaffolds that teachers remove once students demonstrate that they know how to manage their learning experience.

The NCSS C3 Framework also opens opportunities to support self-determination in the classroom. The four dimensions of the Inquiry Arc encourage teachers to create opportunities for students to model self-determined behaviors. These four dimensions are:

- Developing questions and planning inquiries;

- Applying disciplinary concepts and tools;

- Evaluating sources and using evidence; and

- Communicating conclusions and taking informed action.[10]

In addition to problem solving, students respond to and ask compelling and supporting questions allowing for choice-making and decision-making. The expectation that students use inquiry skills and evaluate and use sources to develop informed conclusions or take action on particular topics encourages the advocacy and leadership skills critical to self-determination. The incorporation of the C3 Framework is explained in more detail in Chapter 6 and the sample lesson plans provided in Chapters 11 through 13 incorporate outcomes that align with the framework.

Another way to support self-determination is through instructional strategies that support skills such as problem solving, decision-making, and leadership. Cooperative learning strategies, debates, role-playing, and simulations represent a sampling of strategies that build in support for self-determination skills. Many of these strategies are discussed at length in Chapter 7.

CREATING SELF-ADVOCATES

Teaching students about their rights and responsibilities as citizens is an important step in fostering self-advocacy. Sometimes exceptional learners do not understand why they have an IEP or how it protects their right to a free and appropriate public education. Likewise, their peers without disabilities may perceive accommodations that some students receive as being unfair. Incorporating a legislative or judicial activity that addresses the civil rights of people with disabilities would give students an opportunity to learn how to advocate for others and, in turn, advocate for themselves. It is important to note that any activity that requires students to speak up for their own viewpoints would support self-advocacy skills. Social studies teachers will find a number of opportunities to teach self-advocacy within their existing curriculum.

Beyond the curriculum, social studies teachers have the opportunity to foster self-advocacy for exceptional learners through the IEP. As noted in Chapter 3, the general education teacher is part of the IEP process through participation in team meetings and by supporting and implementing annual goals, accommodations, and modifications. Social studies teachers should consider their role in supporting student self-advocacy within the IEP. If a student is not involved in the IEP meeting, advocate for that student's participation in the process. Become familiar with the *I'm Determined* project (located at http://www.imdetermined.org.) This site supports student involvement in the IEP process and has excellent videos of students demonstrating self-advocacy. Goal setting is an additional skill that supports IEP participation and is also a tool used in the social studies classroom. Teachers who involve their students in service learning projects or project-based learning activities ask students to identify community needs, outline options for addressing those needs, determine possible outcomes related to the options developed, and then implement an action plan. Similarly, exceptional learners need to develop the ability to recognize their own needs and challenges and develop a plan for addressing them within the IEP through annual and postsecondary goals.[11]

DEVELOPING EFFECTIVE SOCIAL SKILLS

What role can social studies play in social skill development? According to Sahin, the ideal context (and content) in which to facilitate social skill development is in the social studies classroom.[12] Social studies provide opportunities for students to situate in the past and, by doing so, understand the motives and actions of others. They also encourage students to become actively engaged in the present. Most importantly, and with particular relevance to early elementary grades, social studies instill the foundational social skills necessary for students

to become informed, engaged, confident, and productive citizens.

So how do we engage our students? An essential cornerstone of engaging social studies is student action. Students become active consumers, if you will, of the content at hand. They analyze, interpret, critique, and discuss. Passivity—most often in the form of teacher-centered instruction dominated by textbooks, lectures with notes, and worksheets—is replaced by rich, sustained, and varied participatory and collaborative opportunities. Hands are raised. Questions are asked. Issues, events, and actions are pondered. Such inquiry-based instruction allows students to formulate and articulate their own opinions while listening to and considering the opinions of their classmates.[13] The inherent participatory and collaborative nature of inquiry-based social studies instruction naturally facilitates the development of an array of social skills including, amongst others, listening, articulating, taking and sharing responsibility, and respecting the opinions of others.[14]

Instruction that supports self-determination and self-advocacy complements social skill development. One of the more commonly used strategies for social skill development in the social studies classroom is cooperative learning. In both social studies and special education literature, cooperative learning supports social skill development.[15] More than mere group work, cooperative learning promotes social interaction through collaboration. Yet for all students—and most particularly exceptional learners who struggle with classroom structures and the inherent expectations embedded in them—cooperative, participatory practices must be well structured. We have identified four key components to structuring meaningful and effective cooperative learning with the exceptional learner in mind. First, the established classroom climate must be premised on tolerance, acceptance, and respect. For exceptional learners to benefit from cooperative learning they must feel welcomed and included as an integral part of the group. Second, pairs and/or groups must be selected with care. Heterogeneous grouping is essential in an inclusive cooperative learning structure. Teachers must avoid grouping students based on similar academic abilities. Assigning roles such as facilitator, recorder, timekeeper, or encourager provides structured opportunities for exceptional learners to participate in a group even if the content is challenging. Third, structured objectives for each member must be made clear. Students need to know what is expected of them, both in terms of collaborative practice (e.g. how to listen, how to communicate one's ideas, etc.) and academic outcomes (e.g. what to produce, how to produce it). Lastly, collaborative learning opportunities must be sustained. The participatory nature of the inquiry-based social studies classroom is perfectly suited for collaborative learning.

In a seminal study by Jenkins, Antil, Wayne, and Vadsey, the authors examined the practices and perceptions of general educators' use of cooperative learning and the impact it had on exceptional learners in their respective classrooms.[16] In general, teachers responded that cooperative learning led to broader student participation, more active learning, and an increase in task initiation and completion. Cooperative learning enhanced listening skills and increased student respect for others and for other points of view. With respect to exceptional learners, cooperative learning increased self-esteem, provided a safe learning environment, and led to increased academic performance. Chapter 7 further addresses specific cooperative learning strategies that support self-determination and social skill development. The combination of Dewey's belief in using schools to model effective citizenship and the approaches outlined in this chapter to address self-determination, self-advocacy, and social skill development, create opportunities for fostering inclusive citizenship in our schools. Self-determination and self-advocacy promote greater student participation in the general education curriculum and lead to successful social skill development.[17] The practice of inclusive citizenship promotes fairness and equity among all citizens, and recognizes how humans have something to offer despite perceived differences or limitations. It also values the right of people to lead their own lives, work with others, and advocate for social justice and acknowledgment as citizens.[18]

Social studies teachers have the curriculum and instructional tools in place to create classrooms premised on advocacy, justice, and the promotion of individual rights. ▧

NOTES

1. John Dewey, "The Democratic Conception in Education," in *Educating the Democratic Mind*, edited by Walter C. Parker (Albany: State University of New York Press, 1996): 25-44.

2. *National Standards for Civics and Government* (Calabasas, CA: Center for Civic Education, 2003): 127.

3. Margo A. Mastropieri and Thomas E. Scruggs, *The Inclusive Classroom: Strategies for Effective Differentiated Instruction*, 4TH edition (Upper Saddle River: Pearson, 2010).

4. Michael L. Wehmeyer, "Self-Determination and Individuals with Severe Disabilities: Re-examining Meanings and Misinterpretations," *Research & Practice for Persons with Severe Disabilities* 30, no. 3 (2006):113-120; Darren Minarik and Danielle Coughlin, "Don't Forget Me! Using Special Educators to Support Interdisciplinary Teaching and Learning," in *Integrative Strategies for the K-12 Social Studies Classroom*, edited by Timothy Lintner (Charlotte: Information Age, 2013): 167-190.

5. Michael L. Wehmeyer and Sharon L. Field, *Self-determination: Instructional and Assessment Strategies* (Thousand Oaks, CA: Corwin Press, 2007); Kathlyn Steedly, Amanda Schwartz, Michael Levin, and Stephen Luke, "Social Skills and Academic Achievement," *Evidence for Education*," 3, no. 2 (2008), http://ecac-parentcenter.org/userfiles/PTI/Resourcepages/SocialSkills/SocialSkills&AcademicAchievement,NICHCY.pdf. Enter "social skills and academic achievement" into the search function on the ECAC home page to locate this resource.

6. *Ibid.*

7. Joseph Zins, Roger Weissberg, Margaret Wang, and Herbert Walberg, *Building Academic Success on Social and Emotional Learning: What Does the Research Say?* (New York: Teachers College Press, 2004).

8. David Test, Catherine Fowler, Paula Kohler, and Larry Kortering, "Evidence-Based Practices and Predictors in Secondary Transition: What We Know and What We Still Need to Know," National Secondary Transition Technical Assistance Center (NSTTAC) (2010): 1-8.

9. Tracey Hall, Nicole Strangman, and Anne Meyer, "Differentiated Instruction and Implications for Udl Implementation," National Center on Accessible Instructional Materials, 2003, http://aem.cast.org/learn/historyarchive/backgroundpapers/differentiated_instruction_udl.

10. National Council for the Social Studies, *Social Studies for the Next Generation: Purposes, Practices, and Implications of the College, Career, and Civic Life (C3) Framework for Social Studies State Standards*, Bulletin No. 113 (Silver Spring, MD: NCSS, 2013).

11. Michael Wehmeyer and Kathy Kelchner, *Whose Future is it Anyway? A Student-Directed Transition Planning Process*, 2nd edition (Zarrow Center: Norman, OK, 2012). http://www.ou.edu/content/education/centers-and-partnerships/zarrow/self-determination-education-materials/whos-future-is-it-anyway.html

12. Cavus Sahin, "An Evaluation of Teachers' Perceptions of Teaching Social Skills to Fifth Grade Students within the Scope of Social Studies Lessons," *International Journal of Progressive Education* 6, no. 1 (2010): 28-46.

13. David E. Harris, "Classroom Assessment of Civil Discourse," in *Education for Democracy: Contexts, Curricula, Assessments*, edited by Walter C. Parker (Charlotte: Information Age, 2002): 211-232.

14. Candy M. Beal and Cheryl Mason Bolick, *Teaching Social Studies in Middle and Secondary Schools*, 6TH edition (Boston, MA: Pearson, 2013).

15. Robert E. Slavin, "Synthesis of Research on Cooperative Learning," *Educational Leadership* 48, no. 5 (1991): 71-81; Paul Nagel, "Moving Beyond Lecture: Cooperative Learning and the Secondary Social Studies Classroom," *Education* 128, no. 3 (2008): 363-368; James E. Schul, "Revisiting an Old Friend: The Practice and Promise of Cooperative Learning for the Twenty-First Century," *Social Studies* 102, no. 2 (2011): 88-93; Robyn M. Gillies and Adrian F. Ashman, "The Effects of Cooperative Learning on Students with Learning Difficulties in the Lower Elementary School," *Journal of Special Education* 34, no. 1 (2000): 19-27; Margaret E. King-Sears, "Best Academic Practices for Inclusive Classrooms," *Focus on Exceptional Children* 29, no. 7 (1997): 1-23; Mastropieri and Scruggs, *The Inclusive Classroom, op. cit.*

16. Joseph R. Jenkins *et al.,* "How Cooperative Learning Works for Special Education and Remedial Students," *Exceptional Children* 69, no. 3 (2003): 279-292.

17. Wehmeyer and Field, *Self-determination, op. cit.*

18. Naila Kabeer, "The Search for Inclusive Citizenship: Meanings and Expressions in an Interconnected World," in *Inclusive Citizenship: Meanings and Expressions*, edited by Naila Kabeer (London: Zed Books, 2005): 1-27; Ruth Lister, "Inclusive Citizenship: Realizing the Potential," *Citizenship Studies* 11, no. 1 (2007): 49-61.

CHAPTER SIX

Instructional Design

How can social studies teachers create an inclusive classroom that unlocks opportunities for all students to gain access to the general curriculum? The process begins with an examination of how we plan our instruction and the tools we use to provide access to the content. This chapter examines the methods for planning and organizing social studies content to create an inclusive classroom setting.

The Covey habit—"begin with the end in mind"—is a good place to start when we consider how to plan instruction.[1] Ultimately, we want students to know certain content for a unit of study and we need to assess their knowledge of this content. Two planning models that "begin with the end in mind" are: (1) Understanding by Design (UbD) and (2) SMARTER planning.[2] The UbD model looks first at student outcomes and how teachers will collect evidence of these outcomes. Essential questions are developed to determine what will be assessed in the unit. The unit is then organized into lessons, strategies, and activities to help students meet the essential unit outcomes. Differentiation comes into play as teachers consider how specific strategies will support the attainment of learning outcomes for exceptional learners.[3]

Similarly, SMARTER planning asks teachers to first consider the essential questions students must answer as well as the central themes of a unit before organizing the content and planning for instruction. Using the SMARTER mnemonic, teachers **S**hape essential questions, **M**ap critical content, **A**nalyze the learning difficulties, **R**each enhancement decisions, **T**each strategically, **E**valuate mastery, and **R**evisit outcomes.[4] After teachers determine the learning challenges, they differentiate lessons and implement evidence-based practices to support acquisition of the critical content.

Both UbD and SMARTER planning provide opportunities for differentiated instruction, which supports the diverse learning needs of students. Differentiation is a reactive approach to planning where the teacher examines the learning needs of individual students, and then introduces necessary strategies and accommodations so students can access the content. A proactive approach to meet the learning needs of all students is Universal Design for Learning (UDL). UDL originates in architectural design. New buildings are designed to be accessible to all who may use doors, ramps, elevators, and restrooms. To navigate a space, there may also be a combination of audio, visual, and tactile queues for a person to utilize.

Just as the concept of UDL removes barriers in architectural design, it also considers potential barriers in course design and instructional delivery, and addresses these barriers before students enter the classroom. Teachers build classroom instruction by considering the multiple needs students possess. A student with a hearing impairment may need captioning to access the dialogue in a video. The same captioning may also support the student who prefers to read or who connects words to pictures to reinforce content comprehension. As illustrated in Figure 6.1, UDL considers multiple ways for students to access the curriculum. Similar to how a person without a disability might use an automatic door or ramp to access a building, all students in a UDL classroom have multiple options for accessing the content.

Figure 6.1 UDL in the Social Studies Classroom

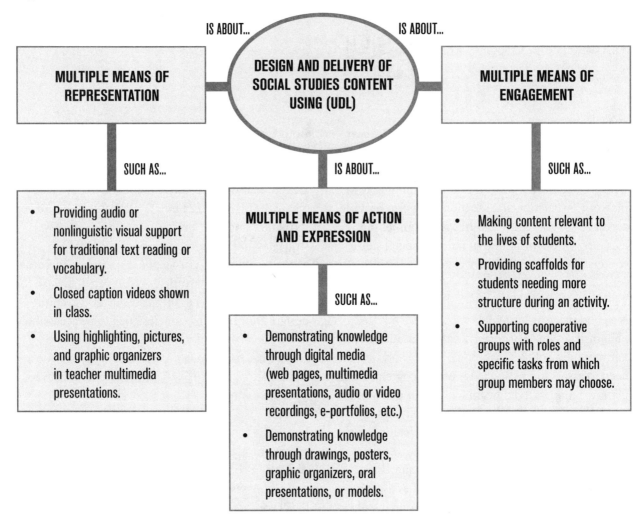

Source: Adapted from "Universal Design For Learning Guidelines Version 2.0," CAST, 2011, http://www.udlcenter.org/aboutudl/udlguidelines. Darren Minarik and Timothy Lintner, "The Push for Inclusive Classrooms and the Impact on Social Studies Design and Delivery," *Social Studies Review* 50, no. 1 (2011): 53.

USING THE FOUR DIMENSIONS OF THE C3 FRAMEWORK TO PLAN INSTRUCTION

NCSS introduced the C3 Framework in 2013 as a guidance document to support social studies educators in the creation of rigorous learning environments that develop engaged and participatory citizens.[5] The C3 encourages teachers who emphasize covering the content and information recall to move toward a focus on engaged higher order thinking. Even though "the C3 Framework is largely silent on the different abilities children bring to their schooling," it still emphasizes the importance of smart, thoughtful, imaginative, and scaffolded teaching that would assist all students

who need help meeting the indicators specified in the Framework.[6] It is important to note that there is some limited evidence exceptional learners are successful when an emphasis is placed on higher order thinking.[7] This is encouraging news and it supports our belief that the C3 Framework fits well with the suggestions offered in this book for designing and implementing instruction. To understand how the C3 Framework supports learning for exceptional learners, let us look at the four dimensions of the Inquiry Arc and potential intersections for teachers to consider as they plan inclusive lessons.

DIMENSION 1:
DEVELOPING QUESTIONS AND PLANNING INQUIRIES

Questions are a critical part of the learning process and all learners need to develop the skills necessary to ask and respond to a variety of questions. Similar in design to Wiggins and McTighe's "essential questions" in UbD or the "essential questions" noted in SMARTER planning, compelling questions in the C3 Framework address enduring themes. They are not necessarily questions that contain a definitive answer; rather, these questions spark interest, curiosity, discussion, and debate. They inspire higher-order thinking and produce additional questions about the topic. In addition, they are frequently interdisciplinary in nature, crossing content areas within social studies and other fields of study. If a teacher poses a compelling question at the beginning of a unit such as, "Was the Cold War really a war?" students are challenged to ask other questions and collect evidence. They examine historical, governmental, geographical, and economic impacts. The students collect essential information and seek out answers rather than the teacher simply providing information to be memorized.

In order to support a thorough response to the compelling question, supporting questions arise such as, "What are the characteristics of war?" "How do I (and others) define war?" "Where did the term 'Cold War' come from, and why is it used to describe this period in history?" Supporting questions are more targeted in nature, filling in pieces needed to develop an informed response to the broader compelling question. Some exceptional learners might ask these questions themselves, while others might generate supporting questions in peer groups. Still others might need the teacher to create explicit prompts, define terms, and use targeted strategies or routines to scaffold the learning process.[8] An important point to remember is that these options are easily built into lessons. Teachers need to challenge all learners with compelling questions and not assume that some students are incapable of responding to such questions. The C3 Framework provides tables containing indicators for the construction of compelling and supporting questions. These indicators are aligned by grade level and serve as excellent supports for teachers

when developing lessons. For instance, Indicator D1.1.9-12 requires students to "explain points of agreement and disagreement experts have about interpretations and applications of disciplinary concepts and ideas associated with a compelling question."[9] D1.3.9-12 is a similar indicator for supporting questions.[10] Both of these indicators express higher order thinking expectations for students answering the compelling and supporting questions about the Cold War. You will find additional examples of C3 Framework indicator alignment throughout the elementary, middle, and high school lessons in Chapters 11 through 13. Numerous compelling and supporting questions are provided in the lessons. For additional compelling and supporting questions beyond the sample lesson plans provided in this text, other suitable questions for exploration are emphasized in the NCSS National Curriculum Standards for Social Studies.

DIMENSION 2:
APPLYING DISCIPLINARY CONCEPTS AND TOOLS

The purpose of Dimension 2 is to provide teachers with a guidance tool for organizing content through the use of conceptual themes rather than providing specific topics. This broad approach was intentional to encourage use of the C3 Framework within existing state standards and to support development of new standards when needed. The content is divided into the four core social studies disciplines, civics, economics, geography, and history. This aligns with the sample classroom tested lesson plans provided in Chapters 11 through 13. As with Dimension 1, indicators for each discipline are broken into benchmarks for second, fifth, eighth, and twelfth grades.

An expectation established by the objectives is that students will reach these target areas individually or with other students. This language in the objectives is accommodating and it provides teachers with the latitude to consider multiple ways to help exceptional learners meet the grade level indicators. So, how does a teacher help exceptional learners understand and apply disciplinary concepts? There are many approaches discussed and modeled in this book that provide the needed assistance for teachers. Specifically, teachers need to write lesson plans that include specific tools to help students break down complex concepts into characteristics, examples, and non-examples.[11] This can be done with Venn diagrams, compare/contrast matrices, concept maps or other devices that allow students to visually sort information.

Dimension 2 poses the sample question, "What does liberty look like?"[12] For some students with exceptional learning needs, prompts are needed to help define the word "liberty" by listing characteristics that best reflect the term. Other students might respond better by examining potential examples of "liberty" first, and then extracting common characteristics that make those examples fit within the concept. It is important for the teacher to be flexible and creative in approaching complex concepts, using peer supports and a variety of strategies to develop understanding. Once there is a better conceptual understanding of "liberty," students could then begin examining the concept through the lens of the four core social studies disciplines. As additional challenging terms or concepts arise, the lessons would need to reflect strategies for supporting student understanding of the new material introduced. Students in a civics lesson who now understand the concept of "liberty" might still struggle with answering the compelling question, "What is the line between liberty and responsibility?" This question introduces the concept of "responsibility" into the discussion and the notion of responsibility within the discipline of civics needs to be understood in order to formulate a response. Similarly, the example of a Dimension 2 compelling question for economics also introduces a new concept into the discussion. Students have to develop a clear definition of "prosperity" before they can answer, "Does more liberty mean more prosperity?"

DIMENSION 3:
EVALUATING SOURCES AND USING EVIDENCE

Dimension 3 begins with the recognition that evaluating sources and using evidence involves "a sophisticated set of skills" and goes on to note that "even the youngest children understand the need to give reasons for their ideas."[13] When teaching exceptional learners, we have to be careful not

to avoid "sophisticated skills" simply because of perceptions we may have about individual abilities. The challenge associated with this dimension is the content being evaluated. Exceptional learners may know the steps for evaluating a source or using evidence to support a claim, but the roadblock to this dimension occurs when students try to understand the sources of information gathered. Students might never evaluate the credibility of the source if their disability makes it challenging to read the information in the first place. Teachers need to plan for making the sources accessible for all learners. This might mean creating a word bank or lower reading level version of a historical document. Teachers will need to examine the accessibility of online sources of information and consider text recognition reading software to improve accessibility. Lessons need to ensure access to the content if we are to be effective in teaching the skills for analyzing and using the content.

DIMENSION 4:
COMMUNICATING CONCLUSIONS AND
TAKING INFORMED ACTION

A critical skill for all learners, the ability to communicate views and take informed action is of particular importance to exceptional learners. As noted in Chapter 5, students who develop self-determined skills and behaviors are more likely to be successful in areas such as employment, education, and independent living after graduating from high school. A big part of self-determination is the ability to communicate effectively and self-advocate. These skills are emphasized in Dimension 4, where students are expected to construct sound arguments using evidence from a variety of sources. The expectation is that students advocate for their beliefs in a variety of formats from print and social media to oral debate. Students are also able to critique the conclusions of others during this process. This dimension encourages students to move from drawing conclusions about an important topic to taking action on those conclusions to inform others. Not only are exceptional learners capable of demonstrating the skills outlined in Dimension 4, it could be argued that these skills are essential if exceptional learners are to be fully included as citizens.

The C3 Framework is a powerful planning tool for teachers wanting to challenge a diverse student population. One criticism noted in Chapter 1 is that research in social studies and special education is limited regarding how exceptional learners perform when participating in inquiry-based lessons. Most of the empirical research examines strategies to support rote memorization of facts rather than higher order thinking skills and application of the content.[14] However, as explained in Chapter 2, the general education setting is where most exceptional learners receive content instruction, and accountability for learning is the same as their peers without disabilities. The reality is that exceptional learners with high incidence disabilities such as learning disabilities have the cognitive ability to be successful and think critically. These students just need accommodations and effective teaching practices in place to provide access to the content. It is our belief that the C3 Framework will encourage teachers to consider ways to address diverse learning needs and it will create more research opportunities to examine the effectiveness of inquiry methods for exceptional learners. This will in turn create a more accessible and effective social studies classroom.

SAMPLE LESSON PLAN STRUCTURE

The lesson plans developed in Chapters 11, 12, and 13 consider aspects of UbD, SMARTER planning, UDL, differentiation, and the C3 Framework in their structure. Each plan begins by asking teachers to list compelling questions to guide design of the lesson and support review and assessment. Included in the lesson plan is a UDL chart (see Figure 6.2) that teachers use to check off approaches addressing representation, engagement, and expression of lesson content. In the sample lesson plan format (see Figure 6.3), there is also a column to consider accommodations and specific strategies for individual learners. This space also provides optional teacher or support personnel roles during the lesson if a co-teacher or paraprofessional is available.

Figure 6.2 Sample UDL Chart for Lesson Plans

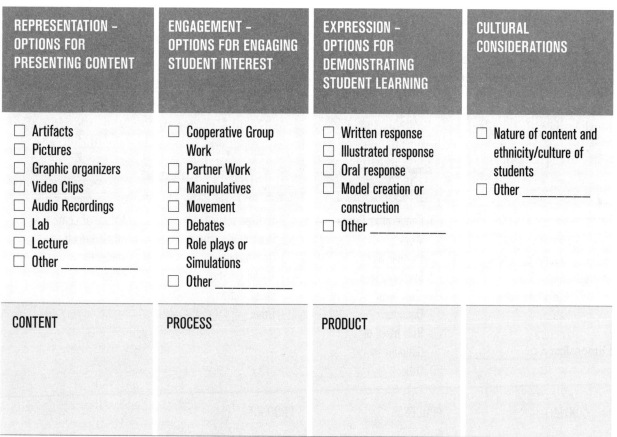

REPRESENTATION – OPTIONS FOR PRESENTING CONTENT	ENGAGEMENT – OPTIONS FOR ENGAGING STUDENT INTEREST	EXPRESSION – OPTIONS FOR DEMONSTRATING STUDENT LEARNING	CULTURAL CONSIDERATIONS
☐ Artifacts ☐ Pictures ☐ Graphic organizers ☐ Video Clips ☐ Audio Recordings ☐ Lab ☐ Lecture ☐ Other _____	☐ Cooperative Group Work ☐ Partner Work ☐ Manipulatives ☐ Movement ☐ Debates ☐ Role plays or Simulations ☐ Other _____	☐ Written response ☐ Illustrated response ☐ Oral response ☐ Model creation or construction ☐ Other _____	☐ Nature of content and ethnicity/culture of students ☐ Other _____
CONTENT	PROCESS	PRODUCT	

Source: Adapted from Glenna Gustafson and Tamara Wallace, "Radford University Lesson Planning Template with UDL," 2010.

Figure 6.3 Sample Lesson Plan Format

GENERAL INFORMATION

Lesson Title: Subject:

Unit: Grade:

Timeframe: Teacher(s):

STANDARDS
- (These include national, state, C3, and Common Core standards)

GOAL OR STANDARD ADDRESSED:
- (Derived from the standards)

OBJECTIVES: KEY KNOWLEDGE, SKILLS, OR ATTITUDES:
Obj. 1: Students will... *(These objectives are measurable and align to your learning plan and activities)*

COMPELLING QUESTIONS:
Q1: *(These guide your review/assessment and examine the bigger picture of a topic)*

SUPPORTING QUESTIONS:
Q1: *(These guide your review/assessment and help guide answers to compelling questions)*

UNIVERSAL DESIGN FOR LEARNING
(How does the lesson address these categories?)

REPRESENTATION – OPTIONS FOR PRESENTING CONTENT	ENGAGEMENT – OPTIONS FOR ENGAGING STUDENT INTEREST	EXPRESSION – OPTIONS FOR DEMONSTRATING STUDENT LEARNING	CULTURAL CONSIDERATIONS
☐ Artifacts ☐ Pictures ☐ Graphic organizers ☐ Video Clips ☐ Audio Recordings ☐ Lab ☐ Lecture ☐ Other _____	☐ Cooperative Group Work ☐ Partner Work ☐ Manipulatives ☐ Movement ☐ Debates ☐ Role plays or Simulations ☐ Other _____	☐ Written response ☐ Illustrated response ☐ Oral response ☐ Model creation or construction ☐ Other _____	☐ Nature of content and ethnicity/culture of students ☐ Other _____
CONTENT	PROCESS	PRODUCT	

Figure 6.3 Sample Lesson Plan Format (cont'd)

LEARNING PLAN:	ROLES, ACCOMMODATIONS, AND DIFFERENTIATION STRATEGIES
(Detailed description of how the lesson is taught with timeframe for activities)	*How will you meet the needs of diverse learners and remove barriers from participation?*
LESSON INTRODUCTION: *(How will you gain student interest and tap into prior knowledge?)*	*(Optional) What are the roles/ responsibilities of the co-teachers in the classroom?*
LESSON PROCEDURES (MAIN BODY OF THE LESSON): *(How will you provide access to the content and engage the learners? What research-based strategies will you use to support learning?)*	*(Optional) How are paraprofessionals and other support personnel included?*
LESSON CLOSURE AND ASSESSMENT: *(How will you review what was learned and assess understanding?)*	
MATERIALS/ EQUIPMENT/TECHNOLOGY: *(What's needed to teach the lesson?)*	

Source: Adapted from Darren Minarik, "Collaborative Lesson Plan Template," 2012.

Figure 6.3 provides a sample outline of the suggested lesson plan sections along with a brief explanation of what to include in each section. This lesson plan format is a good way to start the process of implementing inclusive design principles when planning a unit of study.

PLANNING A LESSON WITH A CO-TEACHER

Mapped out units of study and detailed lesson plans that follow the principles outlined in this chapter are a necessary part of an inclusive social studies classroom. It is not our expectation that developing accessible and inclusive units and lessons will happen immediately. One reality is that the special education teacher will step into the classroom with incomplete knowledge of the content, whereas the social studies teacher will already have a library of units and lessons ready to go and extensive experience with the content. Let's examine a scenario that a social studies teacher is likely to encounter when planning for an inclusive social studies classroom.

Imagine a scenario in which a ninth grade social studies teacher plans a lesson to introduce a unit on ancient river valley civilizations. The original lesson assumes a classroom without a co-teacher or any support personnel because co-teaching was not an option or requirement in the school. It was a successful plan that the teacher had used the previous year. However, this year, a single period has twenty-percent of exceptional learners in it. As a result, a special education teacher is assigned to co-teach the class. The lesson plans will need adjustments to include an additional licensed educator and possibly support personnel. This is where the collaborative process takes shape.

The social studies teacher begins by sharing the unit outline, textbook, Web links, and a series of lessons with the special education teacher. The special education teacher suggests introducing the unit to the class using a Unit Organizer and volunteers to rewrite the outline in this visual format (see Figure 6.4). In addition, the special education teacher volunteers to create visual organizers outlining each daily lesson (see Figure 6.5). The social studies teacher never considered the benefits of sharing the entire unit or a daily lesson to help students visualize what they just learned, what they are currently learning, and what they will learn next. Also, developing the organizers allows the special education teacher to begin learning the content. Both teachers discuss general accommodations or modifications needed to support IEP requirements for individual students. Finally, both teachers consider how to include any support personnel who are in the classroom so that these individuals can assist in structured, meaningful ways.

Figure 6.4 Mapping Out a Unit

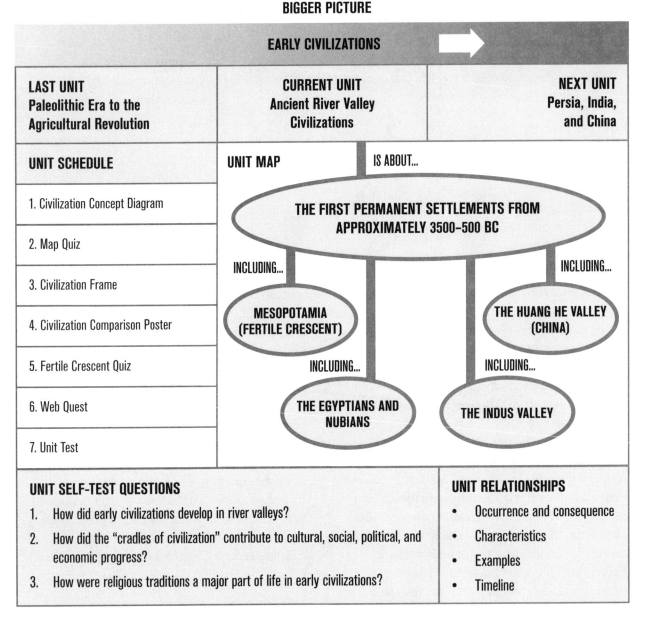

Source: Adapted from Keith Lenz, Janis A. Bulgren, Jean B. Schumaker, Donald D. Deshler, & Daniel A. Boudah, *The Content Enhancement Series: The Unit Organizer Routine* (Lawrence, KS: Edge Enterprises, 1994).

Figure 6.5 Advance Organizer for the Lesson

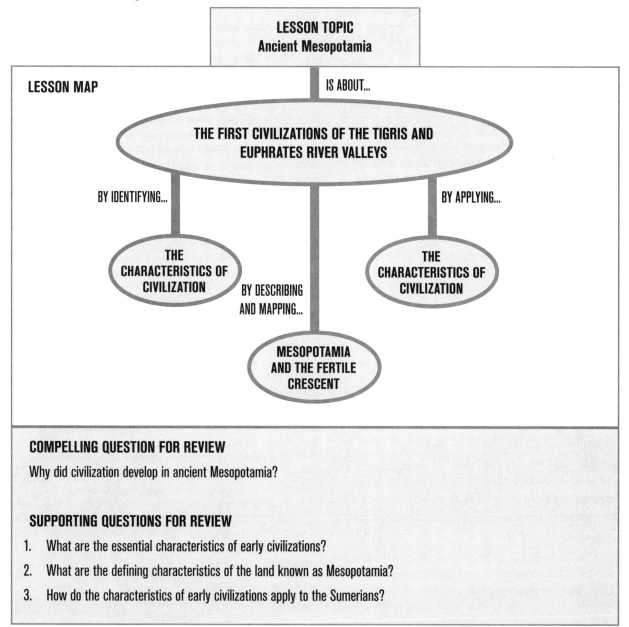

LESSON TOPIC
Ancient Mesopotamia

LESSON MAP

IS ABOUT...

THE FIRST CIVILIZATIONS OF THE TIGRIS AND
EUPHRATES RIVER VALLEYS

BY IDENTIFYING...

BY APPLYING...

THE
CHARACTERISTICS OF
CIVILIZATION

BY DESCRIBING
AND MAPPING...

THE
CHARACTERISTICS OF
CIVILIZATION

MESOPOTAMIA
AND THE FERTILE
CRESCENT

COMPELLING QUESTION FOR REVIEW

Why did civilization develop in ancient Mesopotamia?

SUPPORTING QUESTIONS FOR REVIEW

1. What are the essential characteristics of early civilizations?
2. What are the defining characteristics of the land known as Mesopotamia?
3. How do the characteristics of early civilizations apply to the Sumerians?

Source: Adapted from the Workshop Advance Organizer created by the American Civics Center, LLC, 2015.

There is no need to reinvent the wheel early in the co-teaching relationship. Instead, both teachers begin by enhancing existing lessons and providing extra support for struggling learners. Understanding how to enhance and differentiate content is the expertise that special educators initially bring to the process. This expertise allows the special education teacher to ease into learning the content while still participating in the lesson. In the original lesson the social studies teacher had the students define "civilization" using a text or online resource and then match characteristics listed in the definition to the Sumerians, an early civilization in Mesopotamia. They also did a map exercise where the students defined Mesopotamia and then labeled and colored geographic features of the region. Students were engaged throughout the lesson, using reading and map skills. However, the social studies teacher noted that students who struggled academically in the past had difficulty on tests remembering the definitions of early civilization and Mesopotamia. They also struggled when labeling a map of the region, confusing the locations of the Tigris and Euphrates rivers.

The special education teacher made two suggestions to enhance the lesson and differentiate for the diverse learning needs in the class. The first suggestion was to use an evidence-based graphic organizer to help break down the "always present" characteristics of the concept of "early civilization" for the students, instead of just having them define the term and provide examples. Next, the students would use a mnemonic device to help remember the geographic characteristics of Mesopotamia instead of a more traditional map exercise. Both activities would require a little extra time, but this time spent up front would save time later with less review or remediation needed.

The enhanced lesson described here is located in Chapter 13. It is an example of how the process of implementing universal design begins with one lesson at a time. It is a process that requires patience if it is to be successful. As a basic rule, design all new lessons and units with UDL in mind and commit to reevaluating a few existing units and corresponding lessons each year. It may take a few years of planning and organizing, but eventually all units and lessons will be fully accessible, creating a truly inclusive social studies classroom. 🔊

NOTES

1. Stephen Covey, 7 Habits of Highly Effective People: Powerful Lessons in Personal Change (New York: Free Press, 2004): 95.

2. Grant Wiggins and Jay McTighe, Understanding by Design. 2ND edition (Alexandria, VA: Association for Supervision and Curriculum Development, 2005); Keith B. Lenz, Janis A. Bulgren, Brenda R. Kissam, and Juliana Taymans, "Smarter Planning for Academic Diversity," In Teaching Content to All: Evidence-Based Inclusive Practices in Middle and Secondary Schools, edited by Keith B. Lenz, Donald D. Deshler and Brenda R. Kissam (Boston: Pearson, 2004): 47-77.

3. Tracey Hall, Nicole Strangman, and Anne Meyer, "Differentiated Instruction and Implications for Udl Implementation," National Center on Accessible Instructional Materials, 2003, http://aem.cast.org/learn/historyarchive/backgroundpapers/differentiated_instruction_udl.

4. Lenz, Deshler and Kissam, 2004: 62-73.

5. Michelle M. Herczog, "Implementing the C3 Framework: What is our Task as Social Studies Leaders?" National Council for the Social Studies, http://www.socialstudies.org/c3/implementingforleaders.

6. NCSS, Social Studies for the Next Generation: Purposes, Practices, and Implications of the College, Career, and Civic Life (C3) Framework for Social Studies State Standards, Bulletin No. 113 (Silver Spring, Md: NCSS, 2013): 15.

7. Arthur Lewis and David Smith, "Defining Higher Order Thinking," Theory Into Practice 32, no. 3: 131-137; Alice A. Wilder and Joanna P. Williams, "Students With Severe Learning Disabilities Can Learn Higher Order Comprehension Skills," Journal of Educational Psychology 93, no. 2 (2001): 268-278; Susan De La Paz, Petra Morales, and Philip M. Winston, "Source Interpretation: Teaching Students With and Without LD to Read and Write Historically," Journal of Learning Disabilities 40, no. 2 (2007): 134-144.

8. Janis A. Bulgren, Keith B. Lenz, Donald D. Deshler, and Jean B. Schumaker, The Content Enhancement Series: The Question Exploration Guide (Lawrence, KS: Edge Enterprises, 2001).

9. NCSS, 2013: 24.

10. NCSS, 2013: 25.

11. Janis Bulgren, Jean Schumaker, and Donald Deshler, The Content Enhancement Series: The Concept Mastery Routine (Lawrence, KS: Edge Enterprises, 1993).

12. NCSS, 2013: 30

13. NCSS, 2013: 53

14. Bouck, et al., "The Virtual History Museum," op. cit.

CHAPTER SEVEN

Instructional Strategy

Within the lesson plan, teachers must consider strategies and activities for introducing, delivering, and reviewing content. High stakes testing and teacher accountability has driven demand for teachers to use strategies that are extensively researched and considered best practice. Creating an engaging learning environment is important for all students and is key to creating an inclusive classroom setting.[1] This chapter provides a broad introductory list of strategies for teachers to consider when writing lesson plans that provide for differentiated instruction.[2] We begin with a list of simple strategies to engage students in the learning process when introducing, practicing, or reviewing content. We then examine more specific models to support differentiation of instruction. For additional information about instructional strategies and best practice in social studies and special education instruction, refer to the resources provided in Part III of this book.

WARM UP ACTIVITIES AND INTRODUCING NEW CONTENT

Agree/Disagree: Students are polled on an instructional topic they will learn more about and are asked to take a side. The responses are recorded in a graph or students create a human scale showing where they stand on the topic. Another kinesthetic way to do this activity is to form a circle. When the teacher reads a statement, students who agree step into the circle. Out of discomfort (i.e., shyness, anxiety) or embarrassment (i.e., being on the "wrong side"), some students may be reluctant to participate. It is important to encourage students to do so even if they are unsure about their convictions. For the reluctant student, the teacher may walk them into the circle or stand next to them when creating the human response scale. Such proximity may alleviate anxieties and facilitate participation.

Anticipation Guide: Students are given a series of statements about a topic and respond with yes/no responses. The purpose of this activity is to activate thinking about the topic. The teacher then refers back to the statements as the lesson proceeds.

Artifact Strategy: Teachers select an artifact (e.g. an object, picture, or primary source) and pose a problem or set of clues related to the artifact. Student responses are used to introduce the topic.

Beach Ball: The teacher presents an artifact or concept related to the lesson. Students are divided into small groups and each group gets an inflatable beach ball with prompts written on the ball in different locations. Some suggested prompts are: Identify it, Define it, Describe it, Tell us what it is not, Compare it, Connect it to real life, Tell its history, and Predict its future. Students toss the ball to each other and respond to the prompt closest to the hand they use for writing.

First TRIP: This reading strategy asks students to examine the **T**itle of a reading along with picture and subheading **R**elationships within the reading. The activity is introduced with a series of comprehension questions along with the passage to be read. The students determine the **I**ntent of the questions to help make **P**redictions.

Five plus One: The teacher presents information for five uninterrupted minutes and then the students reflect, respond to questions, and share what they learned. This can also be expanded into a "Ten plus Two" strategy. Both derivations of this strategy facilitate structured learning whereby the teacher can move through and complete a slice of content uninterrupted (which is often difficult to do) and the students can ponder, formulate, and ask thoughtful, relevant questions. Teachers often use this strategy to break up a lecture, or check for comprehension while watching a video.

Foldable: This tool is a 3-dimensional organizer that students create to recall essential lesson content. Examples of how to create foldables are easy to find through a keyword search of "foldables" on the Internet, but a good place to start is http://pinterest.com/learningahoy/foldables-for-the-classroom. After selecting an appropriate foldable, teachers need to demonstrate how to construct one. This step-by-step process assures that the foldable is partitioned (e.g., folded) properly. To better understand what content needs to be included in the foldable, teachers should have a completed foldable on display for students to access.

Forced Choice: Choices are placed around the classroom (no more than six) and students are asked to examine the choices and stand next to their choice. Students can then explain their choice and listen to others' choices. Sometimes this activity is also called "Corners," where choices are placed in the four corners of the room. For example, a second grade teacher completes a unit titled "The Physical Characteristics of South Carolina." She then asks students to decide which physical feature "defines or represents South Carolina best." Around the room she has placed the following responses (and a pictorial representation): The Beach, The Blue Ridge Mountains, The Three Rivers in Columbia. Students then find and explain their response.

PRACTICING TO LEARN CONTENT
Project-Based Learning (PBL): Students apply information they learn about a topic to a real-life or simulated situation. Students divide into groups and are given a project "anchor" or prompt to frame the project. This prompt may include a question to answer by the end of the project. Students choose research tasks where they collect and analyze data and then either write or present their findings. Students are also asked to continually reflect during the project.[3] This reflection allows students to bounce ideas off of each other as well as to monitor both individual and group progress. For example, students are asked to "Create an advertisement for a new type of book bag." In-group tasks are divided: one student draws the prototype; one student researches (via structured Web searches) the various models or types of book bags currently on the market; one student writes the advertisement "pitch," including the book bag's price, and a two-paragraph description of its features; and one student presents this "pitch" to the class. Teachers might incorporate other strategies such as WebQuests to organize the project.

Before, During, After: In this reading strategy, students are assigned a passage and explore the text <u>before</u> reading to activate prior knowledge, monitor comprehension <u>during</u> reading, and summarize <u>after</u> reading the passage.

Expert Jigsaw: This cooperative learning strategy is used when students are asked to locate information on their own and would benefit by working with others. Students are divided into groups with 3 to 6 members in each group. In small groups, students are asked to become "experts" about a particular topic. Then, students are divided into new groups with at least one expert represented from each original grouping. Each expert group member presents information gathered from his or her original group. Students use a graphic organizer to take notes in each group. For instance, heterogeneous student groups might be assigned to learn about characteristics of early river valley civilizations. The civilizations might include the Sumerians, Babylonians, Egyptians, and the Indus River Valley. On a graphic organizer, each group fills out characteristics related to geography, government, cultural innovations, and religious beliefs. Once the groups gather the required information, they separate and divide into new groups that contain at least one person knowledgeable in each civilization assigned. You now have at least one student in each group teaching the other students about their assigned civilization. As an accommodation for exceptional learners, the teacher should divide groups to ensure that any student who needs extra support is paired with another student "expert" to help teach the content to the new group.

Fishbowl Debate: Students are given a topic to debate and are divided into pro (support) and con (against) teams. The teams formulate their debate discussion points and choose two team members to lead the debate. Two chairs are placed in the center of the room facing two other chairs. The chosen debaters sit in the center chairs while the other students form a circle or "fishbowl" around the four students in the center. Students follow debate rules established by the teacher.

Group Investigation: The class is divided into groups with four or five team members in each group. From a list of topics, each team selects a topic to investigate. Team members gather information about the topic, prepare a report, and present their findings to the large group.

KWL: This strategy asks students to write down what they already **K**now about a topic. Then they write down what they **W**ant to know about a topic. Finally, after completing the lesson they write down what they **L**earned about the topic.

Think, Pair, Share: This cooperative learning strategy begins with students individually thinking about a topic or responding to a prompt from the teacher. Then, students pair up and discuss the topic with a partner. Finally, the pairs share their discussions with the class. Other variations include *Think, Pair, Square, Share*, which creates one more grouping of four and *Think, Ink, Pair, Share*, which adds a writing element to the activity.

Work Products: Students are placed in small cooperative learning groups and are given a particular task. Using content they just learned, student groups might create a brochure, bulletin board, mobile, poster, or other work product. Work products are then presented to class as a whole group or students do a gallery walk, visiting each work product put on display. These hands-on, often visually creative displays provide exceptional learners who struggle with reading and writing other (i.e., non text-based) ways to demonstrate their understanding(s) of the social studies content.

REVIEWING CONTENT

Alphabet Review: This activity has many variations, but the basic premise is that students need to select a word beginning with a letter of the alphabet related to the content they just learned. The teacher can assign letters or divide students into groups and make the review a competition to see how many letters in the alphabet each group can fill in with terms and phrases related to the topic.

CROWN: Use this acronym to reflect on the completed lesson. Students **C**ommunicate what they learned. Next, they **R**eact to other student responses. Third, they **O**ffer one sentence to sum up the lesson topic, Then they ask, "**W**here can I apply the information I learned?" Finally, they **N**ote how well the class did today.

Exit Slips: Students receive a slip of paper near the end of a lesson containing a sentence starter or fill-in-the-blank question addressing a key concept from the lesson. The teacher collects the slips to assess what students learned. Similarly, this method also works in the form of entrance slips that students turn in at the beginning of a lesson as a review of previous content.

Grab Bag: At the end of the lesson, each student pulls an object from a bag. They then must connect the object to what they just learned. This object association strategy requires students to use their creativity and is often quite entertaining!

Graffiti Recall: Each student receives a personal roll of adding machine paper. At the end of the unit (or on Friday) students spend 15 minutes drawing what they learned in the form of graffiti on the paper roll. Examples of graffiti include, pictures, symbols, letters, words, and phrases. Students repeat this process, filling up the paper roll throughout the year.

Luck of the Draw: Students put their names into a container. Names are then drawn and students are required to answer questions about the lesson. A popular variation of this lesson asks students to write a question down and place it in a container. A name is selected from one container and then the student selected draws a question from a separate container.

Shapes: Students draw a shape with corners on a piece of paper and are given a prompt. For instance, the teacher asks students to draw a triangle on a sheet of paper and write down three points they want to remember about today's lesson. Another option is to have students draw a square and write down four points that squared with their own beliefs. Then the teacher asks the students to draw a circle and has them write down any questions still circling around in their heads.

Three-Two-One: Ask students to write down three essential terms they have just learned, two ideas they want to learn more about, and one piece of information they mastered. You can vary the requirements for this review based on the content taught. For example, at the end of a unit on The Cold War, students can write three essential terms they learned (containment, proxy wars, geopolitical), two ideas they want to explore deeper (mutually assured destruction, *glasnost*) and one idea or event they mastered (The Berlin Blockade).

GRAPHIC ORGANIZERS

The primary goal of using graphic organizers in social studies classrooms is to present the material both visually and spatially.[4] Graphic organizers assist students in focusing attention on, organizing, and recalling important social studies concepts. As many social studies concepts and constructs can seem confusing and disconnected, using graphic organizers helps visually structure the content, making it accessible and easier to understand for all students.[5]

Exceptional learners benefit from graphic organizers that map out daily lessons, particular units of study, or the entire course.[6] Such organizers should be visual, textual, and read out loud to support the various learning needs in the classroom. Teachers can use graphic organizers to review the previous days content, set up expectations for the current lesson, or foreshadow what is to come in subsequent lessons.[7] As noted earlier, organizers are also fantastic planning tools for teachers. An example of an organizer that supports planning and learning is the Unit Organizer Routine developed by the University of Kansas Center for Research and Learning, though we argue that any organizer, if used appropriately, will assist students in inclusive settings to better understand social studies content. Figure 7.1 reflects a Unit Organizer premised on the Cold War. Teachers either construct the entire organizer with student assistance at the beginning of the unit, or students will complete sections of the organizer as they move through the unit.[8] Teachers always have a draft organizer to use as a guidance document during the co-construction process.

Figure 7.2 provides an example of a daily advance organizer. The lesson topic and content are provided. Supporting questions are included at the end utilizing UbD planning considerations. This visual aide allows students to know what they are about to do, what they just completed, and what will ultimately be assessed.

Using a Venn diagram can visually structure the social studies content. A Venn diagram is used to compare and contrast either known concepts or make analogies between known and new concepts yet to be studied. The Venn diagram provided in Figure 7.3 is premised on the acronym CIRCLES: **C**reate the Venn diagram, **I**ntroduce the concepts/events/people, **R**eveal the characteristics, **C**ompare the characteristics, **L**ocate the present or common characteristics, **E**xplore concept definitions, and **S**ummarize the diagram. Students follow these steps to compare and contrast the concepts "civil disobedience" and "peaceful resistance." Not all Venn diagrams need to be structured this way. Some may be more simple and spontaneous. However, we do recommend the inclusion of a summary statement for all Venn diagrams. Students should be able to interpret and summarize the diagram, either orally or through written expression. Regardless of the complexity, a Venn diagram is a quick, practical, and effective way of visually representing social studies content.

CLASSWIDE PEER TUTORING (CWPT)

One of the most recommended strategies for promoting the achievement of exceptional learners in social studies classrooms is through the use of Classwide Peer Tutoring (CWPT).[9] A simple method of using CWPT is through "content

Figure 7.1 The Unit Organizer

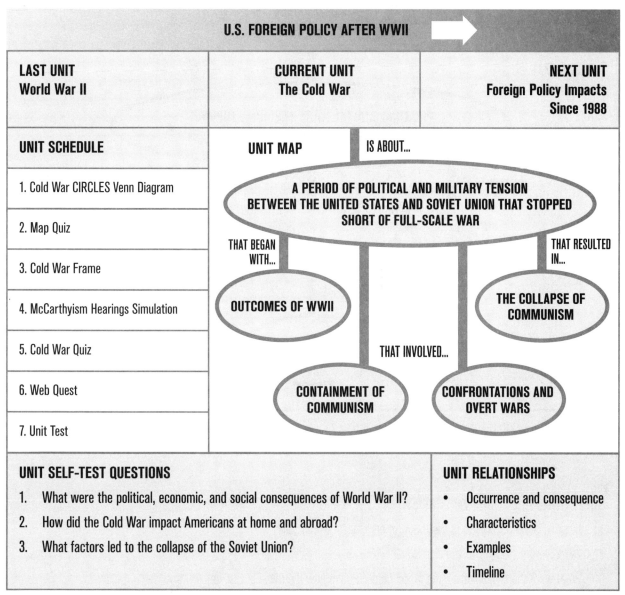

BIGGER PICTURE

U.S. FOREIGN POLICY AFTER WWII		

LAST UNIT World War II	CURRENT UNIT The Cold War	NEXT UNIT Foreign Policy Impacts Since 1988

UNIT SCHEDULE

1. Cold War CIRCLES Venn Diagram
2. Map Quiz
3. Cold War Frame
4. McCarthyism Hearings Simulation
5. Cold War Quiz
6. Web Quest
7. Unit Test

UNIT MAP   IS ABOUT...

A PERIOD OF POLITICAL AND MILITARY TENSION BETWEEN THE UNITED STATES AND SOVIET UNION THAT STOPPED SHORT OF FULL-SCALE WAR

THAT BEGAN WITH...

THAT RESULTED IN...

OUTCOMES OF WWII

THE COLLAPSE OF COMMUNISM

THAT INVOLVED...

CONTAINMENT OF COMMUNISM

CONFRONTATIONS AND OVERT WARS

UNIT SELF-TEST QUESTIONS

1. What were the political, economic, and social consequences of World War II?
2. How did the Cold War impact Americans at home and abroad?
3. What factors led to the collapse of the Soviet Union?

UNIT RELATIONSHIPS

- Occurrence and consequence
- Characteristics
- Examples
- Timeline

Source: Adapted from Keith Lenz, Janis A. Bulgren, Jean B. Schumaker, Donald D. Deshler, & Daniel A. Boudah, *The Content Enhancement Series: The Unit Organizer Routine* (Lawrence, KS: Edge Enterprises, 1994).

sheets." These sheets contain a list of important social studies-related questions and answers. For example, one question might be, "What region of the United States experienced significant population growth of African Americans after the Civil War?" We recommend no more than five questions per content sheet. Teachers can duplicate these sheets and place them in individual student folders. Students are then assigned tutoring pairs.

Though some models advocate for pairings based on disparate academic abilities (i.e. "strong" student paired with a "weaker" student), we advocate that students should have opportunities to work with all classmates irrespective of academic ability. Thus, CWPT groups are dynamic and change throughout the year. Paired partners serve as both tutor (asking questions) and tutee (answering questions).

Figure 7.2 Advance Organizer for a Daily Lesson

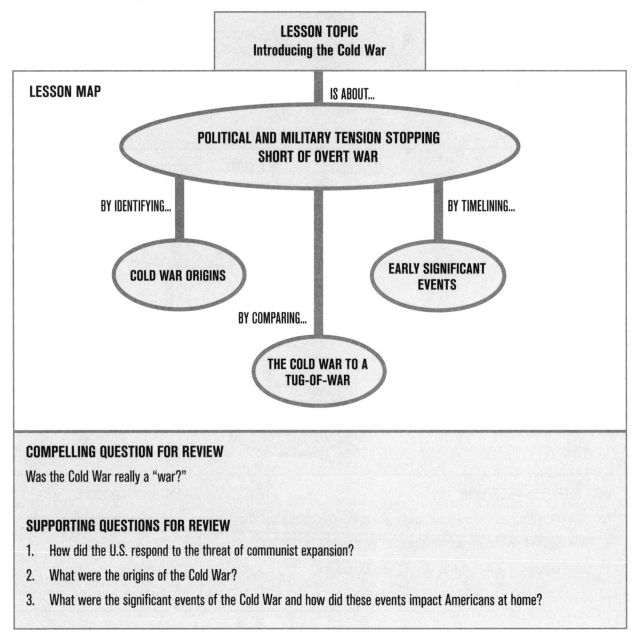

Source: Adapted from the Workshop Advance Organizer created by the American Civics Center, LLC

Next, provide and post directions similar to the following:

TUTORING PROCEDURES
- Pick up your own tutoring folder.
- Get with your partner.
- Take out your Content Sheets.

- Begin asking and answering the questions with your partner.
- Change roles with partner.
- Put all tutoring materials away.[10]

When students are tutoring, describe, post, and enforce the following rules:

Figure 7.3 CIRCLES Venn Diagram

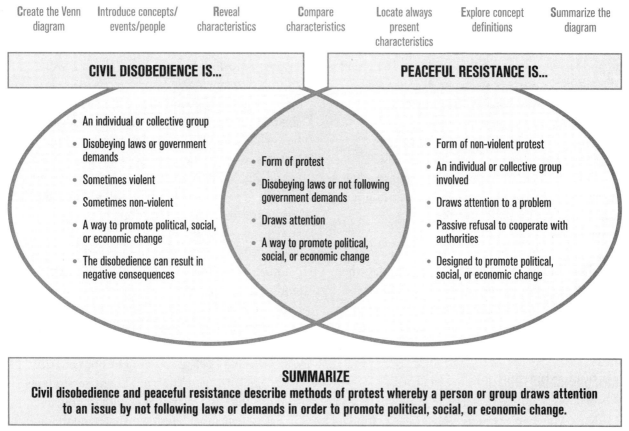

Create the Venn diagram | Introduce concepts/events/people | Reveal characteristics | Compare characteristics | Locate always present characteristics | Explore concept definitions | Summarize the diagram

CIVIL DISOBEDIENCE IS...

- An individual or collective group
- Disobeying laws or government demands
- Sometimes violent
- Sometimes non-violent
- A way to promote political, social, or economic change
- The disobedience can result in negative consequences

- Form of protest
- Disobeying laws or not following government demands
- Draws attention
- A way to promote political, social, or economic change

PEACEFUL RESISTANCE IS...

- Form of non-violent protest
- An individual or collective group involved
- Draws attention to a problem
- Passive refusal to cooperate with authorities
- Designed to promote political, social, or economic change

SUMMARIZE
Civil disobedience and peaceful resistance describe methods of protest whereby a person or group draws attention to an issue by not following laws or demands in order to promote political, social, or economic change.

Source: Adapted from the CIRCLES Venn Diagram created by the American Civics Center, LLC.

RULES FOR PEER TUTORING

- Talk in a quiet voice.
- Cooperate with your partner.
- Do your best.
- Identify and correct any mistakes.[11]

By using the content sheets, all students are receiving the same materials and learning via a similar instructional strategy. CWPT sessions can be implemented several times a week, for 20 to 30 minutes per session. CWPT particularly allows exceptional learners to spend needed time on the more difficult content and move more quickly through content that comes easier to them. Students proceed through the content sheets until each is mastered, assuring individualized practice. When using CWPT, middle school exceptional learners increased their achievement on unit tests from 78%

to 85%. Research in 12 middle school American history classrooms revealed that, when supported by CWPT, exceptional learners scored 20% higher on unit tests than students without disabilities whose instruction was not premised on CWPT.[12]

ROLE PLAYING

As previously stated, while some exceptional learners struggle to make and sustain social connections, others thrive. Many students who struggle with reading and writing excel in dramatic learning.[13] Using drama in the social studies classroom is an excellent way to engage students in experiencing the emotional and physical "life" of social studies.[14] Teachers can assign students group and/or individual roles that allow both collaborative and independent learning. We provide some examples below:

Students explore President Truman's decision to drop the Atomic Bomb on Hiroshima. The teacher divides the class into three groups: those who support Truman's decision, those who oppose it, and Japanese survivors of the attack. To present their "side," students conduct mock interviews, write newspaper editorials, draw political cartoons, or create support/protest placards.

Students act out life in early colonial times, including occupations, expectations, and family life. As an interesting twist, have female students portray male colonists; the male students portray life as a female colonist.

For those students who prefer not to role-play, there are additional complimentary responsibilities (i.e. stage manager, wardrobe coordinator, script writer and/or editor, visual effects supervisor) that allow students to participate in the dramatic process.

MNEMONIC INSTRUCTION

A mnemonic device is designed to improve memory. Mnemonic strategies have been helpful for exceptional learners as they can minimize the effect of general learning weaknesses (i.e., comprehension strategy production, verbal fluency) while enhancing their relative strengths (i.e., particularly visual memory.)[15] There are many mnemonic strategies to support content recall. We have provided a few familiar and successful strategies to consider in this chapter.

The keyword method works by creating similar-sounding proxies (keywords) for unfamiliar words/information. Students then take this keyword and associate it with the information to be recalled. For example, you want your students to remember that an *anarchist* is someone who is essentially "against all forms of government."[16] You first initiate a keyword for "anarchy." Consider using the word "ants," because it sounds like the first part of anarchist and can easily be pictured, both cognitively (in the students head) and visually (through a visual aide). You would then show students a picture of the keyword (ants) toppling government buildings (i.e. the Capitol, the Supreme

Court). When asked for the meaning of anarchist, then, students are taught to think of the keyword, *ants*, think of the picture with the ants toppling government buildings, and retrieve the answer, "against all forms of government." The keyword approach to mnemonic association is a simple yet effective aide in making often difficult and abstract social studies concepts accessible and relevant. In fact, when using the keyword strategy, exceptional learners were able to recall twice as many American presidents. When asked to recall states and their capitals, mnemonically taught students remembered 57% more content than traditionally taught students.[17]

Another method to help students learn social studies content is the use of first-letter acronyms and sentences. For example, students may want to remember the Great Lakes as part of a geography lesson. The acronym HOMES helps them recall that the Great Lakes are **H**uron, **O**ntario, **M**ichigan, **E**rie, and **S**uperior. Likewise, students studying the Civil War might use the acronym SCAR to remember Sherman's march on the cities of **S**avannah, **C**harleston, **A**tlanta, and **R**aleigh. Students also form sentences to help remember important facts. The first-letter sentence, "**F**ine **p**eople **c**heer **f**or **p**eace," is a way to remember the five pillars of Islam: faith, prayer, charity, fasting, and pilgrimage. Similarly, students might recite sentences or lyrics that rhyme to help recall important facts like, "In 1492, Columbus sailed the ocean blue." Encourage students to design their own mnemonic strategies, making this method even more relevant to the individual student.

The first step in using mnemonic strategies is to identify what is the most important content your students need to know. Often, this content is difficult for your students to recall (remember) and to understand (contextualize). Begin by creating a series of keyword visual aide elaborations that assist your students, not just simply with factual recall, but with contextual understanding as well. The visual aids you use do not have to be perfect representations, yet they do need to be simple and understandable.

When using mnemonics in instruction, you need to be extremely explicit about the content to be remembered, the strategy used for retrieving the information, and the precise steps students will take to increase both recall and understanding. Below is an example of a mnemonic strategy for teaching about the "Zimmerman note."

The Zimmerman note was an important reason that the U.S. became involved in World War I. Arthur Zimmerman was the German foreign secretary who sent a coded note to Mexico in 1917 asking Mexico to join Germany in fighting against the United States if the U.S. should enter the war on the side of the Allied Powers. In return, Germany promised to return former Mexican territory in Texas, Arizona, and New Mexico. This note was intercepted and decoded, causing public outrage in the U.S. This incident contributed to the U.S. declaration of war against Germany and its allies.

> To help you remember the Zimmerman note and what it was, remember the keyword for Zimmerman, *swimmer*. What is the keyword for Zimmerman? [students respond]. Good, swimmer. Now, [show picture or slide] remember this picture of a *swimmer* swimming from Germany to Mexico, carrying a *coded note* that reads: "To Mexico: Join us, Germany." Remember this picture of what? [students respond]. Good, a *swimmer* with a *coded note*. So when I ask you about the Zimmerman note, what do you answer? [students respond]. Good, a coded note from Germany to Mexico.[18]

The dialogue between students and teachers can strengthen students' knowledge and understanding of the event, as well as reinforcing the particular steps students take when associating a name with a particular event.

BIG IDEAS

Big ideas are questions or generalizations that anchor the content, making the "smaller bits of information" easier to understand.[19] Big ideas help to organize the content by making meaningful connections between the content and the lives of your students.[20] Ultimately, big ideas provide all students with opportunities to understand the social studies content in the most efficient, appropriate, and accessible way.[21]

How do teachers go about designing instruction based upon big ideas? Begin with a content-based question or topic. What do you want your students to know about this question or topic? What do you want your students to "do" with their new-found understandings? What resources will you need? Lastly, how will you know if your students understand the topic being presented? Such topics can be explored throughout the year, by units, or through individual lessons.[22] Though there are a handful of curricular models on how best to create, organize, and use big ideas to teach social studies to all students, we will focus on just two: The Inside-Out Model, and the Outside-In Model.

Inside-Out Model: A simple way to present your social studies content is through the Inside-Out Model. Here, the big idea—your anchoring concept— is presented first. From this starting point, facts and/or insights are generated that support (i.e. contextualize) your big idea. You start "in the middle" (with your big idea) and move outward. Ultimately, your big idea will be surrounded by "smaller bits of information." Figure 7.4 provides an example using *Big Cities: Is Bigger Better?"* as the anchoring or big idea.

Figure 7.4 Inside-Out Model

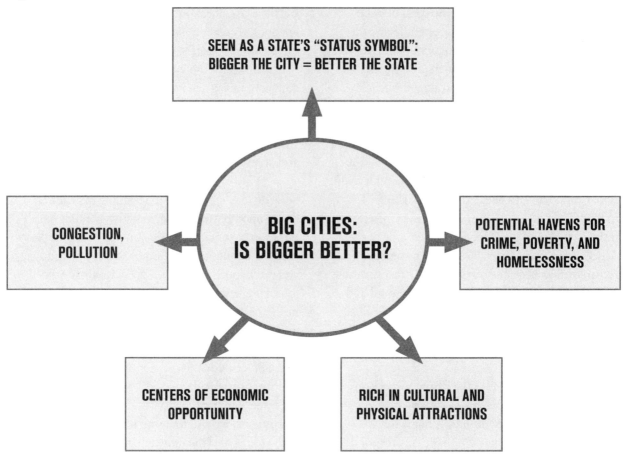

Outside-In Model: This model is the opposite of the Inside-Out Model in which information is generated first that, when combined, forms the big idea. To illustrate our big idea centered on maps, teachers would initially ask students what they know about maps. Students will then provide small, individualized bits of information that, ultimately, lead to the construction of a big idea. Figure 7.5 provides an example of this model.

Both the Outside-In and the Inside-Out models are simple, efficient ways of generating and organizing social studies concepts, ultimately making such information accessible for all students. Though social studies is most often presented as a series of facts and faces, "Knowing a bunch of facts alone does not guarantee that students will be able to think about anything in particular. Facts need to be connected to make sense, and those connections can emerge through the construction of big ideas."[23]

SELF-REGULATED STRATEGY DEVELOPMENT

An approach commonly used to help exceptional learners implement specific strategies is self-regulated strategy development (SRSD).[24] SRSD is a process that teaches students to self-regulate their own learning through the implementation of specific learning strategies that address challenges faced as exceptional learners. First, students learn how to use a specific strategy through direct teacher modeling. Then the teacher gradually releases control of the strategy, allowing the students to model the strategy in small groups before finally using the strategy independently. The teacher provides occasional constructive feedback and positive reinforcement to support the student's move toward independence with the strategy.[25] For example, the teacher might model a specific note-taking strategy to help students organize essential information. After some direct modeling of the note-taking steps, the teacher would then allow students to implement the strategy

Figure 7.5 Outside-In Model

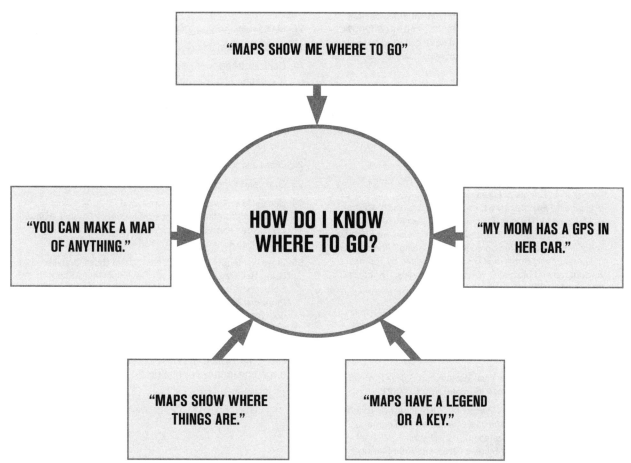

in small groups with occasional teacher feedback. Eventually, students would begin using the strategy independently without prompts from the teacher. The SRSD approach is commonly used to help students become more independent in reading, writing, and comprehension.[26]

It is important to consider a variety of instructional strategies to support the diverse learning needs of the classroom. Teachers should familiarize themselves with effective evidence-based strategies proven to support content-area learning. The introductory list of strategies in this chapter are a good first step for social studies educators who want to create a more inclusive classroom that reaches the needs of exceptional learners.

NOTES

1. Diane Casale-Giannola and Linda Schwartz Green, *41 Active Learning Strategies for the Inclusive Classroom, Grades 6-12* (Thousand Oaks, CA: Corwin, 2012).

2. *Ibid*; Paula Kluth and Sheila Danaher, *From Tutor Scripts to Talking Sticks: 100 Ways to Differentiate Instruction in K-12 Inclusive Classrooms* (Baltimore, MD: Brookes, 2010).

3. William N. Bender, *Differentiating Instruction for Students with Learning Disabilities: New Best Practices for General and Special Educators*, 3RD edition (Thousand Oaks, CA: Corwin, 2012): 51.

4. James A. Duplass, *Teaching Elementary Social Studies: Strategies, Standards, and Internet Resources*, 2ND edition (Boston, MA: Houghton Mifflin, 2008); Nancy Gallavan and Ellen Kottler, "Eight Types of Graphic Organizers for Empowering Social Studies Students and Teachers," *Social Studies* 93, no. 3 (2007): 117-123; James W. Stockard, *Methods and Resources for Elementary and Middle-School Social Studies*, (Long Grove, IL: Waveland, 2001).

5. James McLeskey, Michael S. Rosenberg, and David L. Westling, *Inclusion: Effective Practices for All Students*, 2ND edition (Boston, MA: Pearson, 2010).

6. Janis Bulgren, Donald D. Deshler, and Keith B. Lenz, "Engaging Adolescents with LD in Higher Order Thinking about History Concepts Using Integrated Content Enhancement Routines," *Journal of Learning Disabilities* 40, no. 2 (2007): 121-133; Marcee M. Steele, "Teaching Social Studies to High School Students with Learning Problems," *Social Studies* 98, no. 2 (Spring, 2007): 59-63.

7. Darren W. Minarik and David Hicks, "Toward an Inclusive Social Studies Classroom," in *Practical Strategies for Teaching K-12 Social Studies in Inclusive Classrooms,* edited by Timothy Lintner and Windy Schweder (Charlotte, NC: Information Age, 2011): 47-56.

8. *Ibid.*

9. Charles Greenwood, Joseph Delquadri, and R. Vance Hall, "Longitudinal Effects of Classwide Peer Tutoring," *Journal of Educational Psychology* 81, no. 3 (1989): 371-383; Margot A. Mastropieri, Thomas E. Scruggs, and Lisa Marshak, "Training Teachers, Parents, and Peers to Implement Effective Teaching Strategies for Content Area Learning," in *Advances in Learning and Behavioral Disabilities*, edited by Thomas E. Scruggs and Margot A. Mastropieri (Bingley, UK: Emerald, 2008): 311-329.

10. Mastropieri, Scruggs, and Marshak, *Training Teachers, Parents, and Peers, op. cit.*

11. *Ibid.*

12. *Ibid.*

13. Michael Rohd, "Hope is Vital: Theatre that Solves Problems," *Teaching Theatre* 10, no. 4 (Summer, 1999): 19-21.

14. J. Michael Peterson and Mishael M. Hittie, *Inclusive Teaching: The Journey Towards Effective Schools for All Learners*, 2ND edition (Boston, MA: Pearson, 2010); Dianna A. Michael, "Revitalizing your Social Studies Class with Role-Playing," ERIC Document 237 372, 1983.

15. Mastropieri and Scruggs, 2010.

16. Fontana, Mastropieri, and Scruggs, 2007.

17. Mastropieri, Scruggs, Bakken, Brigham, 1992.

18. Scruggs and Mastropieri, 2011: 41.

19. Duplass, 2008; McLeskey, Rosenberg, and Westling, 2010; Mastropieri and Scruggs, 2010.

20. Brophy, Alleman, and Knighton, 2009.

21. Edwin Ellis, Theresa Farmer, and Jane Newman, "Big Ideas About Teaching Big Ideas," *TEACHING Exceptional Children* 38, no. 1 (2005): 34-40.

22. Grant and Vansledright, 2006.

23. Grant and Vansledright, 2006: 112.

24. Susan De La Paz, Petra Morales, and Philip M. Winston, "Source Interpretation: Teaching Students With and Without LD to Read and Write Historically," *Journal of Learning Disabilities* 40, no. 2 (2007): 134-44.

25. Tanya Santangelo, Karen R. Harris, and Steve Graham, "Using Self-Regulated Strategy Development to Support Students Who Have 'Trubol Giting Thangs Into Werds.'" *Remedial & Special Education* 29, no. 2 (2008): 78-89. doi:10.1177/0741932507311636.

26. Linda H. Mason, Karen R. Harris, and Steve Graham. "Self-Regulated Strategy Development for Students With Writing Difficulties." *Theory Into Practice* 50, no. 1 (2011): 20-27. doi:10.1080/00405841.2011.534922.

CHAPTER EIGHT

Assessing Exceptional Learners in the Social Studies Classroom

As outlined in the Individuals with Disabilities Education Improvement Act (IDEIA 2004), educators must assess exceptional learners in the general education classroom and this assessment must be ongoing. Instructional practices must be aligned to meet the learning needs of such students. To do so, teachers need to maximize and diversify both instruction and assessment.

There are essentially two general categories or philosophies of assessment: traditional assessment and what has been termed authentic or natural assessment. Traditional assessments are what we would commonly call "tests," and are typically paper-and-pencil driven. Authentic or natural assessments are more performance-based and are premised on tasks that are relevant and real. Though varying in scope, substance, and desired outcome, both camps, if you will, have perceptual and practical roots in social studies assessment.

TRADITIONAL ASSESSMENT

The dominant means of assessing social studies at all levels of instruction is the paper-and-pencil exam.[1] Social studies exams typically consist of select response (e.g. true-false, multiple-choice, or matching questions) and constructed response (e.g. short response or essay) questions; seldom do such tests include visual (e.g. maps, paintings, photographs) representations. Advocates of traditional assessment approaches argue that these measurement tools provide objective data, require all students to perform the same task under the same conditions, and make the results easier to understand. Such measurements are easy to construct and, subsequently, easy to administer and score. And in this era of high stakes accountability, such assessments mirror the type of (standardized) exam students will most likely take at the end of the year.

Though convenient and, in some cases essential, more often than not, traditional assessment tools measure memorization and factual recall. Hence, teachers have limited information from which to gauge student comprehension. Rather than guiding instructional decisions, traditional assessments flatly become "another assignment that will become a grade in the grade book."[2]

If using traditional pen-and-paper assessment in the social studies classroom, we recommend making the following modifications to the test format. Such modifications are particularly beneficial to exceptional learners:

- Prepare typewritten or online tests rather than handwritten tests.

- Space test questions out (double space between questions) to reduce interference and confusion.

- Provide ample space for students to respond to open-ended questions.

- Give more tests with fewer questions, rather than fewer, longer tests.

- Define unfamiliar words if they are *not* being tested.

- For true-false questions, have students write out *true* and *false*. You can also have students correct a statement that is false.

- For multiple-choice tests, reduce the number of response options (e.g. from five to four). Teach students how to locate and reduce one or more incorrect multiple-choice responses on their own. We do not recommend reducing response options below four, particularly if the students will see similar test questions on an end-of-year high stakes test. Self-regulated test taking strategies will be of greater long-term value than simply reducing answer choices on tests.

- For matching items, consider using an equal number of response items to questions asked and limiting the number of required matches to eight or fewer. We acknowledge that providing an equal number of response items to questions may lead to guessing. As many high stakes tests contain matching questions, exposing students to this assessment type facilitates question-type familiarity.

- For short or long essays, provide students with specific structural guidance: what should be included in the essay, how long it should be, and how it should be organized. Provide a graphic organizer to help students structure the essay before they begin writing. Have students dictate their responses to a special education teacher or paraprofessional. Encourage students to not only demonstrate knowledge of the content, but also to explain how they could use this knowledge as informed citizens. Teachers might shy away from this more rigorous form of assessment for exceptional learners, but organizational accommodations can create opportunities for all students to demonstrate both knowledge and application of the content.

AUTHENTIC ASSESSMENT

Though traditional assessments do provide teachers with information regarding student comprehension, such assessments are relatively poor indicators of student expertise. Paper-and-pencil exams often provide a singular dimension of student understanding. Using authentic performance-based assessments in the social studies classroom shifts the focus from direct recall to student demonstration of content comprehension.[3] Students construct their own responses rather than selecting correct responses from a test sheet. Teachers can observe student performance on real-life, authentic tasks. Authentic assessment reveals patterns in students' thinking, which would not be evidenced nor easily encouraged via a traditional paper-and-pencil exam. Though there are several ways that students can demonstrate their understanding of the social studies content (e. g. plays, illustrations, oral

presentations), portfolio-based assessment is a tool social studies teachers can use for all students.

Portfolio Assessments: A portfolio is essentially a collection of student work over time and can be used to demonstrate student skills and understandings. A portfolio is more than a mere collection of student papers stored in a file folder: it is a record of students' progress in and processes of learning. The portfolio reflects how a student thinks, questions, interprets, analyzes, prioritizes and creates. It also offers a window into how students interact— intellectually, emotionally and socially—with others.[4] If maintained with fidelity, a portfolio provides a developmental profile of each student as evidenced over the course of a school year.

It is important to provide students choice as to what to include in their portfolio. Though the teacher may require specific artifacts (e.g. standardized exam results, scoring rubrics, various writing samples), the students self-select what they think best represents their understanding of the learning objectives. This way, students evaluate their own work and keep track of their own progress. The ability to self-select and self-monitor spurs both confidence and creativity in students who may heretofore have struggled within these domains.

Below are some suggestions for what a social studies portfolio may contain:

- Daily work samples; ordinary papers that are part of the daily routine.

- A sample of student writing in multiple forms and across multiple contexts.

- Rough drafts or works in progress.

- Finished products, final drafts, and graded papers or projects.

- Evidence of student collaboration (e.g. a think-pair-write-share activity).

- Reflections, such as "I learned" statements.

- Pictures of major products or displays.

- Video and audio recordings of students explaining and reflecting on their work.

- Teacher comments and feedback.

- Creative thoughts, ideas, insights, and personal-growth reflection.[5]

Though portfolio-based assessment provides an opportunity for all students to demonstrate their growth over the course of a year, there are limitations. Maintaining a portfolio takes time. If done correctly, students should be adding to their portfolio at least weekly. Such time allotment must be a systemic and consistent part of the classroom routine. Portfolios are time consuming to construct, organize, and assess. However, they are powerful and practical alternatives to the traditional assessment strategies most often found in the social studies classroom.

Some students may need assistance with artifact selection and portfolio organization. "What should I put in it and how should it look?" As organization is often a concern for exceptional learners, at the beginning of the school year, teachers need to provide explicit verbal and written directions concerning portfolio construction. Such directions should include how to "set-up" or construct the portfolio (i.e., by content area and/or artifact type, etc.) as well as what artifacts to include (i.e., graded papers, rough drafts, and/or non-text artifacts such as maps and/or diagrams, etc.). It is also important to provide students with a written outline of expected portfolio construction and content to serve as a reference throughout the year. Collaboration with special education teachers and paraprofessionals is also important to ensure the proper collection of artifacts. Many special education teachers are already skilled in selecting and collecting artifacts as a way to demonstrate how students meet their IEP goals.

Performance Assessments: We often think of student performances as paper-made top hats, hastily scribbled protest placards, and forgotten lines to important speeches. Performance assessments are those in which students are required to perform a specific skill, like writing a paragraph,

creating a map, or diagramming a cause and effect relationship. Similar to portfolios—but evidenced through different means—performance assessments reveal the depth of student knowledge by allowing them to demonstrate this knowledge in a personal, creative, and relevant way. Below is a brief list of ways students can "perform" their understanding(s) of the social studies content en lieu of traditional writing assignments:

- Presentations (oral, role-playing, skits).

- Projects or demonstrations (displays, models).

- Visual Arts (paintings, drawings, cartoons, photographs).

- Music (singing, playing, composing).

- Dance (ritual or interpretive).

- Technology.[6]

CURRICULUM-BASED MEASUREMENT

As previously noted, teachers can evaluate students' progress via both traditional and authentic assessments. Though both types of assessment vary in design and delivery they ultimately, amongst other outcomes, serve to evaluate student achievement and are used to assign grades. What traditional and authentic assessments do not allow for is the reflection on and subsequent revision of instruction, particularly for struggling students.

At one end of the assessment spectrum are year-end achievement tests. Such tests provide a summative snapshot of student progress for the year. Unfortunately, the test results are often not received for weeks after administration, giving teachers little time (or specific diagnostic information) to make instructional changes to assist those students who scored poorly.

At the other end of the assessment spectrum is progress monitoring, which consists of frequently administered tests that continually ascertain student performance on certain skills. Progress monitoring is designed to estimate and chart the rate of improvement for each student, to identify struggling students and to evaluate instructional effectiveness.

With particular relevance to exceptional learners, progress monitoring upholds the major tenets of IDEIA 2004 by aligning the goals and objectives stated in a student's IEP with progress in the general education classroom.[7] A particular type of progress monitoring that is responsive to the learning needs of all students is called curriculum-based assessment.

Curriculum-based measurement (CBM) allows teachers to systemically monitor student progress throughout the year and, premised on such progress, make appropriate instructional changes when necessary. There are six basic steps to CBM:

STEP 1: CREATING THE PROBES (I.E. TESTS)

The probes are based on the yearly curricular goals and objectives. Each probe includes sample questions/items from every skill taught throughout the academic year. As the year progresses, each probe will include previously taught material. This allows teachers to monitor the retention of these previously taught skills.

At the beginning of the year students will most likely perform poorly on the initial probes as they have learned only a few requisite skills. Remember—the probes include skills to be taught throughout the course of the entire year. It is important for teachers to explain the nature of CBM and to assure students that, as the year progresses and they learn more skills, their performance will increase.

STEP 2: ADMINISTER AND SCORE THE PROBE

Probes can be administered weekly, bi-weekly, or monthly. The same probe is used throughout the year. Probes are administered and scored in the same way to assure fidelity. Though administering and scoring probes is admittedly time consuming, the insights they reveal facilitate nimble, responsive instructional differentiation.

STEP 3: GRAPH THE RESULTS

After the probes have been scored, teachers graph individual student results. The graphs may reflect the number of correct answers or be partitioned into skill sets (e.g. the use of cardinal directions; the identification of a body of water on a map). Graphs need to be accessible and jargon free as the teacher will ultimately share his/her graphs with school personnel and parents. By referencing a student's graph, teachers can quickly note student progress and design corresponding instructional changes when warranted.

STEP 4: SET GOALS

Within the CBM model, teachers indicate the level of expected growth students will demonstrate by the end of school year as well as incremental periods of time (e.g. weekly or monthly goals). Student progress (content/skill attainment) is based on these individual goals, not on norm-referenced criterion. Teachers examine student graphs to chart progress towards goal attainment. If select students are not meeting goal expectations, the teacher makes changes to his/her instructional practice(s).

STEP 5: MAKE INSTRUCTIONAL DECISIONS

The cornerstone to CBM is the ability of teachers to closely and systemically monitor student progress toward skill attainment and make quick and responsive changes to instructional strategies or educational interventions. This instructional flexibility is particularly beneficial for exceptional learners as CBM identifies the particular skills that specific students struggle with. CBM also enables teachers to identify those students who may not be making sufficient progress in the general education classroom and who may benefit from special education services.

STEP 6: COMMUNICATE STUDENT PROGRESS

As briefly mentioned in Step 3, CBM allows student information—in the form of skills-based progress charting—to be easily shared with school personnel and parents. Information can also be shared with the students so they can monitor their own progress.[8] Below is an example of how to use CBM within the context of social studies.

The second grade state social studies curriculum requires that teachers cover particular geographic content throughout the course of the school year (e.g. map location of landforms and bodies of water; use a map legend and cardinal directions; identify natural resources in the local community; distinguish between rural, suburban and urban; and identify on a map the local community, state, nation, and continent). At the beginning of the school year, all students are given probes (i.e., tests) that include sample questions from each content area noted above. The probes may include simple definitions, a blank map, photographs, even a short video supported by content questions. At preset intervals (e.g. weekly, bi-weekly, monthly), the probes are administered and scored. Student progress in each content area is noted and charted. From here, short-term (weekly, unit, etc.) and long-term (by year's end) goals are set for each student for each content (or skill) area. Struggling students are quickly identified and instructional decisions are altered due to the probe results. The CBM information is shared with school personnel, parents, and the students in a collaborative effort to monitor areas of strength and weakness and to adjust instruction accordingly.

We would like to provide a word of caution when assessing the social studies competencies of exceptional learners. As previously mentioned, traditional (i.e., pen-and-paper) assessments are most commonly found in social studies classrooms. Couple this with the fact that the vast majority of exceptional learners struggle with reading and writing.[9] Herein lies the disconnect between assessment strategies used and the abilities of our students. We most often ask our students to read and write knowing that a number of them will invariably struggle. Within such increasingly diverse classrooms, providing authentic assessment opportunities enables all students to demonstrate their understanding(s) of the social studies content.

NOTES

1. Kathy Checkley, *Priorities in Practice: The Essentials of Social Studies, Grades K-8: Effective Curriculum, Instruction, and Assessment* (Alexandria, VA: Association for Supervision and Curriculum Development, 2008).

2. Pokey Stanford and Stacy Reeves, "Assessment That Drives Instruction," *TEACHING Exceptional Children* 37 (2005): 18.

3. Stephen N. Elliott and Lynn S. Fuchs, "The Utility of Curriculum-Based Measurement and Performance Assessment as Alternatives to Traditional Intelligence and Achievement Tests," *School Psychology Review*, 26 (1997): 224-33.

4. Diane Pedrotty Bryant, Deborah Deutsch Smith, and Brian R. Bryant, *Teaching Students with Special Needs in Inclusive Classrooms* (Boston, MA: Pearson, 2008); James W. Stockard, Jr., *Methods and Resources for Elementary and Middle-School Social Studies* (Long Grove, IL: Waveland Press, 2001).

5. Arthur K. Ellis, *Teaching and Learning Elementary Social Studies*, 9TH edition (Boston, MA: Pearson, 2010).

6. Though middle/secondary students are fairly comfortable with PowerPoint, there are other presentation formats that students can use: Prezi (http://www.prezi.com) uses a zoom-in, zoom-out format to create centers or "wheels" of focus. Pictures and video can easily be embedded. Glogster (http://www.glogster.com) is an electronic poster-board program that allows students to create their own single- or tri-fold visual display; The Museum Box (http://www.museumbox.e2bn.org) lets students create their own museum display including text, images, sound, and video; Virtual History Museum (http://www.vhm.msu.edu/site/default.php) is designed specifically for exceptional learners and, similar to the Museum Box, allows students to create a multi-layered virtual display of their historical understandings.

7. Victor Nolet and Margaret J. McLaughlin, *Accessing the General Education Curriculum: Including Students with Disabilities in Standards-Based Reform* (Thousand Oaks: CA: Corwin Press, 2000).

8. For more information about Curriculum Based Instruction, as well as other topics pertinent to addressing the learning needs of exceptional learners, see http://www.iris.peabody.vanderbilt.edu.

9. Janet W. Lerner and Beverley Johns, *Learning Disabilities and Related Mild Disabilities*, 12TH edition (Belmont, CA: Wadsworth, 2012).

CHAPTER NINE

Technology to Assist Exceptional Learners

The use of technology has the potential to create rich and relevant learning experiences for all students.[1] Appropriate use of technology has proven to increase recall, engagement, and test results of exceptional learners.[2] Relevant to social studies, the National Council for the Social Studies (NCSS) guidelines for technology assert the need to take advantage of the increased role of social media in students' lives to promote "a rich tradition of innovative use of technology in the teaching and learning of social studies."[3] Technology creates constructivist opportunities whereby learning is active, student-centered, and enhances the critical and conceptual thinking of all students at all levels.[4]

Though the use of technology is desired in the social studies classroom and can benefit the learning experiences of all students, social studies teachers lag behind their content area colleagues in using innovative teaching techniques enhanced via technology.[5] Lamentingly, Martorella described technology as the "sleeping giant in the social studies curriculum" with "few serious attempts to rouse him."[6] As social studies teachers move towards the incorporation of technology into their classrooms, Doolittle and Hicks caution: "If integrating technology means nothing more than enhancing the traditional delivery system of social studies content, where laptops replace notebooks, where PowerPoint slides replace handwritten overheads, where e-textbooks replace hardcopy textbooks, then we will be no closer to the NCSS vision of transformative, powerful social studies instruction."[7] We concede, however, that the absence of technology in the social studies classroom may be influenced more by the lack of resources provided by individual districts rather than the individual teacher's reluctance to use it.

As previously stated, more and more exceptional learners are accessing the general education social studies classroom. Yet such classrooms are under-utilizing available technologies that would benefit students who may struggle with traditional means of content delivery (e.g. lecture, note-taking, independent reading). So, how can social studies educators access and use appropriate technology to enhance the learning opportunities of all students?

Though social studies advocates have called for diversified instructional tools that promote activity-based learning, and are rooted in the analysis and evaluation of primary sources, the dominant means of much social studies instruction is text (i.e. textbook) based.[8] Many students struggle with deciphering the alphabetic code, and thus struggle with reading and writing individual words. Other students read at a slow pace that often correlates into difficulty with text comprehension. Some students experience difficulties in writing. Such challenges are common to many exceptional learners.[9] Literacy-assistive technologies can help students adapt and hopefully overcome many of the barriers that restrict their understanding of and engagement with the social studies content.[10]

AUDIO AND DIGITAL TEXT

As referenced above, the textbook remains the dominant means of instructional delivery in the social studies classroom. Coupled with the fact that many social studies textbooks are filled with difficult and often nuanced passages, reading comprehension becomes difficult for many students. A simple way to make the text more accessible is to translate it from text to audio. Text to audio converters take printed information (in text or PDF formats) and convert the file to digital audio. Text converters like YAKiToMe (http://www.yakitome.com) and NextUp (http://www.nextup.com/TextAloud/audio-books.html) are either free or inexpensive tools to assist struggling readers. Such files can be easily

Table 9.1 Partial List of Digital and Audio Sources

NAME	BRIEF DESCRIPTION	URL
Amazon eBooks	Books, newspapers, magazines, blogs and other documents for the Kindle. A large collection for purchase.	http://www.amazon.com
Audible and AudibleKids	Books, magazines, radio shows, podcasts, and speeches in audio format. Books can be loaded to most music players or stored on CD. Requires yearly membership or purchase of individual titles.	http://www.audible.com
Barnes and Noble	Books, newspapers, magazines, blogs, and other documents for the Nook and iPad. Books can be shared for free.	http://www.barnesandnoble.com
Bookshare	Includes children and popular literature and textbooks. Free to individuals with a print disability or to institutions serving individuals with print disabilities.	http://www.bookshare.org
Google Books	Free access to out-of-copyright books; limited access (e.g., a page) to copyrighted books. Books can be searched. Offers links to libraries where books are available or sites where they can be purchased.	http://www.books.google.com
iTunes	Children's and young adult books for purchase. Requires free iTunes software; books play on computer and digital music players and devices.	http://www.itunes.com
Librivox	Audio versions of books (some young adult fiction) in the public domain; read by volunteers and available as MP3 files.	http://www.librivox.org
Project Gutenburg	Books are in the public domain or authors have granted copyright for single use. Books can be read on computer, iPhone, Kindle, Sony Reader, or other portable devices. Includes a large collection of children's literature.	http://www.gutenberg.org
Simply Audiobooks	Audio books available for download, purchase, or rental. Geared toward adults and adult interests, but includes children and young adult literature. Includes a collection of history books.	http://www.simplyaudiobooks.com

Source: Adapted from Cynthia M. Okolo, Carrie Anna Bouck, Anne Heutsche, Carrie Anna Courtad, & Carol Sue Englert, "Technology in the Social Studies for Students with Disabilities," in *Practical Strategies for Teaching K-12 Social Studies in Inclusive Classrooms*, edited by Timothy Lintner and Windy Schweder (Charlotte: NC: Information Age, 2011): 67-87.

downloaded onto a portable digital music player.[11] Other accessibility options are provided through the National Center on Accessible Educational Materials (http://aem.cast.org). Rather than listening to or reading the material exclusively during instruction, students now have unlimited access to the lesson. Such access allows students to replay and therefore "reread" parts of the lesson that may have been initially confusing or hurriedly presented. Reading repetition not only builds processing skills but also increases content comprehension.

As digital texts become increasingly popular in today's classrooms, exceptional learners can readily take advantage of this accessible and flexible delivery tool. The advent of the Kindle, the Nook, and the iPad has had—and will continue to exert—an increase in digital textbook demand. Table 9.1 provides an abridged collection of both digital and audio text sources teachers can use to assist student comprehension of the social studies content.

It should be noted that "merely putting text in alternative formats for listening or displaying on an electronic device may not have an appreciable effect on students' understanding of that text."[12] The impact of such devices comes in how they are used. Though audio and digital devices may be an important and beneficial accommodation for some students, they may not be beneficial for all.

Many exceptional learners possess organizational deficiencies. Using graphic organizers can assist students in connecting the information by visualizing the relationship between seemingly disparate facts.[13] Graphic organizers have been shown to increase note taking frequency, content comprehension, and classroom participation for exceptional learners.[14] Though social studies instruction has often relied upon paper-based graphic organizers, many are included in interactive software.[15] Programs such as Inspiration (http://www.inspiration.com), Kidspiration (http://www.inspiration.com/Kidspiration), and FreeMind (http://freemind.sourceforge.net/wiki/index.php/Main_Page) allow teachers to change text and image representations, convert information into concept maps, and embed audio and text. Organizational templates are available for teachers to modify based on students' individual needs.[16]

Writing is another area of deficiency for exceptional learners. The National Assessment of Educational Progress (NAEP) concluded that, when compared to their non-disabled peers, exceptional learners struggled with sentence structure, word choice, spelling, revision, and general mechanics.[17] There are a handful of software programs available that can assist students in the planning, revising, editing, and processing of written work. *Draft Builder* and *Co-Writer* (both from http://www.donjohnston.com) help with structure organization and assist students with spelling and grammar revision. *Ginger* (http://www.gingersoftware.com) identifies a misspelled word and predicts the word that the student may have intended to use. Though a bit more complex than the packages mentioned heretofore, *Boardmaker* (http://www.mayer-johnson.com) allows students to place a corresponding picture over unfamiliar text, thus making the connection between word and image.

INFORMATION REPOSITORIES

Many museums and educational entities house videos, primary source materials, lesson plans and classroom-based activities. Such resources can enhance the social studies content by providing students with essential foundational or background knowledge about select social studies topics. Table 9.2 provides select sites to support social studies content through the use of video.

VIDEO AND FILM

For students who struggle with social studies text comprehension, supplementing instruction through video and film provides the visual details that may be lost in text negotiation. Such mediums help students create "visual representations" of social studies that often lead to deeper and more layered understandings. As students are entwined in and with the digital age, video and film presents a captivating and engaging instructional medium that leads to heightened levels of motivation.[18]

There are many different means of accessing video and film to include in social studies instruction as an alternate format to printed text. Commercial outlets such as Netflix (http://www.netflix.com) and Redbox (http://www.redbox.com) offer a range of films that can be used in the social studies classroom. Streaming video is another popular and accessible means of downloading short segments of video to a computer for instant classroom use. Discovery Education Streaming (http://www.discoveryeducation.com) offers more than 9,000 full-length videos and 71,000 content-specific video segments. YouTube is another powerful medium for contextual social studies content.[19]

Just as social studies teachers need to be purposeful in their use of audio and digital text tools, the same careful considerations apply when using video and

Table 9.2 Sources for Teaching with Video

TITLE	BRIEF DESCRIPTION	URL
The Center for Media Literacy	Offers guidelines and videos for teaching media literacy within the content areas, including social studies. Provides students and teachers guidance in evaluating the impact of images, words, and video on understanding the world.	http://www.medialit.org
Discovery Channel	Offers lesson plans and other ideas to accompany TV shows on the Discovery Channel.	http://www.discoveryeducation.com/teachers/free-lesson-plans/index.cfm
History Channel Classroom	Contains teaching guides for History Channel productions.	http://www.history.com/shows/classroom
Khan Academy	Provides free interactive video lessons in Economics, World History, and Civics.	http://www.khanacademy.org
Modern History in the Movies	Chronological list of movies, with descriptions and a link to further information.	http://www.fordham.edu/halsall/mod/modsbookmovies.html
Movies to Study Early Modern History By	Description of movies, organized by era and location.	http://faculty.nipissingu.ca/muhlberger/2155/MOVIES.HTM
National Geographic	Collection of videos distributed by National Geographic and a listing of TV shows on the National Geographic Channel.	http://www.nationalgeographic.com
Public Broadcasting Service (PBS)	Lessons and activities to support PBS shows and videos for purchase.	http://www.pbs.org/teachersource
Teaching History through Films	Teaching film guides to several popular movies.	http://xolotl.org/mediapede/filmhistory
Teach with Movies	Lesson plans and discussion questions for nearly 300 movies, listed by topic and by age.	http://www.teachwithmovies.org

Source: Cynthia M. Okolo, Carrie Anna Bouck, Anne Heutsche, Carrie Anna Courtad, & Carol Sue Englert, "Technology in the Social Studies for Students with Disabilities," in *Practical Strategies for Teaching K-12 Social Studies in Inclusive Classrooms*, edited by Timothy Lintner and Windy Schweder (Charlotte: NC: Information Age, 2011): 67-87.

film. To best support social studies instruction of exceptional learners, it is suggested that teachers:

- Show short segments of videos and films lasting no more than 7-10 minutes. Students are more likely to focus and understand important events if the information is presented in specific segments. Too much information can be overwhelming. Video streaming repositories like Discovery Education Streaming (http://www.discoveryeducation.com) learn360 (http://www.learn360.com), TeacherTube (http://www.teachertube.com) and YouTube (http://www.youtube.com) offer an array of concise reference videos.

- Assist students in integrating their understandings of the video or film with other means of information (e. g. textbook, primary sources, websites). Pause to discuss the differences and/or similarities between the sources and how they may complement or alter interpretations.

- Encourage note-taking. Students can use notes for future recall when completing an activity or studying for a test. Graphic organizers are excellent at assisting students to organize thoughts on to paper.

- Pause the video or film at key moments. Discuss with the students their interpretations. Have students then predict what may happen next.[20]

- Provide subtitles for video or film to enhance understanding of what is being said during the segment.

WEBSITES

There are a number of websites available that can support social studies engagement for exceptional learners. Though the use of such technology (e.g., the Internet) remains intermittent in many social studies classrooms, it does have the potential to transform how content is both approached and understood.

Teachers need to be judicious in their site-selection. The following guidelines can assist teachers in selecting sites that are particularly appropriate for exceptional learners:

- Select sites that are interactive and allow students to predict, participate, and problem-solve.

- Choose sites that are graphic-rich.

- Access sites that are audio-rich (sites that "talk").

- Look for sites that are easily navigated (a "busy" site is a distraction).

- Choose sites whose content is presented in small, partitioned segments rather than a series of rolling narratives.

- Select sites that allow for text enhancement (magnification) or have embedded text readers.

- If possible use sites that are identified as W3C Web accessible.

Table 9.3 provides an admittedly brief selection of websites that can be used in the social studies classroom to support learning for all students.

THE VIRTUAL HISTORY MUSEUM

The often abstract nature of social studies, coupled with the reliance on passive seatwork and challenging textbooks, makes comprehension, processing and engagement elusive. This is particularly true for exceptional learners as they search for ways to negotiate and respond to the content being presented. The Virtual History Museum (VHM) (http://vhm.msu.edu/site/default.php) is a free web-based history learning environment that emphasizes, not only the social studies content, but processing and higher order thinking skills as well. "[VHM] provides supports and scaffolds to students with disabilities in an effort to increase their participation and achievement in social studies, especially United States and world history. VHM assists students in understanding social studies content through methods of analysis and interpretation of evidence and artifacts, exploring multiple perspectives, and enabling students to publish their own interpretations of events in social studies."[21]

VHM is a web-based "real" museum in which the teacher (and eventually the student) effectively becomes the museum's curator. The teacher culls exhibits for students to examine, interpret, and

Table 9.3 Partial List of Websites

NAME	BRIEF DESCRIPTION	URL
iCivics	Provides students with multiple scenario-based opportunities to analyze, prioritize, and problem-solve issues and events related to holding political office.	http://www.icivics.org
BrainPOP	A series of simple, easy to follow vignettes covering multiple content areas. A short quiz follows each segment.	http://www.brainpop.com
President for a Day	This interactive site allows students to assume the role of President. Students make decisions and problem-solve their way through a "typical day" in the life of the President.	http://www.pbskids.org/democracy/presforaday/
The Great Corn Adventure	Students learn about the history, uses, and economic importance of corn. Timelines and graphs are used to support learning.	http://www.urbanext.uiuc.edu/corn
Geosense	Locate countries on an interactive map. These timed exercises can be done via individual or multi-player format.	http://www.geosense.net
The Underground Railroad	Follow Harriet Tubman as she makes her way North. Students predict scenarios posed. Rich in primary sources (e.g. photographs, music, maps), this site engages students on multiple levels.	http://www.nationalgeographic.com/railroad/j2.html
Holocaust Survivors	Rich in both audio and video formats, students click to access primary-source material relevant to Holocaust survivors.	http://www.holocaustsurvivors.org
You Be the Historian	Students uncover clues to understand colonial life through the historical records of the Springer family of New Castle, Delaware. Students are ultimately asked to draw conclusions about colonial life.	http://americanhistory.si.edu/springer/
Museum Box	This site allows students to create a digital museum of historical artifacts and "display" them in their own format.	http://museumbox.e2bn.org

analyze. Exhibits are created using artifacts (e.g. documents, photographs, music, video) that contextualize a historical moment in time. Artifacts already available in the museum can be used or additional artifacts can be downloaded from the Web.

The VHM project benefits classroom teachers' ability to construct meaning of and to social studies for all students in three ways. First, there are a number of representational tools (e.g., Compare/Contrast charts, Cause and Effect tables, Venn diagrams, KWL charts) that allow teachers to present—and students to organize and process—information. Second, the VHM facilitates differentiated instruction by supporting any browser and being compatible with all major screen-reading software. Lastly, simple drop-down menus make the VHM easy to use and easy to incorporate into the social studies classroom.

VOICETHREAD

VoiceThread (http://www.voicethread.com) is an interactive, multimedia slide show tool that enables students to hold text-based and voice-over conversations around imported images, documents, and videos. Teachers can add either text or voiced comments to individual slides. Teachers can make individual VoiceThreads private, with "conversations" between teacher and student exclusive. VoiceThreads can also be made public, either restricted to fellow classmates or accessible to anyone around the world.[22]

VoiceThread can benefit exceptional learners in two ways. First, it allows students to understand and present content in and through multiple formats—text, image, and video. Such differentiation decreases the reliance on literacy-based presentations and offers students multiple means of expression. Second, by design, VoiceThread promotes the "collaborative development of knowledge by providing students the opportunity to share their voice, quite literally, and express opinions regardless of ability."[23] Through engagement around shared topics of interest, students gain confidence in their ability to interact and express themselves in collaborative settings.

VoiceThread facilitates conversational collaborations that are perfectly suited for the social studies classroom.[24] Here, simple conversations can turn into debates, whereby students assess and respond to the information presented. Not only are collaboration, discussion, and debate cornerstones to social studies theory and practice writ large, such practices have both immediate and long-lasting benefits for exceptional learners as well.

Both The Virtual History Museum and VoiceThread support the principles of Universal Design for Learning (UDL), a cornerstone for curriculum development benefiting all students.[25] Students are *engaged* through the use of interactive technologies; an engagement not often found in the more traditional (i.e., paper-and-pencil) approaches to social studies delivery. Students are able to *express* themselves in a format most suited to their comfort and ability levels. Students may prefer to express themselves through writing, art, or dance. With VoiceThread, students can literally express themselves through their own voices. The third principle of UDL, *representation*, allows students to demonstrate their understanding(s) of social studies through multiple means. Both VHM and VoiceThread allow students to individualize their representations through the use of text, images, video, and voice. Such individualism opens up an array of possibilities for students to "show what they know" about social studies. At its core, UDL supports the active participation of students, whereby information is accessed and presented in ways that encourage creativity and deeper, more individualized interpretation of the content at hand. 🖾

NOTES

1. Roberta Devlin-Sherer and Nancy B. Sardone, "Digital Simulation Games for Social Studies Classrooms," *The Clearing House,* 28 (2010): 587-595; Vivian H. Wright and Elizabeth K. Wilson, "Using Technology in the Social Studies Classroom: The Journal of Two Teachers," *The Journal of Social Studies Research,* 33 (2009): 133-154.

2. Terry G. Cronis and David Ellis, "Issues Facing Special Educators in the New Millennium," *Education,* 120 (2000): 639-649; Ted S. Hasselbring, "A Possible Future of Special Education Technology," *Journal of Special Education Technology,* 16 (2001): 15-21; Jane Hauser and David B. Malouf, "A Federal Perspective on Special Education Technology," *Journal of Learning Disabilities,* 29 (1996): 504-512.

3. National Council for the Social Studies, "Technology Position Statement and Guidelines," 2013; see http://www.socialstudies.org/positions/technology.

4. Margaret S. Crocco, "Leveraging Constructivist Learning in the Social Studies Classroom: A Response to Mason, Berson, Diem, Hicks, Lee, and Dralle," *Contemporary Issues in Technology and Teacher Education,* 1 (2001): 386-394.

5. Nancy E. Atkins and Ellen Vasu, "Measuring Knowledge of Technology Usage and Stages of Concern About Computing: A Study of Middle School Teachers," *Journal of Technology and Teacher Education*, 8 (2000): 279-302; Kara G. Dawson, Glenn Bull, and Colleen Swain, "Considerations for the Diffusion of Technological Innovations in Social Studies Teaching and Learning," *Theory and Research in Social Education,* 28 (2000): 587-595.

6. Peter Martorella, "Technology and Social Studies—Or: Which Way to the Sleeping Giant?" *Theory and Research in Social Education*, 25 (1997): 511.

7. Peter E. Doolittle and David Hicks, "Constructivism as a Theoretical Foundation for the Use of Technology in Social Studies," *Theory and Research in Social Education,* 31 (2003): 75.

8. M. Priscilla Myers and Tom Savage, "Enhancing Student Comprehension of the Social Studies Material," *The Social Studies,* 1 (2005): 18-24.

9. Jack M. Fletcher, G. Reid Lyon, Lynn S. Fuchs, and Marcia A. Barnes, *Learning Disabilities: From Identification to Intervention* (New York, NY: Guiliford Publications, 2006); Susan Mayes and Susan Calhoun, "Frequency in Reading, Math, and Writing Disabilities in Children with Clinical Disorders," *Learning and Individual Differences,* 16 (2006): 145-157.

10. Cynthia M. Okolo, Emily Bouck, Anne Heutsche, Carrie Anna Courtad, and Carol Sue Englert, "Technology in the Social Studies for Students with Disabilities," in *Practical Strategies for Teaching K-12 Social Studies in Inclusive Classrooms*, edited by Timothy Lintner and Windy Schweder (Charlotte, NC.: Information Age, 2011): 67-88.

11. *Ibid.*

12. *Ibid:* 72

13. Karen Madden, "Teaching Students with Disabilities Literacy though Technology," *Language and Literacy Spectrum* 22 (2012): 30-42.

14. Sean Smith and Cynthia Okolo, "Response to Intervention and Evidence-Based Practice: Where does Technology Fit?" *Learning Disability Quarterly* 33, no. 4 (2010): 257-272.

15. Nancy Gallavan and Ellen Kottler, "Eight Types of Graphic Organizers for Empowering Social Studies Students and Teachers," *The Social Studies* 93, no. 3 (207): 117-123.

16. Madden, 2012.

17. Smith and Okolo, "Response to Intervention and Evidence-Based Practice: Where does Technology Fit?" *op. cit.*

18. Russell Gersten, Scott K. Baker, Joyce Smith-Johnson, and Joseph A. Peterson, "Eyes on the Prize: Teaching Complex Historical Content to Middle School Students with Learning Disabilities," *Exceptional Children*, 72 (2006): 264-280.

19. For a more comprehensive overview of film in the social studies classroom, see William B. Russell III, *Teaching Social Issues with Film* (Charlotte, NC.: Information Age, 2009).

20. Ralph Ferretti, Charles A. MacArthur, and Cynthia M. Okolo, "Teaching for Historical Understanding in Inclusive Classrooms," *Learning Disability Quarterly,* 24 (2001): 59-71; Okolo et al., "Technology in the Social Studies Classroom for Students with Disabilities," *op. cit.*

21. Emily Bouck, Carrie Anna Courtad, Anne Heutsche, Cynthia M. Okolo, and Carol Sue Englert, "The Virtual History Museum: A Universally Designed Approach to Social Studies Instruction," *Teaching Exceptional Children*, 42 (2009): 15.

22. Stein Brunvand and Sara Byrd, "Using Voice Thread to Promote Learning Engagement and Success for All Students," *Teaching Exceptional Children* 43, no. 4 (2011): 28-37.

23. Brunvand and Byrd, 2011: 36.

24. Adam Friedman and John Lee, "Using Voice Thread as a Debate Tool," paper presented at the James F. Ackerman Colloquium on Technology and Citizenship Education, West Lafayette, Indiana, June 2009.

25. Bouck *et al,* "The Virtual History Museum: A Universally Designed Approach to Social Studies Instruction," *op. cit.;* Afton Gillis, Katie Luthin, Howard P. Parette, and Craig Blum, "Using VoiceThread to Create Meaningful Receptive and Expressive Learning Activities for Young Children," *Early Childhood Education Journal* 40, no. 4 (2012): 203-211.

CHAPTER TEN

Classroom Management

For students to be successful, not just in social studies, but also in all aspects of school life, their behavior must align with the policies and practices of the teacher. Unfortunately, disconnects sometimes exist between behavior and expectation, particularly for exceptional learners. The U.S. Department of Education reported that exceptional learners are twice as likely to be suspended when compared to their non-disabled peers.[1] Over a third of exceptional learners are suspended or expelled from school at some point. In some school districts, exceptional learners were 2-3 times more likely to be disciplined than their non-disabled peers.[2]

Many exceptional learners have social and behavioral challenges that are separate from their academic struggles. Often, these social and behavioral issues affect academic performance. Others who demonstrate social and behavioral challenges in the classroom do so as a direct result of their academic frustrations or the environment in which they are educated. Many act out as a means of self-defense against others "finding out" about their disability; this behavior is their only form of communication. This becomes concerning for school personnel as students enter school with multiple challenges manifested in a variety of ways.

For many students with and without exceptionalities, school is full of social challenges. Social conventions dictate that students interact and collaborate. Behavioral expectations require students to conform to prescribed rituals and routines. Academic requirements ask students to complete tasks that are undoubtedly important yet are often too difficult. For example, students are asked to read a series of primary sources about the Battle of Lexington and Concord. The passage is long, the language esoteric and unfamiliar. The purpose of the reading starts to fade. Resiliency and persistence become hard to

maintain. Often out of sheer frustration, the primary sources are put down. The student stops reading. Consequential behavior may arise. We are not advocating that teachers give exceptional learners a free pass when confronted with social, behavioral or academic expectations. We merely suggest that teachers be mindful of and attentive to the interplay between academic expectation and social and behavioral outcomes.

SOCIAL CHALLENGES

Social skills are necessary for students to successfully function inside and outside of school.[3] Deficits in social skills are often the most devastating types of problems students have, as they make social interaction with others difficult. Challenges associated with social skills impact approximately one-third of exceptional learners.[4] Students who have problems with social relationships may lack sensitivity to others, be unsure of "what to do" in social situations, be impulsive, and possess a low tolerance for frustration.[5] It should be noted that some students who suffer underdeveloped social skills excel academically. Similarly, some exceptional learners shine in social settings.

Some students are truly unfamiliar with social conventions and thus display inappropriate behavior. For example, Sarah is an exceptional learner who constantly blurts out the answer to each and every question asked by the teacher. Unfortunately, the vast majority of responses she provides are incorrect. Her fellow classmates roll their eyes and some snicker. Though the teacher stressed answering questions with greater confidence and allowing others to participate as well, Sarah still does not understand the impact of her impulsive behavior.

In another example, Arturo is identified with an emotional/behavioral disorder and is verbally abusive to many of his classmates. Arturo recognizes that his behavior is inappropriate and is "in tune" to the displeasure of his teacher and fellow classmates. He is able to use appropriate language in certain circumstances, particularly during social studies, his favorite subject. Yet during recess, the instances of inappropriate language increase. Arturo understands the difference between appropriate and inappropriate language, yet chooses to exhibit appropriate language only in certain contexts. His understanding of social conventions differs from Sarah's.

What can teachers do to assess and support proper social skills? The easiest way of assessing social skills is by direct observation of social behavior in naturalistic settings (e.g. the classroom, car line, recess, lunch room). We encourage teachers to keep a running record of student interaction (or lack thereof), noting setting, frequency, duration, and resultant outcomes. Though admittedly time-consuming, teachers can identify certain situations in which concerning behavior has been consistently noted and keep running records exclusive to these environments. Also, teachers can use the one-teach, one-observe model of co-teaching where one teacher provides content while the other collects data on individual students. Having this information handy is valuable in targeting social settings that may need to be modified and teaching social skills that may be lacking.

Though there are several ways classroom teachers can teach social skills, we advocate a simple four-step process: modeling, shaping, coaching, and modeling/reinforcement.[6] Teachers need to model what proper social behavior looks like. While modeling a given social convention (i.e. working in pairs), the teacher reinforces the behavior by stating, "Now, when I work with a partner, I will work quietly, respectfully, and will do my share of the work." The teacher then pulls a student to the front of the room and provides a brief skit of what working together should "look like." Teachers also need to shape the desired social behavior. This is done through positive reinforcement. "Becky and Javon, thank you both for working so quietly and respectfully on your map project. I can tell you both are working very hard and your map is accurate with nice detail and color." Next, teachers use verbal cues to coach students towards proper skill development. "Class, remember that when you are working with your partner, you are to work quietly, respectfully, and equally hard." The teacher approaches Monica and Alisa who are off-task. "Please remember what is expected of you when you work with your partner." Sometimes verbal cues can be in the form of questions, allowing students to share their own understanding of expected behaviors. "What is expected of you when you work with a partner?" Lastly, to assure that the desired social skill will be practiced throughout the school year, the teacher uses a combination of modeling and reinforcement.

BEHAVIORAL CHALLENGES

We have all seen, heard of, or experienced classrooms that were out of control. Though there is no reliable data that states how many classrooms suffer from a lack of effective management policies and procedures, educators would likely agree that even one classroom is one too many.

Most school and classroom behavioral challenges are related to a handful of specific behaviors or actions, most notably tardiness, disrespect, being unprepared, excessive talking, calling or blurting out, and instances of verbal and or physical acting out. Many of these behaviors can be prevented through a system of proactive measures that reduces the likelihood of misbehavior before the opportunity to do so arises.[7]

FUNCTIONAL BEHAVIORAL ASSESSMENT (FBA)

The Individuals With Disabilities Education Improvement Act of 2004 (IDEIA 2004) requires that if a child's behavior interferes with his or her learning or the learning of others, the school-based IEP team can consider strategies and supports to address the behavior. If, in fact, the child's behavior is deemed to impact his or her learning and the learning of others, the IEP team must evaluate the child through a functional behavioral assessment in order to design a Behavior Intervention Plan (BIP) of positive behavioral supports to address the behavior in question.[8]

A functional behavioral assessment involves examining factors that contribute to a child's behavior. In doing so, information is gathered to (1) measure student behavior; (2) determine why, where, and when such behavior occurs; (3) identify the context (e.g. instructional, social, environmental) that may influence the behavior; and (4) plan appropriate interventions.[9] The typical model used in FBA is the ABC model: antecedent, behavior, and consequence.

Figure 10.1 ABC Model

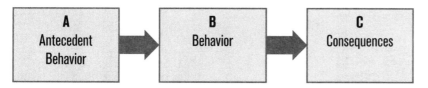

Here is an example of how to apply the ABC model to student behavior. When the teacher asks Karl to read from the board (antecedent), he begins to complain, disturbing the other students. As he reluctantly walks to the board, he hits Ben on the arm (behavior). The teacher admonishes Karl, asking him to sit down (consequence). Through observation and data collection, the teacher records each occurrence of the behavior and recognizes a pattern (every time Karl is asked to approach the board, he disrupts the class). Based upon the FBA, a behavioral support plan is made that focuses on changing the environment (procedural, physical), teaching appropriate behavioral skills, and establishing consequences that make such behaviors less likely to be repeated.[10] The FBA provides baseline behavioral information (ABC model) that allows teachers and school-based personnel to create positive behavioral supports that work towards the elimination of undesirable behavior.

POSITIVE BEHAVIORAL SUPPORT (PBS)

Positive behavioral supports are strategies to change and, ultimately, eliminate an undesirable behavior. Remember that, as part of IDEIA 2004, positive behavior support strategies can be considered in the IEP if behavior impedes learning. A positive behavioral support may be, in the case of Karl noted above, that he is asked to read from the board only after the teacher has prepared him to do so. If his resultant behavior is acceptable (e.g. no verbal and/or physical outbursts), Karl is rewarded with a positive consequence. The teacher would also begin teaching Karl to self-monitor and self-regulate his behavior, and make a conscious effort to recognize Karl's desired behaviors when they are modeled in different settings.

When implementing positive behavioral supports or interventions there are certain strategies to consider. First, teach the student a desired replacement behavior through modeling. If the student constantly gets out of her desk, teach the student when, and when it is not, appropriate to do so and provide the student with an acceptable way to move around the room. Secondly, modify the environment. For example, if a student is constantly distracting neighbors during a test, consider moving the student to the front table or a quiet space during subsequent tests. Lastly, positively reinforce appropriate behavior and limit negative consequences.

Heretofore, we have isolated positive behavioral supports to individual teachers in individual classrooms. Yet the PBS model has been expanded to include the whole school. The goal of School-Wide Positive Behavior Support (SWPBS) is to create proactive structures that reduce the likelihood of misbehavior by consistently reinforcing positive behavior. There are three stages to the SWPBS model. Stage One defines and identifies the problems to be addressed by the SWPBS program. These may be more sweeping (Respect) or particular (No Running in the Hallway). In Stage Two, the designated PBS plan is articulated to faculty, staff, and students and implemented in all school-based settings. Identified "target areas" (e.g., hallways) are given extra attention. Lastly, in Stage Three, the PBS program is monitored and information is gathered (e.g., the number of instances students were running down the hallways). These findings are regularly shared with faculty and staff and the program is modified as warranted. An excellent source to learn more about positive behavioral supports and school-wide positive behavioral supports can be found at http://www.pbis.org.

NOTES

1. U.S. Department of Education Office of Civil Rights: Civil Rights Data Collection: Data Snapshot: School Discipline (2014). http://www2.ed.gov/about/offices/list/ocr/docs/crdc-discipline-snapshot.pdf

2. National Center for Learning Disabilities, *The State of Learning Disabilities, Third Edition (2014).* http://www.ncld.org/wp-content/uploads/2014/11/2014-State-of-LD.pdf

3. Margo A. Mastropieri and Thomas Scruggs, *The Inclusive Classroom: Strategies for Effective Differentiated Instruction,* 4TH edition (Upper Saddle River, NJ: Merrill, 2010).

4. Linda K. Elksnin and Nick Elksnin, "The social-emotional side of learning disabilities," *Learning Disability Quarterly* 27, no. 1 (2004): 3-8; Kytja K. S. Voeller, "Techniques for Measuring Social Competence in Children," in *Frames of Reference for the Assessment of Learning Disabilities: New Views on Measurement Issues 1994.* Edited by G. Reid Lyon (Baltimore: Paul H. Brookes Publishing, 1994): 523-554.

5. Dheepa Sridhar and Sharon Vaughn, "Bibliotherapy for All: Enhancing Reading Comprehension, Self-Concept, and Behavior," *TEACHING Exceptional Children* 33 (Nov-Dec 2000): 74-92.

6. Mastropieri and Scruggs, *The Inclusive Classroom, op. cit.*

7. Michael S. Rosenberg, David L. Westling, and James McLeskey, *Special Education for Today's Teachers: An Introduction,* 2ND edition (Upper Saddle River, NJ: Pearson, 2011).

8. George Sugai and Robert H. Horner, "Including the Functional Behavioral Assessment Technology in Schools," *Exceptionality* 8 (1999-2000): 145-48; U.S. Department of Education, *2000;* Janet W. Lerner and Beverley Johns, *Learning Disabilities and Related Mild Disabilities,* 12TH edition (Belmont, CA: Wadsworth Cengage, 2011).

9. Spencer J. Salend, *Creating Inclusive Classrooms: Effective and Reflective Practices,* 7TH edition (Boston, MA: Pearson, 2011).

10. Mastropieri and Scruggs, *The Inclusive Classroom, op cit.*

CHAPTER ELEVEN

Elementary Lesson Plans

The premise of elementary social studies is to create varied opportunities for student exploration and engagement. Over and above covering the prescribed content, elementary social studies classrooms should push students to think, to question, to collaborate and to confidently raise one's hand and contribute.

We have provided a series of four lesson plans that serve to achieve these aims and outcomes. Each lesson plan is tied to a specific content area (Economics, Geography, History, and Civics) and is based on the Universal Design for Learning and C3 frameworks. Lessons also include optional guidelines for shared responsibilities within an inclusive (i.e. co-taught) classroom, but are easily taught without a co-teacher or paraprofessional present.

In order to address the learning needs of all students, each lesson plan includes multiple tools to teach elementary social studies. Such tools include graphic organizers, individual and whole group instruction, paired or whole group collaboration, discussion and debate, individual and small group presentations, interactive technology, writing activities, and kinesthetic learning.

ELEMENTARY ECONOMICS LESSON PLAN

Economics. It can be a rather daunting word (and concept) for young learners. Students usually think of economics as buying and selling, money, what banks do or, generally, aren't really sure what economics is in the first place!

A seminal elementary economic concept is the definition of and difference between consumers and producers. We argue that young learners are both consumers and producers every day; they just lack the terminology to define their actions. Thus, as with any good social studies lesson, it is important to link the concept to the lives of your students.

We have provided an interactive and engaging lesson that focuses only on consumers. The link provided is a simple interactive overview of what a consumer is and what role(s) he/she plays. The video supports voice-to-text narration, which is perfect for students who struggle with reading. Having students collaboratively use the newspaper, not only reinforces the concept of informational text, but frames the concept of consumer and consumerism with a real-work context. Lastly, students individually complete an activity sheet whereby they write or illustrate three items that they consume. This affords differentiation of expression. The more differentiated opportunities you can provide students to engage with economic concepts, the more likely they are to perceive economics as more than just money.

LESSON TITLE: BEING A CONSUMER	SUBJECT: ECONOMICS
Unit: Goods and Services	Grade: 2
Timeframe: 35 minutes	Teacher(s):

STANDARDS:

This lesson promotes the following objectives of the *National Social Studies Standards*, the *C3 Framework for Social Studies State Standards*, and the *Common Core State Standards for English Language Arts and Literacy in History/Social Studies.*

NATIONAL SOCIAL STUDIES STANDARDS[†]

Theme ❼ **PRODUCTION, DISTRIBUTION, AND CONSUMPTION** (Early Grades):
Questions for Exploration: Why Can't People Have Everything That They Want? (p. 50)

C3 FRAMEWORK FOR SOCIAL STUDIES STATE STANDARDS[††]

- D1.4.K-2. Make connections between supporting questions and compelling questions. (p. 25)

- D2.Eco.5.K-2. Identify prices of products in a local market. (p. 37)

- D3.1.K-2. Gather relevant information from one or two sources while using the origin and structure to guide the selection. (p. 54)

- D4.2.K-2. Construct explanations using correct sequence and relevant information. (p. 60)

- D4.5.K-2. Ask and answer questions about explanations. (p. 61)

COMMON CORE STATE STANDARDS FOR ENGLISH LANGUAGE ARTS AND LITERACY IN HISTORY/SOCIAL STUDIES[†††]

Anchor Reading Standards:
Key Ideas and Details
1. Read closely to determine what the text says explicitly and to make logical inferences from it; cite specific textual evidence when writing or speaking to support conclusions drawn from the text. (p. 60)

GOAL
The students will examine the characteristics of a consumer.

OBJECTIVES
Obj. 1: Students will recognize the ways in which they and their families act as consumers.

Obj. 2: Students will be introduced to the definition of a consumer.

Obj. 3: Students will apply their understanding of a consumer.

---

†   This and subsequent references in this chapter to the National Social Studies Standards are citations of National Council for the Social Studies (NCSS), *National Curriculum Standards for Social Studies: A Framework for Teaching, Learning, and Assessment* (Silver Spring, MD: NCSS, 2010).

††   This and subsequent references in this chapter to the C3 Framework for Social Studies State Standards are citations of National Council for the Social Studies (NCSS), *The College, Career, and Civic Life (C3) Framework for Social Studies State Standards: Guidance for Enhancing the Rigor of K-12 Civics, Economics, Geography, and History* (Silver Spring, MD: NCSS, 2013).

†††   This and subsequent references in this chapter to the Common Core State Standards for English Language Arts and Literacy in History/Social Studies are citations of National Governors Association Center for Best Practices (NGA) and Council of Chief State School Officers (CCSSO), *Common Core State Standards for English Language Arts and Literacy in History/Social Studies, Science, and Technical Subjects* (Washington, DC: NGA and CCSSO, 2010).

COMPELLING QUESTIONS

Q1: Is everything we consume for sale?

Q2: Will we ever run out of things to consume?

SUPPORTING QUESTIONS

Q1: What do consumers do?

Q2: Who can be a consumer?

Q3: As a consumer, what are some items you have bought or would like to buy?

Q4: Why do you want to buy them?

MATERIALS/EQUIPMENT/TECHNOLOGY

- "Consumers" video website (http://www.econedlink. org/lessons/index.php?lid=457&type=educator)

- Newspaper supermarket advertisements

- "We are Consumers" activity sheet. (Adapted from EconEdLink: http://www.econedlink.org/lessons/ docs_lessons/457_we_are_consumers1.pdf)

UNIVERSAL DESIGN FOR LEARNING

REPRESENTATION – OPTIONS FOR PRESENTING CONTENT	ENGAGEMENT – OPTIONS FOR ENGAGING STUDENT INTEREST	EXPRESSION – OPTIONS FOR DEMONSTRATING STUDENT LEARNING	CULTURAL CONSIDERATIONS
☐ Artifacts ☒ **Pictures** ☒ **Graphic organizers** ☒ **Video Clips** ☐ Audio Recordings ☐ Lab ☐ Lecture ☐ Other _____	☐ Cooperative Group Work ☒ **Partner Work** ☒ **Manipulatives** ☐ Movement ☐ Debates ☐ Role plays or Simulations ☐ Other _____	☒ **Written response** ☒ **Illustrated response** ☒ **Oral response** ☐ Model creation or construction ☐ Other _____	☐ Nature of content and ethnicity/culture of students ☒ **Other** Are there some goods and services all people around the world consume? (e.g. food, clothes). Do parents around the world all buy their children shoes?
CONTENT	PROCESS	PRODUCT	

LEARNING PLAN

	ROLES, ACCOMMODATIONS, AND DIFFERENTIATION STRATEGIES
LESSON INTRODUCTION 1. Begin with a warm-up activity. As the students transition into social studies, a brief unit overview is provided. ("For the past several days, we have been exploring the difference between a 'good' and a 'service.'") Content clarification questions are asked and examples of goods and services are provided. (3 minutes)	**INTRODUCTION** Have both co-teachers lead transition into social studies and monitor on-task behavior.
2. Introduce the lesson for the day. Write "Consumer" on the board. (2 minutes)	A co-teacher writes "Consumer" on the board.

LESSON PROCEDURES

1. Ask students if they have ever bought a good or service. State that, when you buy a good or service – whether it is an ice cream cone or a haircut – you are a consumer. Define consumer: "A consumer is a person who buys and uses goods and services." Write the definition on the board. Have students read the definition out loud as a whole class. Provide examples ("If you buy a puppy, are you a consumer?" "If I dig a hole, am I a consumer?" "If you buy a ticket to Walt Disney World, are you a consumer?") Display a regular notebook to the class. "If I need a notebook and go to the store to buy it, I am a consumer." Display other artifacts to support contextualization. Gauge concept understanding. (5 minutes)

   One co-teacher leads the introduction while the other co-teacher writes the definition on the board. Both co-teachers offer additional content contextualization if needed.

2. Show the video "Consumers." The video supports interaction and voice-over-text. Students can follow along silently or read out loud as a whole class. Stop the video at appropriate intervals to ask content/clarification questions (frame 4 and 5). Allow students to either verbally predict or physically select (via interactive White Board) what goods and services they can consume (e.g., buy) (frame 7). (10 minutes)

   A co-teacher accesses and navigates the website. The other co-teacher moves through the room assuring that all students are on-task.

3. Pair students by proximity. Provide each pair a single sheet of supermarket advertisements from the local newspaper. Ads can be from the same paper or from different papers (or different days of the same paper). Students will circle all the goods and services they can consume (e.g., buy). (5 minutes)

   Both co-teachers distribute materials and monitor student behavior and task completion.

4. Students will individually complete the "We are Consumers" activity sheet (see Figure 11.1). Teachers can collect the activity sheets and group them by similar responses. (7 minutes)

   Both co-teachers distribute the activity sheet and monitor student behavior and task completion. Co-teachers assist with handwriting and spelling when warranted.

LESSON CLOSURE AND ASSESSMENT

1. Students will answer the compelling and supporting questions identified at the beginning of the lesson in a large group as a review. (2 minutes)

2. Have select students reach into a Grab Bag and state if their item (e.g. pencil, notebook paper, a book, eraser, crayons, etc.) can be consumed (i.e., bought). Reiterate that this makes them a consumer. (2 minutes)

Figure 11.1 We are Consumers! Activity Sheet

Name: Date:

WE ARE CONSUMERS!

Draw pictures or write about three goods and/or services you like to consume or buy.

I AM A CONSUMER OF ...

Draw a circle around your favorite.

Adapted from EconEdLink (http://www.econedlink.org/lessons/docs_lessons/457_we_are_consumers1.pdf)

ELEMENTARY GEOGRAPHY LESSON PLAN

The next lesson for elementary social studies focuses on map skills, specifically the reinforcement of cardinal directions through the use of a compass rose. With the advent of GPS, we often hear students say, "I don't need a map. I know exactly where to go. I have a GPS." We casually counter this argument by asking, "If your GPS unit doesn't work, how are you going to find your way?" Silence.

In the absence of a GPS, how do young learners know where to go? The first step is learning the cardinal directions. We have provided a simple introductory lesson to cardinal directions through the introduction of a compass rose. The supporting video provides both a definition of a compass rose and multiple visual representations. Movement (kinesthetic learning) is an effective teaching strategy for all learners. We have created an opportunity for students to understand cardinal directions by modeling teacher movement. Students are up, out of their desks, and interacting with the content through movement. The "Let's Go On a Road Trip" activity sheet supports student independent practice. For struggling readers and writers, this sheet can be done with assistance from a paired student, teacher, or co-teacher.

SAMPLE LESSON PLAN

LESSON TITLE: WHICH WAY TO GO?	SUBJECT: GEOGRAPHY
Unit: Map Skills	Grade: 1
Timeframe: 45 minutes	Teacher(s):

STANDARDS

This lesson promotes the following objectives of the *National Social Studies Standards, the C3 Framework for Social Studies State Standards*, and the *Common Core State Standards for English Language Arts and Literacy in History/Social Studies.*

NATIONAL SOCIAL STUDIES STANDARDS

Theme ❸ **PEOPLE, PLACES, AND ENVIRONMENTS** (Early Grades):
Knowledge
Learners will understand: "Tools such as maps, globes, and geospatial technologies in investigating the relationships among people, places and environments." (p. 35)

C3 FRAMEWORK FOR SOCIAL STUDIES STATE STANDARDS

D1.4.K-2. Make connections between supporting questions and compelling questions. (p. 25)

D2.Geo.2.K-2. Use maps, graphs, photographs and other representations to describe places and the relationships and interactions that shape them. (p. 41)

D3.1.K-2. Gather relevant information from one or two sources while using the origin and structure to guide the selection. (p. 54)

D4.2.K-2. Construct explanations using correct sequence and relevant information. (p. 60)

Anchor Speaking and Listening Standards:
Comprehension and Collaboration
1. Prepare for and participate effectively in a range of conversations and collaborations with diverse partners, building on others' ideas and expressing their own clearly and persuasively. (p. 22)

GOAL
The students will demonstrate their knowledge of a compass rose.

OBJECTIVES
Obj. 1: Students will use basic map skills including a map legend and cardinal directions.

Obj. 2: Students will apply their understanding of a compass rose.

COMPELLING QUESTIONS
Q1: How do we know which direction to go?

SUPPORTING QUESTIONS
Q1: What does a compass rose do?

Q2: How could you use a compass rose?

Q3: What are the cardinal directions on a compass rose?

MATERIALS/ EQUIPMENT/TECHNOLOGY
- TeacherTube video "Compass Rose" (http://www.teachertube.com/viewVideo.php?video_id=120576) To view this clip you will need to create and/or log in to TeacherTube (www.teachertube.com) and select "Download Video" from the left.

UNIVERSAL DESIGN FOR LEARNING

REPRESENTATION – OPTIONS FOR PRESENTING CONTENT	ENGAGEMENT – OPTIONS FOR ENGAGING STUDENT INTEREST	EXPRESSION – OPTIONS FOR DEMONSTRATING STUDENT LEARNING	CULTURAL CONSIDERATIONS
☐ Artifacts ☐ Pictures ☐ Graphic organizers ☒ **Video Clips** ☐ Audio Recordings ☐ Lab ☒ **Lecture** ☐ Other _____	☐ Cooperative Group Work ☐ Partner Work ☐ Manipulatives ☒ **Movement** ☐ Debates ☐ Role plays or Simulations ☐ Other _____	☒ **Written response** ☐ Illustrated response ☒ **Oral response** ☐ Model creation or construction ☐ Other _____	☐ Nature of content and ethnicity/culture of students ☒ **Other:** How do you think children around the world, who do not know what a compass rose is, know which direction they are going?
CONTENT	PROCESS	PRODUCT	

	ROLES, ACCOMMODATIONS, AND DIFFERENTIATION STRATEGIES

LESSON INTRODUCTION

INTRODUCTION

1. Begin with a warm-up activity. As the students transition into social studies, a brief unit overview is provided. ("For the past several days, we have been exploring what maps do and what can be found on a map" [e.g. maps help to find places and contain physical features like mountains and roads]). (3 minutes)

Have both co-teachers lead the transition into social studies and monitor on-task behavior.

2. Introduce the lesson for the day. Write "Compass Rose" on the board. Display on the board (via website or paper-based) a simple four-point labeled compass rose. (2 minutes)

A co-teacher writes "Compass Rose" on the board and displays an image of a compass rose. The other co-teacher introduces the lesson.

LESSON PROCEDURES

1. Ask students if they know which direction they will be going when they leave school today. Solicit a few responses. State that it is important to know which direction we are going so we can find our destination and don't get lost. State that students will be introduced to a tool that allows them to know which way they are traveling on a map–the compass rose. Define compass rose: "A compass rose shows directions on a map. The compass rose has four main directions: North, South, East and West. These are called cardinal directions. You can use the compass rose to give or follow directions." (5 minutes)

One co-teacher leads the introduction while the other co-teacher monitors behavior. Both co-teachers offer additional content contextualization if needed.

2. Show the TeacherTube video "Compass Rose." At the end of the video, ask students if they can recall any of the cardinal directions mentioned (North, South, East or West). Ask why it is called a compass rose (because it "looks like a rose.") Also state that, for today, we will be focusing on the cardinal directions and not the intermediate (Northwest, Southeast, etc.) directions. Answer any content clarification questions as warranted. (7 minutes)

A co-teacher accesses and moves through the website activity. The other co-teacher moves through the room assuring that all students are on-task. Both co-teachers facilitate discussion and answer any content clarification questions.

3. Ask students to stand up next to their seats/desks. Model the compass rose by extending arms above the head and saying "North"; by lowering arms towards the ground and saying "South"; by extending the right arm to the right and saying "East"; and extending the left arm to the left and saying "West." (It is important that teachers actually face north in the classroom!) Ask students to follow along. Repeat once more with students. Move the right arm to the right and ask, "What direction is this?" Students respond. Do this for the remaining three cardinal directions. Ask students to retake seats. (10 minutes)

Both co-teachers model movement. One co-teacher asks directional questions.

4. Distribute "Let's Go On a Road Trip" activity sheet (see Figure 11.2). Remind students to use the compass rose to assist in answering questions. Read directions aloud. Allow students to work individually. Review as whole group. (10 minutes)

Both co-teachers distribute the activity sheet and monitor student behavior and task completion. Co-teachers assist with handwriting and spelling when warranted.

LESSON CLOSURE AND ASSESSMENT

1. Students will answer the compelling and supporting questions identified at the beginning of the lesson in a large group as a review. (2 minutes)

2. The teacher identifies and labels (by putting a sticky note on the classroom wall) "North." The teacher then asks students to go "stand next to the West wall." The process is repeated for East and South. (3 minutes)

Figure 11.2 Let's Go On A Road Trip activity sheet

Name: Date:

LET'S GO ON A ROAD TRIP!
Directions: Write NORTH, SOUTH, EAST, or WEST when answering the questions.

In which section of the United States is the 🚗 ?

_____

In which section of the United States is the 🚌 ?

_____

In which section of the United States is the 🚂 ?

_____

In which section of the United States is the 🚍 ?

_____

Adapted from: http://site.k8websites.com

ELEMENTARY HISTORY LESSON PLAN

One of our favorite topics of Westward Expansion is the California Gold Rush. There is so much to cover: motives and miseries, inventions and investments, travel and triumphs. It is a fascinating slice of American history. We have designed a single-lesson introduction to mining life during the Gold Rush. Though this lesson was designed for 45 minutes, it can easily be extended into a second lesson period.

To set the stage, we chose a brief video of the Gold Rush. Make sure to ask students analysis/ interpretation/perception questions. Ultimately, you will ask your students if, based on the living and working condition of Gold Rush miners, they would choose to travel west in search of gold. The lesson also provides an admittedly cursory content section. We suggest that you supplement what is provided with information gleaned from additional sources (e.g. textbook, primary sources, internet). The heart of the lesson provides opportunities for students to engage in the analysis, interpretation, and synthesis of text and visual primary sources. This allows multiple means of content engagement. The collaborative activity sheet pushes students to holistically conceptualize the Gold Rush by, once again, allowing multiple perspective (i.e. sensory) points.

SAMPLE LESSON PLAN

LESSON TITLE: MINING LIFE DURING THE CALIFORNIA GOLD RUSH	SUBJECT: U.S. HISTORY
Unit: Reasons for Moving West	Grade: 5
Timeframe: 45 minutes	Teacher(s):

STANDARDS

This lesson promotes the following objectives of the *National Social Studies Standards*, the *C3 Framework for Social Studies State Standards*, and the *Common Core State Standards for English Language Arts and Literacy in History/Social Studies.*

NATIONAL SOCIAL STUDIES STANDARDS

Theme ❷ TIME, CONTINUITY, AND CHANGE (Middle Grades):

Knowledge

Learners will understand:

That learning about the past requires the interpretation of sources, and that using varied sources provides the potential for a more balanced interpretive record of the past. (p. 31)

Processes

Learners will be able to:

Identify and use a variety of primary and secondary sources for reconstructing the past, such as documents, letters, diaries, maps, textbooks, photos, and other sources. (p. 32)

C3 FRAMEWORK FOR SOCIAL STUDIES STATE STANDARDS

D1.5.3-5. Determine the kinds of sources that will be helpful in answering compelling and supporting questions, taking into consideration the different opinions people have about how to answer the questions. (p. 25)

D2.Hist.16.3-5. Use evidence to develop a claim about the past. (p. 49)

D3.3.3-5. Identify evidence that draws information from multiple sources in response to compelling questions. (p. 55)

D3.4.3-5. Use evidence to develop claims in response to compelling questions. (p. 55)

D4.1.3-5. Construct arguments using claims and evidence from multiple sources (p. 60)

COMMON CORE STATE STANDARDS FOR ENGLISH LANGUAGE ARTS AND LITERACY IN HISTORY/SOCIAL STUDIES

Anchor Reading Standards

Key Ideas and Details

1. Read closely to determine what the text says explicitly and to make logical inferences from it; cite specific textual evidence when writing or speaking to support conclusions drawn from the text. (p. 60)

Integration of Knowledge and Ideas

7. Integrate and evaluate content presented in diverse formats and media, including visually and quantitatively, as well as in words. (p. 60)

Anchor Speaking and Listening Standards

Comprehension and Collaboration

1. Prepare for and participate effectively in a range of conversations and collaborations with diverse partners, building on others' ideas and expressing their own clearly and persuasively. (p. 22)

GOAL

The students will examine the living and working conditions of miners during the California Gold Rush.

OBJECTIVES

Obj. 1: Students will be introduced to further information regarding the westward expansion of the United States.

Obj. 2: Students will examine and analyze primary sources (narratives, photographs) of mining life during the California Gold Rush.

Obj. 3: Students will identify the benefits and detriments of mining life.

Obj. 4: Students will apply their understanding(s) of mining life by completing the "Put Yourself There: California Gold Rush" activity sheet.

COMPELLING QUESTIONS

Q1: If life was so difficult and the chances for "striking it rich" so limited, why do you think folks continued to mine?

Q2: Would you have been caught up in the "Gold Rush Fever" and travelled west?

Q3: Who actually struck it rich? Was it skill or luck?

SUPPORTING QUESTIONS

Q1: What was life like for Gold Rush miners?

Q2: What tools and/or techniques were used to mine gold?

Q3: What hazards and/or hardships did miners face?

Q4: How (or to whom) would miners sell their gold to?

MATERIALS/ EQUIPMENT/TECHNOLOGY

- "The Gold Rush" video (http://www.watchknowlearn.org/Video.aspx?VideoID=20874&CategoryID=5423)

- Excerpts of a letter written by General David Willock (http://www.rootsweb.ancestry.com/~momarion/march17.htm)

- Excerpts from "The Lousy Miner" poem (http://twain.lib.virginia.edu/roughingit/map/minlousy.html)

- Images of miner life and work (Figure 11.5)

  ▶ A California Gold Rush Mining Town: http://cali49.com/hwy49/2013/11/21/pc-hang-town-placerville-cal?rq=Hangtown

  ▶ Miners Hoping to Strike it Rich: http://www.learnnc.org/lp/editions/nchist-antebel-lum/5425

  ▶ Miners Pause in their search for gold: https://www.pinterest.com/pin/115756652892125752/

- "Put Yourself There: The California Gold Rush" activity sheet.

UNIVERSAL DESIGN FOR LEARNING

REPRESENTATION – OPTIONS FOR PRESENTING CONTENT	ENGAGEMENT – OPTIONS FOR ENGAGING STUDENT INTEREST	EXPRESSION – OPTIONS FOR DEMONSTRATING STUDENT LEARNING	CULTURAL CONSIDERATIONS
☐ Artifacts ☒ **Pictures** ☐ Graphic organizers ☒ **Video Clips** ☐ Audio Recordings ☐ Lab ☒ **Lecture** ☒ **Other**: Primary sources	☐ Cooperative Group Work ☒ **Partner Work** ☐ Manipulatives ☐ Movement ☐ Debates ☐ Role plays or Simulations ☐ Other _____	☒ **Written response** ☐ Illustrated response ☒ **Oral response** ☐ Model creation or construction ☐ Other _____	☐ Nature of content and ethnicity/culture of students ☒ **Other:** Why did a number of immigrants work in the gold mines?
CONTENT	PROCESS	PRODUCT	

LEARNING PLAN

	ROLES, ACCOMMODATIONS, AND DIFFERENTIATION STRATEGIES
LESSON INTRODUCTION 1. Begin with a warm-up activity. As the students transition into social studies, a brief unit overview is provided. ("For the past several days, we have been exploring issues surrounding Westward Migration.") A few content review questions are asked based upon previous lessons. (2 minutes)	**INTRODUCTION** Have both co-teachers lead the transition into social studies and monitor on-task behavior.
2. Introduce the lesson for the day. Write "Gold Rush: Are you Coming?" on the board. (1 minute)	A co-teacher writes "Gold Rush: Are you Coming?" on the board.

LESSON PROCEDURES

1. (The teacher will use the Ten Plus Two model: Lecturing for 10 minutes then fielding student questions for two minutes.) Start by showing a brief video about the California Gold Rush. After the video, ask "Why would folks be willing to leave their homes, and often their families, and travel West in search of gold?" "What hardships did these folks face before they even arrived in California to search for gold?" (10 minutes)

   One co-teacher leads the introduction while the other co-teacher readies the video. At the end of the video, both co-teachers ask extension questions and answer any content questions the students may have.

2. State that, at the beginning of the California Gold Rush (1848), it was not uncommon for miners to "scratch the surface" and find up to $2,000 of gold a day. Yet the average miner was lucky to find $10.00 a day. As more and more miners rushed to California, less and less gold was found. By 1852, most of the gold that lay just below the surface was gone and panning for gold was no longer profitable. Most miners lived in tents and cooked food over an open fire. Meals typically consisted of beans, bacon or whatever game could be found. Mining towns consisted of rickety wooden buildings that often caught fire. Many mining towns were completely destroyed by fire. Heavy rains and snow during the winter made mining difficult at best. Many miners stopped mining and went into the bigger cities (San Francisco). Every miner was assured of one thing – getting sick. Food was scarce and not very nutritious. Sanitation was poor and miners seldom bathed or washed their clothes. Medical doctors were few and far between. Yet given these harsh conditions, people continued to flock to California in hopes of striking it rich. (10 minutes) (This brief overview is to be supplemented with additional information gleaned from the social studies textbook or other resources). Student questions will be fielded. (2 minutes)

   One co-teacher leads the lecture/discussion. The other co-teacher monitors student behavior and offers additional content contextualization if needed.

3. The students will independently read excerpts from a letter written by General David Willock (see Figure 11.3). Ask students to briefly summarize Willock's description of mining life. Students will independently read The Lousy Miner poem (see Figure 11.4). Ask students to briefly describe how the miner is feeling and why he/she may feel this way. (10 minutes).

   As one co-teacher introduces the next activity, the other distributes copies to the students. Both co-teachers ask and field student comprehension and extension questions.

4. Provide each student a set of three Gold Rush images (see Figure 11.5 collectively). Guide students to specifically look at representations of living and working conditions of the miners. (5 minutes)

   Co-teachers share in the distribution of copied photographs.

5. Pair students by proximity. Provide each student a copy of the "Put Yourself There: The California Gold Rush" activity sheet (see Figure 11.6). Based upon the video, the two text-based primary sources, and the series of four primary source photographs, students are to collaboratively complete the activity sheet. (10 minutes)

   As one co-teacher introduces and explains the activity, the other co-teacher distributes the material. During the activity, both co-teachers circulate throughout the room, offering guidance and monitoring for on-task behavior.

LESSON CLOSURE AND ASSESSMENT

1. Students will answer the compelling and supporting questions identified at the beginning of the lesson in a large group as a review. (2 minutes)

2. As an extension activity, students will write a three paragraph letter home describing 1) the conditions of the mining town; 2) a description of a "typical" day spent mining; and 3) what they plan to do once (or if) they "strike it rich." Students can also draw their representation of mining life.

Figure 11.3 Excerpts from a letter written by General David Willock, March 17, 1850

DEFINITIONS

maimed: to be seriously wounded
*The soldier was **maimed** due to the attack.*

shoulder: to carry a heavy load; to transport
*The strongest person had to **shoulder** the supplies.*

composed: what is included; what something is made up of
*The lunch was **composed** of sandwiches and fruit.*

canopy: something that hangs or spreads overhead.
*The **canopy** of stars was particularly bright last night.*

John Sharp and John J. Hawkins are among the dead. Dr. A. G. Anderson and Wm. Muldrow's old black man, George, were victims; and many, indeed, who left the States within the last year, now lie beneath the sands of California. Many poor fellows fall in the struggle, and many more will be maimed for life. It is not uncommon for a man to shoulder from 60 to 80 pounds, composed of [supplies], blankets, and mining tools, and march away over mountains and canyons, at the rate of 15 or 20 miles per day, and when they have found a place that suits their views, they fall to work, with no shelter, day or night, save the canopy of heaven; and then their food generally consists of pickled pork and bread and sugar and coffee, and necessarily so, for they cannot pack a variety of food.

Figure 11.4 Excerpts from The Lousy Miner (date and author unknown)

It's four long years since I reached this land,
In search of gold among the rocks and sand;
And yet I'm poor, when the truth is told,
I'm a lousy miner,
I'm a lousy miner in search of shining gold.

I was covered with lice, coming on the boat,
I threw away my fancy swallow-tailed coat,
And now they crawl up and down my back;
I'm a lousy miner,
I'm a lousy miner, a pile is all I lack.

Oh, land of gold, you did me deceive,
And I intend in thee my bones to leave;
So farewell home, now my friends grow cold,
I'm a lousy miner,
I'm a lousy miner in search of shining gold

Figure 11.5 Select images of the California Gold Rush Mining and Camping Life

A California Gold Rush Mining Town

White and Chinese Miners Hoping to Strike It Rich During the California Gold Rush, 1852

Miners Pause in Their Search for Gold in the Sierra Nevada Mining Camp, 1851

Figure 11.6 Put Yourself There: The California Gold Rush activity sheet

Name: Date:

PUT YOURSELF THERE: THE CALIFORNIA GOLD RUSH

Based upon the video, poem, diary entry, and the photographs provided, list three to five phrases describing what you see, hear, taste, touch and smell.

SIGHT

What do you see? People? Words? Buildings? Animals? Interesting Items? Do these things give you clues about how life was like back then?

SMELL

What smells are around you? People? Animals? Machinery? Do they make you think of something good or bad?

SOUND

What do you hear? People? Animals? Nature? Sounds from inside or outside of buildings? Sounds can indicate something good, bad or sad.

TOUCH

How and what do you feel? What is the environment like? Hot? Cold? Wet? Are there "things" that you can touch? What do they feel like?

TASTE

What do you taste? Are things edible?

ELEMENTARY CIVICS LESSON

Not just the word itself, but the concept of "government" can be confusing to young learners. Though students experience "the hand of government" daily, they struggle to understand what, exactly, government does. Add to the mix the layers of government—local, county, state, and federal—and their respective roles, and students come to view government as something wholly separate from their lives and experiences.

The goal of this lesson is to provide students an opportunity to understand how decisions are made. Students brainstorm, tabulate and then vote on three initiatives they want for their school. A formal "petition" is written and sent to the principal. In turn, the principal addresses the class and discusses they way in which decisions are rendered. Parallels are made between the decision-making process of a principal and the President.

SAMPLE LESSON PLAN

LESSON TITLE: THE ROLES OF THE PRINCIPAL AND THE PRESIDENT	SUBJECT: CIVICS
Unit: The Roles of Government	Grade: 2
Timeframe: Multiple days	Teacher(s):

STANDARDS

This lesson promotes the following objectives of the *National Social Studies Standards*, the *C3 Framework for Social Studies State Standards*, and the *Common Core State Standards for English Language Arts and Literacy in History/Social Studies*.

NATIONAL SOCIAL STUDIES STANDARDS

Theme ⑩ **CIVIC IDEALS AND PRACTICES** (Early Grades)

Knowledge
Learners will understand:
The importance of gathering information as the basis for informed civic action. (p. 63)

Processes
Learners will be able to:
Ask and find answers to questions about how to plan for action with others to improve life in the school, community, and beyond. (p. 64)

C3 FRAMEWORK FOR SOCIAL STUDIES STATE STANDARDS

- D1.4.K-2. Make connections between supporting questions and compelling questions. (p. 25)

- D2.Civ.5.K-2. Explain what governments are and some of their functions. (p. 32)

- D3.1.K-2. Gather relevant information from one or two sources while using the origin and structure to guide the selection. (p. 54)

- D4.2.K-2. Construct an argument with reasons. (p. 60)

Reading Standards for Informational Text:
Key Ideas and Details
1. Ask and answer such questions as *who, what, where, when, why,* and *how* to demonstrate understanding of key details in a text. (p. 13)

GOAL

Students will understand the decision-making process and powers of the principal.

OBJECTIVES

Obj. 1: Students will participate in group collaboration and consensus-building.

Obj. 2: Students will petition their principal for collaborative wants.

Obj. 3: Students will ask their principal about his/her decision-making process.

COMPELLING QUESTIONS

Q1: How are important decisions made?

SUPPORTING QUESTIONS

Q1: What is the role of the principal at your school?

Q2: What, specifically, does your principal do for you?

Q3: In what way(s) is the principal like a President?

MATERIALS/EQUIPMENT/TECHNOLOGY

- Paper for drafting the "Letter of Petition."

UNIVERSAL DESIGN FOR LEARNING

REPRESENTATION – OPTIONS FOR PRESENTING CONTENT	ENGAGEMENT – OPTIONS FOR ENGAGING STUDENT INTEREST	EXPRESSION – OPTIONS FOR DEMONSTRATING STUDENT LEARNING	CULTURAL CONSIDERATIONS
☐ Artifacts ☐ Pictures ☐ Graphic organizers ☐ Video Clips ☐ Audio Recordings ☐ Lab ☐ Lecture ☒ **Other:** Scenario	☒ **Cooperative Group Work** ☐ Partner Work ☐ Manipulatives ☐ Movement ☐ Debates ☐ Role plays or Simulations ☐ Other _____	☒ **Written response** ☐ Illustrated response ☒ **Oral response** ☐ Model creation or construction ☐ Other _____	☐ Nature of content and ethnicity/culture of students ☐ Other _____
CONTENT	PROCESS	PRODUCT	

LESSON INTRODUCTION

1. Begin with a warm-up activity. As the students transition into social studies, a brief overview is provided. ("For the past several days, we have been exploring the many roles of the President.") A few content review questions are asked based upon previous lessons. (2 minutes)

2. Introduce the lesson for the day. (2 minutes)

INTRODUCTION

Have both co-teachers lead the transition into social studies and monitor on-task behavior.

A co-teacher introduces the procedures, expectations, goals and objectives for the lesson.

LESSON PROCEDURES

* Note that principal participation needs to be secured prior to the lesson.

1. Write on the board the following question: How is our principal like our President? State, "In many ways, the school's principal is much like our President. Both listen to people. Both solve problems. Both have to make decisions. And, often, both have to say 'no' to a request that is made." (2 minutes)

One co-teacher writes the guiding question on the board while the other facilitates discussion.

2. Ask students "If you can have or change any three things here at school, what would they be?" Field ample student responses and put responses on the board. Students will subsequently vote for the top three needs or desires they want at their school. Based on voting, the teacher will narrow responses to the top three. (15 minutes)

One co-teacher opens the discussion while the other tallies student votes. Both teachers facilitate student voting and the final list of wants.

3. The teacher will state, "As a class, we are going to take these wants to our principal." The teacher will draft a "Letter of Petition" stating the collective wants of the class (e.g. "We the class of Ms. Smith do hearby petition you, Principal Jones, to 1) [insert want]; 2) [insert want]; and 3) [insert want]. We respectfully request a verbal response by [insert date]. Gratefully, the class of Ms. Smith." (10 minutes)

One co-teacher drafts the petition as the other co-teacher assists with answering questions and monitoring on-task behavior.

4. When the petition is drafted, have all students sign it. Designate two students to physically deliver the petition to the principal. (10 minutes)

One co-teacher passes around the petition for students to sign. The other co-teacher selects two student representatives and escorts them to the principal's office.

5. The teacher will work with the principal to establish a date on which the principal will physically address the students. The principal should 1) thank the students for their petition; 2) state that he/she has thoroughly read the petition; and 3) has made a decision based upon the individual requests made. The principal will discuss the rationale behind each decision. Students are free to ask the principal questions about the decision-making process. (20 minutes)

Both co-teachers monitor student behavior during the principal's discussion.

6. Lastly, compare the role(s) and qualifications of the principal and the President (the President is elected by citizens 18 years of age or older, serves a set term, and must be at least 35 years old; the principal is hired or appointed, can serve for years, needs to have a college degree and special education license, and there is no age restriction). (5 minutes)

A chart or Venn diagram could be used for this comparison if students need an additional visual.

LESSON CLOSURE AND ASSESSMENT

1. Students will answer the compelling and supporting questions identified at the beginning of the lesson in a large group as a review. (5 minutes)

2. Students will draw a triangle on a sheet of paper and, at each point, reiterate how the role of the school principal is similar to the role of the President.

CHAPTER TWELVE
Middle Level Lesson Plans

Middle level social studies promotes interdisciplinary, interrelational, and interpersonal understandings. It is in the middle grades that students see the connections between other content areas, other perceptions, and other practices. It is also a critical period of transition when students consider connections between their present lives and future experiences as responsible and participatory citizens.

We provide four lesson plans that, in various forms and through various means, push middle level students towards deeper, more complex understandings of the social studies content. Each lesson plan provides multiple means of content representation, rich opportunities for student engagement, and promotes varied avenues for student expression. The lessons include guidelines for shared responsibilities within an inclusive (i.e. co-taught) classroom, but are easily taught without a co-teacher or paraprofessional present.

Students will explore middle level social studies by defining critical terms and concepts, comparing characteristics and providing examples, evaluating primary texts, synthesizing a series of visual images, engaging through written and oral responses, collaborating in small group settings, and participating in whole group simulation.

MIDDLE LEVEL ECONOMICS LESSON PLAN

Entrepreneurship is a foundational part of the United States economy, with new and existing business ventures creating opportunities for investment and job growth. Asking students to examine future career opportunities is an important step in determining what abilities, skills, education, and work ethic are needed to promote career success and fiscal responsibility. For exceptional learners who are turning 14 years old, addressing topics in economics also begins the process of developing postsecondary goals related to education, training, employment, and independent living.

This lesson examines three types of business organizations found in the United States and asks students to compare these organizations and consider how their own career interests may or may not fall within these business types. The lesson begins by defining key terms. Students draw a picture to help define the term "entrepreneur." Students use a three main idea flow chart and a modified version of the FRAME linking steps to organize the characteristics and examples for each business type. They use online resources or a text to locate examples for each business type. On a separate day, the students expand their knowledge of each organization by listening to local guest speakers, asking questions, and taking notes on a KWL organizer. They also create an informational brochure for future entrepreneurs considering what business type to choose.

LESSON TITLE: ENTREPRENEURSHIP	SUBJECT: ECONOMICS
Unit: U.S. Economic System	Grade: 7 or 8
Timeframe: 90 minutes	Teacher(s):

STANDARDS

This lesson promotes the following objectives of the *National Social Studies Standards, the C3 Framework for Social Studies State Standards*, and the *Common Core State Standards for English Language Arts and Literacy in History/Social Studies.*

NATIONAL SOCIAL STUDIES STANDARDS[†]

Theme ❼ **PRODUCTION, DISTRIBUTION, AND CONSUMPTION** (Middle Grades):

Knowledge

Learners will understand:

How markets bring buyers and sellers together to exchange goods and services. (p. 51)

C3 FRAMEWORK FOR SOCIAL STUDIES STATE STANDARDS[††]

- D1.4.6-8 Explain how the relationship between supporting questions and compelling questions is mutually reinforcing. (p. 25)

- D2.Eco.7.6-8. Analyze the role of innovation and entrepreneurship in a market economy. (p. 37)

- D3.3.6-8. Identify evidence that draws information from multiple sources to support claims, noting evidentiary limitations. (p. 55)

- D4.2.6-8. Construct explanations using reasoning, correct sequence, examples, and details with relevant information and data, while acknowledging the strengths and weaknesses of the explanations. (p. 60)

COMMON CORE STATE STANDARDS FOR ENGLISH LANGUAGE ARTS AND LITERACY IN HISTORY/SOCIAL STUDIES[†††]

Anchor Reading Standards:

Key Ideas and Details

1. Read closely to determine what the text says explicitly and to make logical inferences from it; cite specific textual evidence when writing or speaking to support conclusions drawn from the text. (p. 60)

Anchor Speaking and Listening Standards:

Comprehension and Collaboration

1. Prepare for and participate effectively in a range of conversations and collaborations with diverse partners, building on others' ideas and expressing their own clearly and persuasively. (p. 22)

3. Evaluate a speaker's point of view, reasoning, and use of evidence and rhetoric. (p. 22)

---

† This and subsequent references in this chapter to the national social studies standards are citations of National Council for the Social Studies (NCSS), *National Curriculum Standards for Social Studies: A Framework for Teaching, Learning, and Assessment* (Silver Spring, MD: NCSS, 2010).

†† This and subsequent references in this chapter to the C3 Framework for Social Studies State Standards are citations of National Council for the Social Studies (NCSS), *The College, Career, and Civic Life (C3) Framework for Social Studies State Standards: Guidance for Enhancing the Rigor of K-12 Civics, Economics, Geography, and History* (Silver Spring, MD: NCSS, 2013).

††† This and subsequent references in this chapter to the Common Core State Standards for English Language Arts and Literacy in History/Social Studies are citations of National Governors Association Center for Best Practices (NGA) and Council of Chief State School Officers (CCSSO), *Common Core State Standards for English Language Arts and Literacy in History/Social Studies, Science, and Technical Subjects* (Washington, DC: NGA and CCSSO, 2010).

GOAL

The student will demonstrate knowledge of the structure and operation of the United States economy by describing the types of business organizations and the role of entrepreneurship.

OBJECTIVES

Obj. 1: Students will define business, entrepreneurship, proprietorship, partnership, and corporation.

Obj. 2: Students will compare and contrast proprietorship, partnership, and corporation and provide examples for each.

Obj. 3: Students will explain why entrepreneurs consider one business type over another.

Obj. 4: Students will identify one or more of their own career interests and how these interests might fit within the business types.

COMPELLING QUESTION

Q1: Why might entrepreneurs choose one business type over another when creating a new business venture?

SUPPORTING QUESTIONS

Q1: What are the characteristics of an entrepreneur? Proprietorship? Partnership? Corporation?

Q2: What type of business might you be interested in organizing or working for when you finish school?

MATERIALS/EQUIPMENT/TECHNOLOGY

- Main-idea flow chart (Figure 12.1, p. 108) or similar graphic organizer
- KWL chart
- Access to the Internet or area phone books
- Local business leaders for guest speakers

UNIVERSAL DESIGN FOR LEARNING

REPRESENTATION – OPTIONS FOR PRESENTING CONTENT	ENGAGEMENT – OPTIONS FOR ENGAGING STUDENT INTEREST	EXPRESSION – OPTIONS FOR DEMONSTRATING STUDENT LEARNING	CULTURAL CONSIDERATIONS
☒ **Artifacts** ☐ Pictures ☒ **Graphic organizers** ☐ Video Clips ☐ Audio Recordings ☐ Lab ☐ Lecture ☐ Other _____	☒ **Cooperative Group Work** ☒ **Partner Work** ☐ Manipulatives ☒ **Movement** ☐ Debates ☐ Role plays or Simulations ☒ **Other:** Guest Speaker	☒ **Written response** ☐ Illustrated response ☒ **Oral response** ☐ Model creation or construction ☒ **Other:** Brochure	☐ Nature of content and ethnicity/culture of students ☒ **Other:** Identifying area businesses with specific cultural ties
CONTENT	PROCESS	PRODUCT	

LEARNING PLAN

LESSON INTRODUCTION

1. Begin with a bell ringer activity. Have the word "business" visible for the students as they enter the room. Ask them to write down what words or phrases (characteristics of businesses, types/names of businesses) come to mind when they see or hear the word "business." (2 minutes)

   While one co-teacher greets the students as they enter and takes roll, the other co-teacher and/or support professional monitors on-task behavior with the first activity. A co-teacher might provide examples to some students to help them think of other examples to write down.

2. Solicit student responses and relate their responses to today's lesson about the three business types. The teacher reveals an agenda for the lesson along with the compelling and supporting questions to be answered by the end of the lesson. (5 minutes)

   Both co-teachers call on students and relate their responses to today's lesson topic.

LESSON PROCEDURES

1. Ask the students to draw a picture (stick figure) of a person. Reveal the word "entrepreneur." Ask, why do we have businesses? Why do you think a person would start a business? Utilizing student responses, guide students to write down the following terms/phrases around the stick figure: profit–make money; produce goods; sell goods; take a risk; an owner or co-owner. Have the students use the words to form a definition of entrepreneur. Explain that the word "entrepreneur" will be used to describe a person who helps start a business in one of the three business types we will learn about in this lesson. (5 minutes)

   All teachers/support personnel monitor and facilitate this step.

2. The students receive copies of a three-main-idea graphic organizer (GO) and are introduced to the Framing Routine as a tool to support taking and organizing notes on essential content to be learned. The teacher explains how the GO will help clearly list the characteristics and examples of three business types in the U.S. economy (see Figure 12.1). (5 minutes)

   One co-teacher leads the introduction to the graphic organizer while the other co-teacher (and any support personnel) hand out copies to each student and assign the students to partners or triads. The co-teacher and support personnel move through the classroom ensuring that all students are on-task and support any students with handwriting if necessary.

3. The students pair up and co-construct the GO with the teacher using a modified version of the FRAME linking steps. Students begin by Focusing on the Key Topic (Types of Business) and write this in the GO followed by a statement explaining what today's topic is about. (5 minutes)

   The co-teacher and support personnel monitor completion of the GO section.

4. The teacher then Reveals the three business types as the three main ideas of the GO. Students write sentence stems for each business type (A Proprietorship is...). (10 minutes)

   Support personnel or a co-teacher assist with writing in the information for select students or helping students find information in the text about the three business types.

5. Next the students reveal characteristics for each business type and form sentences for each. "A proprietorship is a type of business with (1) one owner who (2) takes all the risk and (3) gets all of the profit." (10 minutes)

Continued support or the co-teacher switches roles to complete the next section of the GO with the students.

6. The next step is to have the students analyze the characteristics of each business type and provide examples that meet those characteristics. Students can use laptops or tablets to search for examples or the co-teachers can bring in phone books. (20 minutes)

The co-teacher hands out tablets or laptops and makes sure all students are on task. Support personnel are helping individual students with specific accommodations related to reading.

7. Next the students <u>M</u>ake a "So what?" summary statement explaining why it might be important to know about these three business types. Students are asked to share their statements. (10 minutes)

Student pairs/triads collaboratively self-monitor completion of each section during the entire GO activity.

8. Option A to <u>E</u>xtend Understanding: In small groups, the students use the GO and the research they collected about business types to create a colorful brochure (tri-fold) explaining one of the three business types to potential entrepreneurs. (15 minutes)

Both co-teachers facilitate this activity and support individual needs.

9. Option B to <u>E</u>xtend Understanding: The students meet a guest speaker representing each of the three business types over the course of the unit. The co-teacher leads the students through a KWL chart (see Figure 12.2), asking the students to list what they know already about a particular business type and questions they want to ask the guest speaker. As the speaker responds to questions, the students will fill in what they learned from the speaker. (30 minutes–for each class period that has a guest speaker)

One co-teacher sets up the KWL chart and the other co-teacher facilitates the discussion with the guest speaker.

LESSON CLOSURE AND ASSESSMENT

1. Students are asked to independently write down responses to the compelling question introduced at the beginning of the lesson. A few students are asked to share their responses and everyone turns in their responses at the end of class. (5 minutes)

Some students might orally dictate their understanding to a co-teacher or support personnel who will write down the response on paper. Both co-teachers will check for understanding.

2. The students are then asked to identify some of their own career interests. Which business type might your career choice fall within? Why? (5 minutes)

This information can be used as data for the IEP for any students turning 14.

Figure 12.1 Main-idea Flow Chart on Types of Business

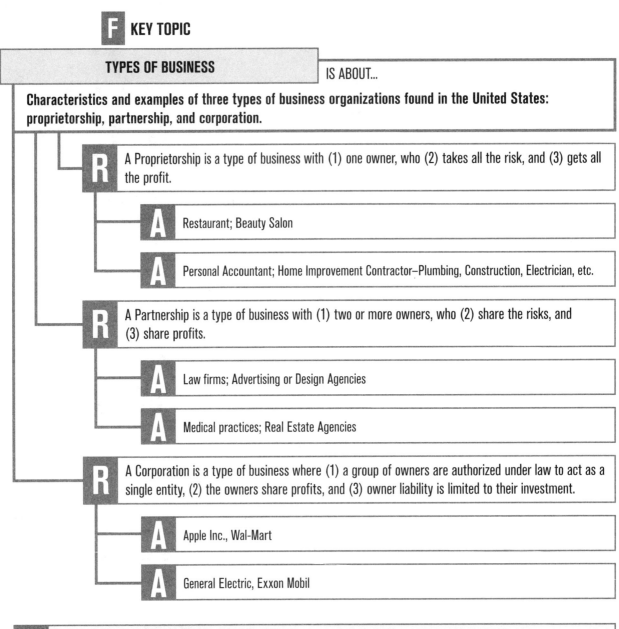

F KEY TOPIC

TYPES OF BUSINESS   IS ABOUT...

Characteristics and examples of three types of business organizations found in the United States: proprietorship, partnership, and corporation.

R A Proprietorship is a type of business with (1) one owner, who (2) takes all the risk, and (3) gets all the profit.

A Restaurant; Beauty Salon

A Personal Accountant; Home Improvement Contractor–Plumbing, Construction, Electrician, etc.

R A Partnership is a type of business with (1) two or more owners, who (2) share the risks, and (3) share profits.

A Law firms; Advertising or Design Agencies

A Medical practices; Real Estate Agencies

R A Corporation is a type of business where (1) a group of owners are authorized under law to act as a single entity, (2) the owners share profits, and (3) owner liability is limited to their investment.

A Apple Inc., Wal-Mart

A General Electric, Exxon Mobil

M So what?
Learning more about various types of business organizations helps us understand how businesses we see in every-day life are formed and makes us consider our own possible career interests.

E XTEND UNDERSTANDING

Adapted from Edwin Ellis The Content Enhancement Series: The Framing Routine *(Lawrence, KS.: Edge Enterprises, 1998); Edwin Ellis* Makes Sense Strategies: 3 Main Idea Flow Chart *(Tuscaloosa, Al., 2008).*

Figure 12.2 KWL Chart

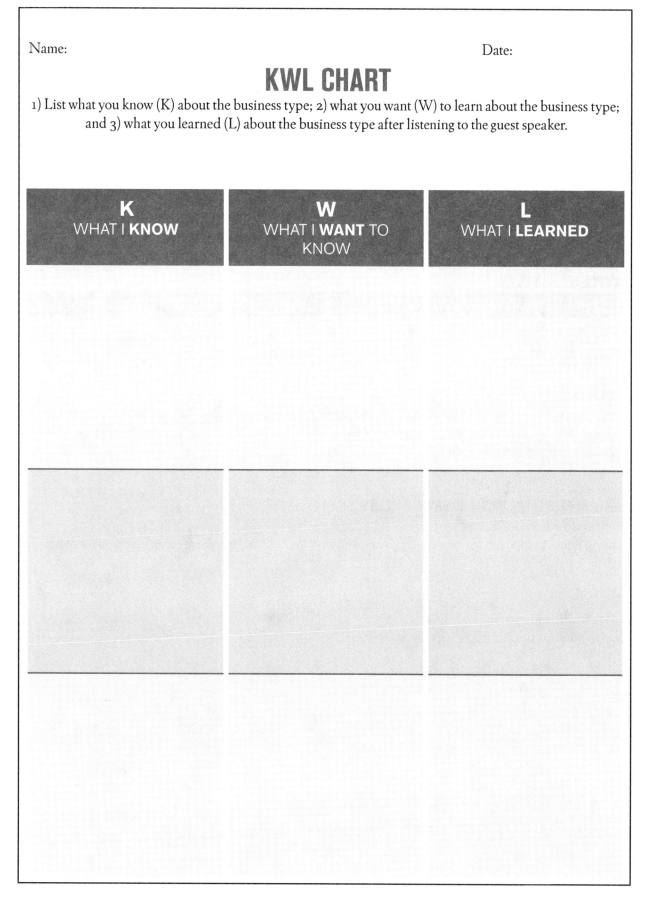

Name: Date:

KWL CHART

1) List what you know (K) about the business type; 2) what you want (W) to learn about the business type; and 3) what you learned (L) about the business type after listening to the guest speaker.

K WHAT I **KNOW**	W WHAT I **WANT** TO KNOW	L WHAT I **LEARNED**

MIDDLE LEVEL GEOGRAPHY LESSON PLAN

From turmoil to triumph, devastation to discovery, one thing is certain—the world is ever changing. How can students explore change through Geography? One of the Five Themes of Geography is Human-Environment Interaction: the relationship between people and their environment and the way humans both adapt and change it. It is important for middle level students to expand their notions of geography beyond maps and location. Students need to see geography in general and human-environment interaction in particular as a set of interdependent relationships that often have profound ramifications.

A geography lesson premised on the theme of Human-Environment Interaction is a perfect way to get hands in the air, voices heard, and positions taken.

This lesson starts by showing students two images and asking them to discuss their perceptions in relation to human interaction with the environment. Students are then asked to generate ways in which humans interact with the environment on a daily and seasonal basis. Student pairings provide opportunities for collaboration as they work on an activity sheet using photographs as visual prompts. Student presentations conclude the lesson.

SAMPLE LESSON PLAN

LESSON TITLE: HUMAN-ENVIRONMENT INTERACTION	SUBJECT: WORLD GEOGRAPHY
Unit: The Five Themes of Geography	Grade: 7
Timeframe: 60 minutes	Teacher(s):

STANDARDS

This lesson promotes the following objectives of the *National Social Studies Standards, the C3 Framework for Social Studies State Standards*, and the *Common Core State Standards for English Language Arts and Literacy in History/Social Studies.*

NATIONAL SOCIAL STUDIES STANDARDS

Theme ❸ **PEOPLE, PLACES, AND ENVIRONMENTS** (Middle Grades)

Questions for Exploration
How do human actions change the environment, and how does the environment influence the lives of people? (p. 34)

Knowledge
Learners will understand:
Human modifications of the environment. (p. 35)

Processes
Learners will be able to:
Evaluate the consequences of human actions in environmental terms. (p. 36)

- D1.2.6-8. Explain points of agreement experts have about interpretations and applications of disciplinary concepts and ideas associated with a compelling question (p. 24)

- D2.Geo.8.6-8. Analyze how relationships between humans and environments extend or contract spatial patterns of settlement and movement. (p. 43)

- D3.3.6-8. Identify evidence that draws information from multiple sources to support claims, noting evidentiary limitations. (p. 55)

- D4.2.6-8. Construct explanations using reasoning, correct sequence, examples, and details with relevant information and data, while acknowledging the strengths and weaknesses of the explanations. (p. 60)

COMMON CORE STATE STANDARDS FOR ENGLISH LANGUAGE ARTS AND LITERACY IN HISTORY/SOCIAL STUDIES

Anchor Reading Standards:
Integration of Knowledge and Ideas
7. Integrate and evaluate content presented in diverse formats and media, including visually and quantitatively, as well as in words. (p. 60)

Anchor Speaking and Listening Standards:
Comprehension and Collaboration
1. Prepare for and participate effectively in a range of conversations and collaborations with diverse partners, building on others' ideas and expressing their own clearly and persuasively. (p. 22)

2. Integrate and evaluate information presented in diverse media and formats, including visually, quantitatively, and orally. (p. 22)

GOAL
The students will demonstrate knowledge of human-environment interaction.

OBJECTIVES
Obj. 1: Students will be introduced to the key aspects of human-environment interaction.

Obj. 2: Students will generate aspects of human-environment interaction witnessed in their own town or community.

COMPELLING QUESTIONS
Q1: How do people interact with their environment?

Q2: Can altering the physical environment by humans be justified?

SUPPORTING QUESTIONS
Q1: What is a simple definition of human-environment interaction?

Q2: What are the three seminal or key aspects to human-environment interaction?

Q3: How has the physical environment been altered by humans in your community?

MATERIALS/EQUIPMENT/TECHNOLOGY
- Visual references:

  ▶ Deforestation (http://s1.ibtimes.com/sites/ www.ibtimes.com/files/styles/v2_article_large/ public/2013/11/15/amazon-deforestation. jpg?itok=SvQzfUGZ)

  ▶ Discovery Green Park (http://tvblogs. nationalgeographic.com/?s=Discovery+Green+Park)

  ▶ Central Park (https://thepulseandthesound.files. wordpress.com/2012/08/urban-parks.jpeg);

  ▶ Women Tending Crops in Benin (http://news. stanford.edu/news/2011/december/images/solardrip_ crops_news.jpg).

UNIVERSAL DESIGN FOR LEARNING

REPRESENTATION – OPTIONS FOR PRESENTING CONTENT	ENGAGEMENT – OPTIONS FOR ENGAGING STUDENT INTEREST	EXPRESSION – OPTIONS FOR DEMONSTRATING STUDENT LEARNING	CULTURAL CONSIDERATIONS
☐ Artifacts ☒ **Pictures** ☒ **Graphic organizers** ☐ Video Clips ☐ Audio Recordings ☐ Lab ☒ **Lecture** ☐ Other_____	☐ Cooperative Group Work ☒ **Partner Work** ☐ Manipulatives ☐ Movement ☐ Debates ☐ Role plays or Simulations ☐ Other_____	☒ **Written response** ☐ Illustrated response ☒ **Oral response** ☐ Model creation or construction ☐ Other_____	☐ Nature of content and ethnicity/culture of students ☒ **Other:** Describe some ways that other cultures interact with their environment that are both similar to and different from American culture.
CONTENT	PROCESS	PRODUCT	

LEARNING PLAN

LEARNING PLAN	ROLES, ACCOMMODATIONS, AND DIFFERENTIATION STRATEGIES
LESSON INTRODUCTION 1. Begin with a warm-up activity. Display both images (see Figure 12.3 collectively). Ask students, "In what ways did humans interact with their environment to produce such different results?" (5 minutes)	**INTRODUCTION** One co-teacher leads the discussion while the other takes roll.
2. Introduce the lesson for the day. Write "Human-Environment Interaction" on the board. (1 minute)	One co-teacher introduces the lesson while the other co-teacher writes "Human Environment Interaction" on the board.
LESSON PROCEDURES 1. Begin lesson by providing a content overview of Human-Environment Inter-action. Defined as "The relationship between people and their environment; how people adapt to the environment and how they change it." (5 minutes)	One co-teacher leads the content overview presentation.
2. Create a t-chart on the board titled "Human-Interaction Comparison." Label the left side "Daily" with the right side labeled "Seasonal." Have students generate ways in which people affect their environment every day (e.g. driving, using water, disposing of trash, building houses and roads). Ask students to then generate a list of the ways that people affect their environment through seasonal activities (e.g. watering lawns, burning leaves, skiing, hunting or fishing). Ask students to discuss differences. Ask, "What types of activities can be harmful to the environment under what conditions?" (10 minutes)	One co-teacher creates the t-chart on the board while the other co-teacher provides directions. Both co-teachers field student responses. One co-teacher writes responses on the board. Both co-teachers field student opinion responses.

3. Review the definition of human-environment interaction. State that there are three ways in which humans and their environment affect each other: **We Depend On It:** People depend on the environment for natural resources, travel, and recreation; **We Modify It:** People modify their environment by heating and/or cooling their houses, building dams, rivers, and lakes, deforestation, building new businesses, creating biking/hiking trails; and **We Adapt To It:** We adapt to the environment by wearing clothes suitable for summer (e.g. shorts) and winter (e.g. coats and sweaters), by building bridges, and building raised homes along coastlines. (10 minutes)	One co-teacher leads discussion while the other monitors student engagement.
4. Heterogeneously pair students. Provide each student with a copy of the Human-Environment Interaction Analysis activity sheet (see Figure 12.4). State that students are to work with their pair partner to generate responses to the questions posted on the activity sheet. (10 minutes)	One co-teacher provides pairing directions. Both co-teachers distribute materials. Both co-teachers monitor student/pair progress and offer any assistances as warranted.
5. A representative from each pair will share one or two responses with the class. (10 minutes)	Both co-teachers offer additional insights or probes based on responses.

LESSON CLOSURE AND ASSESSMENT

1. Students will answer the compelling and supporting questions identified at the beginning of the lesson in a large group as a review.

2. Ask students what action they can take to stop what they may perceive to be an environmental injustice. (10 minutes)

Figure 12.3 Images of Human-Environment Interaction

Amazon Deforestation: Clear-cutting in the Amazon to Make Room for Human Development

Discovery Green Park: the Largest Urban Public Park in Houston, Texas

Figure 12.4 Human Environment Interaction Analysis Sheet

Name: Date:

HUMAN ENVIRONMENT INTERACTION ANALYSIS
Use each image to answer the questions below.

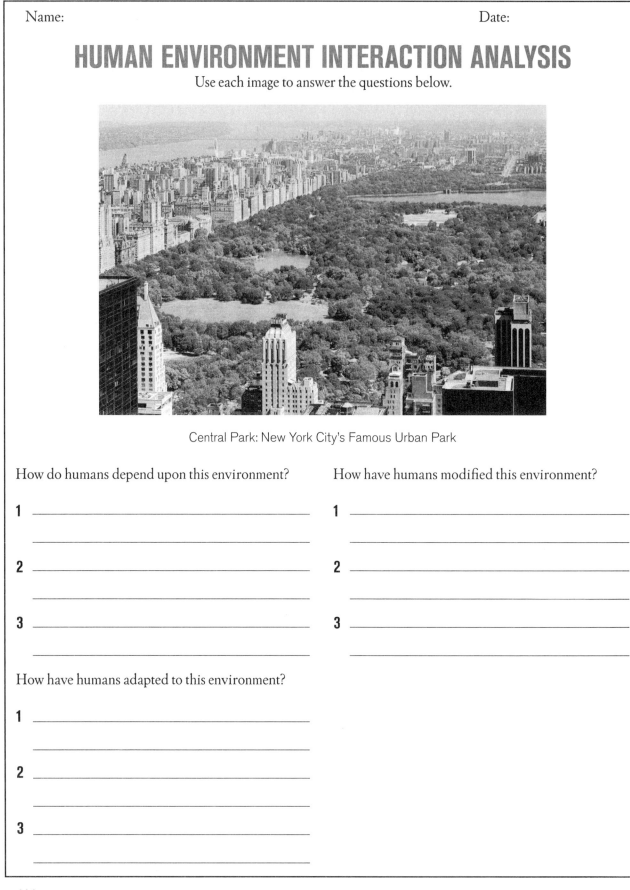

Central Park: New York City's Famous Urban Park

How do humans depend upon this environment?

1 _____

2 _____

3 _____

How have humans modified this environment?

1 _____

2 _____

3 _____

How have humans adapted to this environment?

1 _____

2 _____

3 _____

Women Tending Crops in Rural Benin

Due to human-environment interaction...

How will these humans depend upon their environment?

1 _____
_____

2 _____
_____

3 _____
_____

How will these humans adapt to their environment?

1 _____
_____

2 _____
_____

3 _____
_____

How will these humans modify their environment?

1 _____
_____

2 _____
_____

3 _____
_____

MIDDLE LEVEL HISTORY LESSON PLAN

One of the vexing and timeless questions in United States history is who *really* fired the first shot at the Battle of Lexington and Concord? Putting patriotism and centrism aside for a moment, there are conflicting "interpretations" about the first shot. This lesson explores the first shot scenario through the use of primary source documents and visual images. Not only are students engaging with the historical content in their quest to conclude who really did fire the first shot, they are also wrestling with concepts such as bias, persuasion, interpretation, representation, and historical accuracy.

Using the website *Historical Scene Investigation* as our lesson guide, students read a series of primary source narratives, two from the British perspective and two from the Colonists. As students peruse through these documents they complete a Detectives Log indicating the date, author, and summary conclusions. Students are then shown two paintings depicting the Battle of Lexington and Concord. From here, students are asked to corroborate their text-based conclusions (according to the texts provided, who fired the first shot?) with the portrayals represented in the two accompanying paintings (according to the paintings, who fired the first shot?)

SAMPLE LESSON PLAN

LESSON TITLE: WHO REALLY FIRED THE FIRST SHOT?	SUBJECT: U.S. HISTORY
Unit: American Revolution	Grade: 8
Timeframe: 60 minutes	Teacher(s):

STANDARDS

This lesson promotes the following objectives of the *National Social Studies Standards, the C3 Framework for Social Studies State Standards*, and the *Common Core State Standards for English Language Arts and Literacy in History/Social Studies.*

NATIONAL SOCIAL STUDIES STANDARDS

Theme ❷ **TIME, CONTINUITY, AND CHANGE** (Middle Grades)
Knowledge
Learners will understand:
That learning about the past requires the interpretation of sources, and that using varied sources provides the potential for a more balanced interpretive record of the past. (p. 31)

C3 FRAMEWORK FOR SOCIAL STUDIES STATE STANDARDS

- D1.5.6-8. Determine the kinds of sources that will be helpful in answering compelling and supporting questions, taking into consideration multiple points of views represented in the sources. (p. 25)

- D2.Hist.13.6-8. Evaluate the relevancy and utility of a historical source based on information such as maker, date, place of origin, intended audience, and purpose. (p. 48)

- D3.2.6-8. Evaluate the credibility of a source by determining its relevance and intended use. (p. 54)

- D4.1.6-8. Construct arguments using claims and evidence from multiple sources, while acknowledging the strengths and limitations of the arguments. (p. 60)

Anchor Reading Standards:

Integration of Knowledge and Ideas

8. Delineate and evaluate the argument and specific claims in a text, including the validity of the reasoning as well as the relevance and sufficiency of the evidence. (p. 60)

Anchor Writing Standards:

Text Types and Purposes

1. Write arguments to support claims in an analysis of substantive topics or texts using valid reasoning and relevant and sufficient evidence. (p. 63)

Research to Build and Present Knowledge

8. Gather relevant information from multiple print and digital sources, assess the credibility and accuracy of each source, and integrate the information while avoiding plagiarism. (p. 63)

Anchor Speaking and Listening Standards

Presentation of Knowledge and Ideas

4. Present information, findings, and supporting evidence such that listeners can follow the line of reasoning and the organization, development, and style are appropriate to task, purpose, and audience. (p. 22)

GOAL

The students will conclude who fired the first shot at the Battle of Lexington and Concord.

OBJECTIVES

Obj. 1: Students will be exposed to key issues and/or events that led to the American Revolution.

Obj. 2: Students will examine and analyze primary sources (e.g. narratives, paintings) describing and depicting the Battle of Lexington and Concord.

Obj. 3: Students will evaluate sources for bias.

Obj. 4: Students will use primary sources to complete the Historical Scene Investigation: Battle of Lexington and Concord activity sheet.

COMPELLING QUESTIONS

Q1: Who *really* fired the first shot at the Battle of Lexington and Concord?

Q2: When historical sources are inconsistent, what does this mean for historians?

Q3: Why is history often biased or sometimes inaccurate?

Q4: How can we know what really happened in the past?

SUPPORTING QUESTIONS

Q1: Why did the Lexington townsfolk feel compelled to stop the British?

Q2: What inference can be drawn by "hiding behind a stone wall?"

MATERIALS/EQUIPMENT/TECHNOLOGY:

* Visual references:

  ▶ http://t1.gstatic.com/images?q=tbn:ANd9GcQqmt2AesRxRRQ1GYmct7lMBd5tSd6F3WDZTocG2AOWy8a_WErs

  ▶ http://www.sonofthesouth.net/revolutionary-war/battles/revolutionary-war-minutemen.jpg

* Lesson adapted from Historical Scene Investigation (http://web.wm.edu/hsi/?svr=www)

UNIVERSAL DESIGN FOR LEARNING

REPRESENTATION – OPTIONS FOR PRESENTING CONTENT	ENGAGEMENT – OPTIONS FOR ENGAGING STUDENT INTEREST	EXPRESSION – OPTIONS FOR DEMONSTRATING STUDENT LEARNING	CULTURAL CONSIDERATIONS
☐ Artifacts ☒ **Pictures** ☒ **Graphic organizers** ☐ Video Clips ☐ Audio Recordings ☐ Lab ☐ Lecture ☒ **Other:** Primary source narratives	☒ **Cooperative Group Work** ☐ Partner Work ☐ Manipulatives ☐ Movement ☐ Debates ☐ Role plays or Simulations ☒ **Other:** Group presentations	☒ **Written response** ☐ Illustrated response ☒ **Oral response** ☐ Model creation or construction ☐ Other _____	☐ Nature of content and ethnicity/culture of students ☒ **Other:** Would British history textbooks have a different representation of the Battle of Lexington and Concord?
CONTENT	PROCESS	PRODUCT	

LEARNING PLAN

LEARNING PLAN	ROLES, ACCOMMODATIONS, AND DIFFERENTIATION STRATEGIES
LESSON INTRODUCTION 1. Begin with a warm-up activity. Ask students whom they think fired the first shot in the Battle of Lexington and Concord. Field a few responses. Ask how did students come to their conclusions? What evidence did they use? (5 minutes)	One co-teacher leads the discussion while the other takes roll.
2. Introduce the lesson for the day. Write "Who *Really* Fired the First Shot?" on the board. (1 minute)	One co-teacher introduces the lesson while the other co-teacher writes "Who Really Fired the First Shot?" on the board.
LESSON PROCEDURES 1. Distribute a copy of the Case File (see Figure 12.5) and the Detectives Case Log (see Figure 12.6) to each student. State that, for the remainder of the period, they are going to become historical detectives. Their "case" is to find out who fired the first shot in the Battle of Lexington and Concord. They will be using a series of primary source narratives and visual representations as their clues. State that students will read a document, then answer the questions on the Detectives Logs pertinent to that document. Divide students into heterogeneous groups of 4-5 students per group (7 minutes)	Both co-teachers distribute materials. One co-teacher provides directives. Both co-teachers answer any logistical questions that may arise. Both co-teachers quickly divide the class into groups.
2. Ask students to read Document 1 (3 minutes). When finished reading, model along with students how to complete Document 1 in the Detectives Log. (3 minutes)	One co-teacher leads the modeling, while the other circulates to assure accurate student completion. Both answer any logistical questions that may arise.

3. Follow the same steps as noted in #2 above for the remaining three documents. (15 minutes)	Both co-teachers follow processes noted in Step #2 above.
4. When students have completed their Detectives Log, ask "Based upon the information presented so far, who fired the first shot?" (As two documents state that the British fired first and two state that the Colonists fired first, students should say that the information is inconclusive). Facilitate discussions regarding bias, persuasion, and possible historical inaccuracies. (10 minutes)	Both co-teachers facilitate discussion and offer extension questions as warranted.
5. Show two visual representations of the Battle of Lexington and Concord (see Figure 12.7 collectively). Have students recall from the narratives key physical features (e.g. "in the town square," and "hiding behind a wall.") Ask students if the narratives and visual representations "tell the same story." Ask, "Based upon the text and now the two visual representations, who fired the first shot?" Facilitate discussion. (5 minutes)	Both co-teachers facilitate discussion and offer extension questions as warranted.
6. Working in their groups, ask students to see if consensus can be reached as to who fired the first shot. (5 minutes)	Both co-teachers monitor group work and provide assistance as warranted.
7. Each group will designate a spokesperson and state the group decision. (5 minutes)	Both co-teachers monitor the group presentation and offer clarification and/or extension questions when warranted.

LESSON CLOSURE AND ASSESSMENT

1. Students will answer the compelling and supporting questions identified at the beginning of the lesson in a large group as a review. (5 minutes)

2. As an extension, students can write a two-paragraph "witness statement" from the perspective of an onlooking civilian. Students can also draw a cartoon depicting the bravery, savagery, or cowardice of either side.

Figure 12.5 Case Files

DOCUMENT 1

Letter by Joseph Warren, President *pro tem* of the Massachusetts Provincial Council, sent to Benjamin Franklin, the colonial representative in London

To the inhabitants of Great Britain: In Provincial Congress, Watertown, April 26, 1775:

On the night proceeding the nineteenth of April …the Town of Lexington…was alarmed, and a company of [colonists] mustered on the occasion; that the [British] troops, on their way to Concord, marched into the town of Lexington, and the [colonists], on their approach, began to disperse; the [British troops] rushed on with great violence and first began hostilities by firing on [the colonists], whereby they killed eight and wounded several others; that the [British] continued their fire until [the colonists], who were neither killed nor wounded, had made their escape.

DOCUMENT 2

We Nathaniel Mulliken, Philip Russell, (Followed by the names of 32 other men present on Lexington Green on April 19, 1775)… do testify and declare, that on the nineteenth of April, about one or two o'clock in the morning, being informed that…a body of [British troops] were marching from Boston towards Concord…we were alarmed and having met at the place of our company's parade (Lexington Green), were dismissed, with orders to be ready to attend at the beat of the drum. About five o'clock in the morning, hearing our drum beat, we proceeded towards the parade, and soon found that a large body of [British] troops were marching towards us. While our backs were turned, we were fired on by [the British], and a number of our men were instantly killed and wounded, not a gun was fired by any person in our company to our knowledge before [the British] fired on us, and continued firing until we had all made our escape. Lexington, April 25, 1775.

Sworn by 34 minutemen on April 25 before three Justices of the Peace.

DOCUMENT 3

Entry for April 19th 1775, from the diary of Lieutenant John Barker, an officer in the British army.

At 2 o'clock we began our march by wading through a very long ford up to the middles; about five miles on this side of a town called Lexington, which lay in our road, we heard there were some hundreds of [colonists] collected together intending to oppose us and stop our going on; at 5 o'clock we arrived [in Lexington], and saw a number of people, I believe between 200 and 300, formed in a common in the middle of town; we still continued advancing, keeping prepared against an attack though without intending to attack [the colonists]; but on our coming near them [the colonists] fired on us two shots, upon which our men without any orders, rushed upon them, fired and put them to flight; several of them were killed, we could not tell how many, because they were behind walls and into the woods.

DOCUMENT 4

Ensign Jeremy Lister, youngest of the British officers at Lexington, in a personal narrative written in 1782.

To the best of my recollection about 4'oclock in the morning on the 19th of April, the five front companies were ordered to load, which they did….It was at Lexington when we saw [the colonists] drawn up in regular order. Major Pitcairn of the Marines called them to disperse, but their not seeming willing, he desired us to mind our places which we did when [the colonists] gave us a fire, the run off to get behind a wall. I believe we killed and wounded either 7 or 8 men.

Figure 12.6 Detectives Log

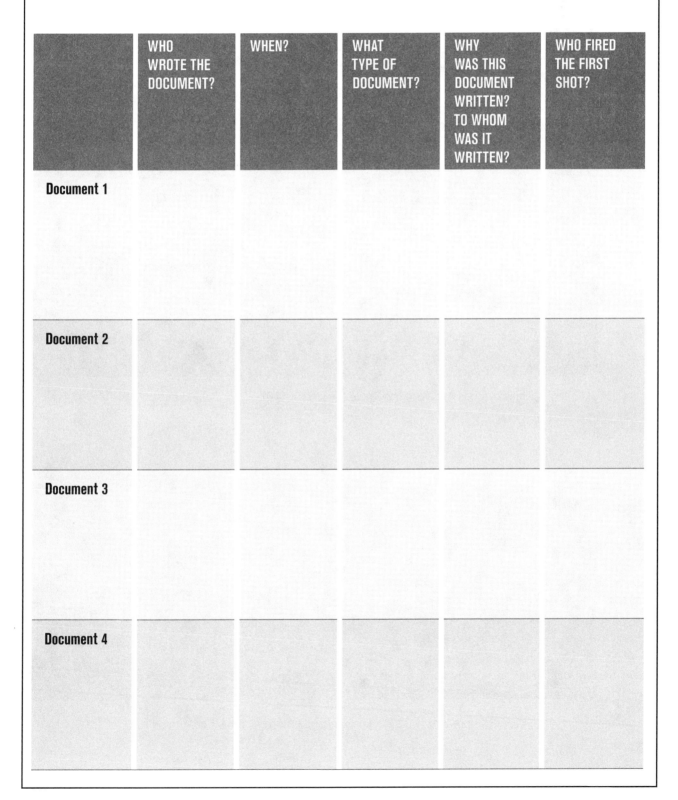

HSI: HISTORICAL SCENE INVESTIGATION
WHO FIRED THE FIRST SHOT AT LEXINGTON AND CONCORD?

	WHO WROTE THE DOCUMENT?	WHEN?	WHAT TYPE OF DOCUMENT?	WHY WAS THIS DOCUMENT WRITTEN? TO WHOM WAS IT WRITTEN?	WHO FIRED THE FIRST SHOT?
Document 1					
Document 2					
Document 3					
Document 4					

Figure 12.7 Images representing the Battle of Lexington and Concord

British Troops Are Marching While the Colonists Fire from Behind a Wall

British Troops Are in the Background and Colonists in the Foreground

MIDDLE LEVEL CIVICS LESSON PLAN

Though the concept of democracy was introduced and illustrated in elementary school, it is in the middle grades that students start to begin linking the notion of democracy to their own lives and experiences. As students start to question (and practice) democracy and democratic ideals, they often do so within the context of their own understandings of democracy's origins. Simply, it is often assumed that democracy "started" in America. This lesson plan pushes our students back in time to examine the origins of ancient Athenian democracy.

The opening discussion offers students an opportunity to wrestle with the ambiguous concept of democracy by situating it within the context of their own understandings. "What does democracy mean to you?" An animated and engaging video provides relevant supplementary content. Yet the heart of this lesson is the hands-on simulation. Here, students experience the "selectivity" of Athenian democracy, as only a few students will be "qualified" to participate (i.e. vote). The ensuing discussion asks students to articulate their impression of Athenian democracy as witnessed through their level of participation (ranging from full to none at all) in the simulated voting process. Lastly, students express their opinion of Athenian democracy in the form of an illustrated petition.

Learning is active. Connections are real and relevant. Understanding emerges through participation. These allowances afford all students multiple opportunities to engage with the content and express their understandings of democracy's early origins.

SAMPLE LESSON PLAN

LESSON TITLE: ATHENIAN DEMOCRACY	SUBJECT: WORLD HISTORY (CIVICS)
Unit: Ancient Greece	Grade: 6
Timeframe: 60 minutes	Teacher(s):

STANDARDS

This lesson promotes the following objectives of the *National Social Studies Standards, the C3 Framework for Social Studies State Standards*, and the *Common Core State Standards for English Language Arts and Literacy in History/Social Studies.*

NATIONAL SOCIAL STUDIES STANDARDS

Theme ❻ **POWER, AUTHORITY, AND GOVERNANCE** (Middle Grades)
Questions for Exploration
How are power, authority, and governments alike and different across groups and nations? (p. 46)

C3 FRAMEWORK FOR SOCIAL STUDIES STATE STANDARDS

- D1.1.6-8. Explain how a question represents key ideas in the field. (p. 24)

- D2.Civ.14.6-8. Compare historical and contemporary means of changing societies and promoting the public good. (p. 34)

- D3.3.6-8. Identify evidence that draws information from multiple sources to support claims, noting evidentiary limitations. (p. 55)

- D4.1.6-8. Construct arguments using claims and evidence from multiple sources, while acknowledging the strengths and limitations of the arguments. (p. 60)

Anchor Writing Standards:

Text Types and Purposes

1. Write arguments to support claims in an analysis of substantive topics or texts using valid reasoning and relevant and sufficient evidence. (p. 63)

Anchor Speaking and Listening Standards:

Comprehension and Collaboration

1. Prepare for and participate effectively in a range of conversations and collaborations with diverse partners, building on others' ideas and expressing their own clearly and persuasively. (p. 22)

Presentation of Knowledge and Ideas:

4. Present information, findings, and supporting evidence such that listeners can follow the line of reasoning and the organization, development, and style are appropriate to task, purpose, and audience. (p. 22)

GOAL

Students will demonstrate an understanding of early ancient Athenian Democracy.

OBJECTIVES

Obj. 1: Students will describe which segments of society were included in early Athenian democracy.

Obj. 2: Students will simulate early Athenian democracy through role-play.

Obj. 3: Students will discuss the outcome(s) of Athenian democracy regarding the perpetuation of power and the exclusion of women.

COMPELLING QUESTIONS

Q1: Who gets to vote in a democracy? Why not let everyone vote?

Q2: Who decides who votes?

Q3: Why is democracy not always democratic?

SUPPORTING QUESTIONS

Q1: What are three pillars or seminal aspects of Athenian democracy?

Q2: What aspects of Athenian and American democracy do you find appealing?

Q3: Can you think of parallels between early Athenian democracy and early democracy in the United States?

MATERIALS/EQUIPMENT/TECHNOLOGY:

- Video: Athenian Democracy: Solon and Cleisthenes (http://study.com/academy/lesson/athenian-democracy-solon-and-cleisthenes.html)

- Lesson adapted from Lesson Zoom (http://www.classroomzoom.com/lessons/dl/?id=374&fgid=)

UNIVERSAL DESIGN FOR LEARNING

REPRESENTATION – OPTIONS FOR PRESENTING CONTENT	ENGAGEMENT – OPTIONS FOR ENGAGING STUDENT INTEREST	EXPRESSION – OPTIONS FOR DEMONSTRATING STUDENT LEARNING	CULTURAL CONSIDERATIONS
☐ Artifacts ☐ Pictures ☐ Graphic organizers ☒ **Video Clips** ☐ Audio Recordings ☐ Lab ☒ **Lecture** ☐ Other _____	☐ Cooperative Group Work ☐ Partner Work ☐ Manipulatives ☐ Movement ☐ Debates ☒ **Role plays or Simulations** ☐ Other _____	☐ Written response ☒ **Illustrated response** ☒ **Oral response** ☐ Model creation or construction ☐ Other _____	☐ Nature of content and ethnicity/culture of students ☒ **Other:** Describe similarities and/ or differences between Athenian and American democracy.
CONTENT	PROCESS	PRODUCT	

LEARNING PLAN

	ROLES, ACCOMMODATIONS, AND DIFFERENTIATION STRATEGIES
LESSON INTRODUCTION 1. Begin with a warm-up activity. Ask students, "When you think of Democracy what words or images come to mind?" (2 minutes)	One co-teacher leads the discussion while the other takes roll.
2. Introduce the lesson for the day. Write "Athenian Democracy" on the board. As this lesson is procedurally detailed, assure that directions are clear and clearly understood. (3 minutes)	One co-teacher introduces the lesson while the other co-teacher writes "Athenian Democracy" on the board.
LESSON PROCEDURES 1. Fictitiously state that you are undecided about what type of project you wish to assign for the current unit. State that you have thought about a report, a play, or some form of electronic, internet-based display. You have decided to be democratic and let the "will of the people" decide. (3 minutes)	One co-teacher leads the content overview presentation.
2. To provide content contextualization, show the video "Athenian Democracy: Solon and Cleisthenes." (11 minutes)	One co-teacher loads and displays the video. Both co-teachers provide content contextualization as warranted.
3. State that democracy was truly a radical idea for Ancient Greece in 500 B.C. For well over 500 years, the Greek city-states had been ruled by small groups of aristocratic (influential) men who, in essence, made all of the decisions. Slowly, rulers such as Solon, Cleisthenes, and Pericles instituted a (restricted) form of democracy. All common male citizens were allowed to vote, yet foreigners, slaves, and women could not. (5 minutes)	One co-teacher leads the content overview yet both co-teachers offer additional contextualization as warranted.

4. Distribute role cards (see Figure 12.8) in this order: 1). Ecclesia cards should be given to half of the males in the class. 2). Metic and Servant cards should be equally distributed to the remaining half of male students. (No females should receive any cards). State that only those who carry the Ecclesia card may have a say in what type of impending project they want. Though males holding the Metic and Servant cards may want to contribute, and surely female students will as well, reiterate that only the Ecclesia are entitled to vote. Hold a vote on the project choices, allowing only the Ecclesia to vote. (10 minutes)

Both co-teachers distribute the simulation cards. One co-teacher leads the discussion/voting while the other monitors for student engagement.

5. When this initial round of voting is over, ask "How was or wasn't this a democratic way of deciding what project we were all going to do?" "What 'segment of society' was not allowed to participate?" "Why do we call it democracy when it wasn't very democratic at all?" (10 minutes)

Both co-teachers facilitate the discussion.

6. As an extension, students will create a "petition" to Cleisthenes advocating for the continuance of this form of democracy (as supported by the Ecclesia), or advocating for a change in policy (as supported by the Metic, Servants, and Women). Petitions need to have a single-line slogan, offer at least two points why Cleisthenes should keep or change the policy, and an illustrated representation. (10 minutes)

One co-teacher provides directions. Both co-teachers monitor and offer guidance as warranted.

7. Select students will share their petitions to the class. (5 minutes)

Both co-teachers facilitate discussion.

LESSON CLOSURE AND ASSESSMENT

1. Students will answer the compelling and supporting questions identified at the beginning of the lesson in a large group as a review. (3 minutes)

2. As an extension, students complete a Venn diagram (see Figure 12.9) comparing and contrasting Athenian and American democracy.

Support provided to individual students to prepare a response for one of the essential questions. This can be done with a peer-tutoring structure or with a teacher or paraprofessional providing guidance.

Figure 12.8 Role Cards

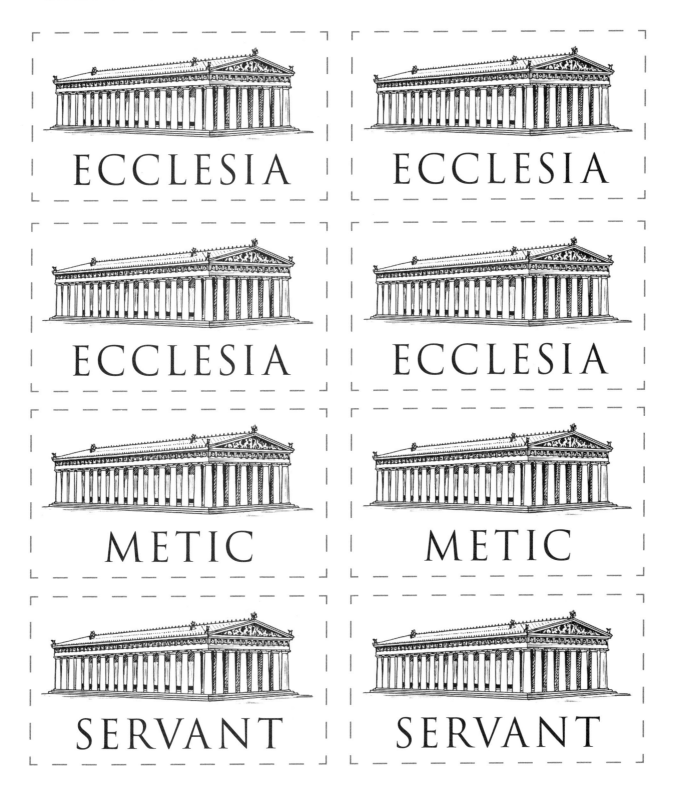

Figure 12.9 Venn Diagram: Contrasting Athenian and American Democracy

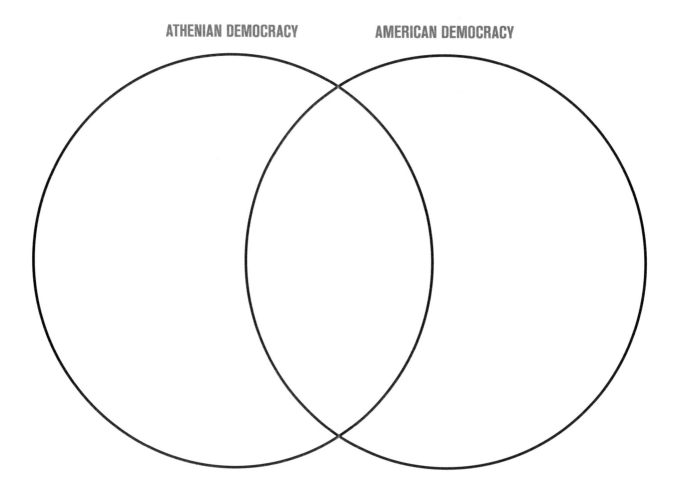

CHAPTER THIRTEEN

High School Lesson Plans

High school serves as a period of transition for all students as they complete academic requirements for graduation and experience social and emotional growth in preparation for postsecondary life. For exceptional learners in the secondary general curriculum, transition is also a part of their IEP, where measurable postsecondary goals are established in education, training, employment, and independent living. Students complete a course of study and participate in a coordinated set of transition activities to support movement toward these postsecondary goals. Involvement in the IEP process for exceptional learners becomes even more critical at the secondary level as decisions are being made that affect postsecondary life. This involvement in the IEP process requires students to develop self-determination skills. As noted in Chapter 5, social studies teachers have the ability to foster self-determination in exceptional learners, which in turn leads to positive academic and social outcomes in school and supports positive postsecondary education and employment outcomes.

Like earlier sections addressing elementary and middle school, we developed examples of secondary lesson plans in each of the following content areas: Economics, Geography, History, and Civics/U.S. Government. Each plan provides models for implementing several instructional strategies discussed in earlier chapters and utilizes the lesson plan format incorporating elements of the C3 Framework, Universal Design for Learning (UDL), differentiation, and collaboration with other teachers and support personnel. The lessons are easily taught without an available co-teacher or paraprofessional. Also, each plan supports self-determination skills through the instructional strategies and topics selected.

SECONDARY ECONOMICS LESSON PLAN

Supply and demand is a fundamental principle of free market economies in addition to being a fun topic to teach. This lesson addresses the concept of supply and demand using a variety of instructional strategies. The lesson begins by using a video clip to engage the students in the topic and activate prior knowledge. Notes are organized into a matrix to make them easier to read and study. Co-teachers are encouraged to use parallel teaching during the note taking to provide more individualized instruction.

When students are asked to read supply and demand scenarios, they are encouraged to use visual graphs to demonstrate their understanding in addition to verbally explaining how the laws of supply and demand apply. Participation is encouraged in large group and small group settings throughout the lesson. Finally, the review in this lesson uses a sorting activity, kinesthetic vocabulary review, and an exit slip to gauge understanding.

LESSON TITLE: SUPPLY AND DEMAND	SUBJECT: ECONOMICS
Unit: U.S. Market Economy	Grade: 9-12
Timeframe: 90 minutes (or two days)	Teacher(s):

STANDARDS

This lesson promotes the following objectives of the *National Social Studies Standards*, the *C3 Framework for Social Studies State Standards*, and the *Common Core State Standards for English Language Arts and Literacy in History/Social Studies*.

NATIONAL SOCIAL STUDIES STANDARDS[†]

Theme ❼ **PRODUCTION, DISTRIBUTION, AND CONSUMPTION** (High School)

Knowledge

Learners will understand:

Entrepreneurial decisions are influenced by factors such as supply and demand, government regulatory policy, and the economic climate. (p. 51)

C3 FRAMEWORK FOR SOCIAL STUDIES STATE STANDARDS[††]

- D1.2.9-12 Explain points of agreement and disagreement experts have about interpretations and applications of disciplinary concepts and ideas associated with a compelling question. (p. 24)

- D2. Eco.3.9-12. Analyze the ways in which incentives influence what is produced and distributed in a market system. (p. 37)

- D3.1.9-12. Gather relevant information from multiple sources representing a wide range of views while using the origin, authority, structure, context, and corroborative value of the sources to guide the selection. (p. 54)

- D4.2.9-12. Construct explanations using sound reasoning, correct sequence (linear or non-linear), examples, and details with significant and pertinent information and data, while acknowledging the strengths and weaknesses of the explanation, given its purpose (e.g., cause and effect, chronological, procedural, technical). (p.60)

COMMON CORE STATE STANDARDS FOR ENGLISH LANGUAGE ARTS AND LITERACY IN HISTORY/SOCIAL STUDIES[†††]

Anchor Reading Standards

Integration of Knowledge and Ideas

7. Integrate and evaluate content presented in diverse formats and media, including visually and quantitatively, as well as in words. (p. 60)

[†] This and subsequent references in this chapter to the national social studies standards are citations of National Council for the Social Studies (NCSS), *National Curriculum Standards for Social Studies: A Framework for Teaching, Learning, and Assessment* (Silver Spring, MD: NCSS, 2010).

[††] This and subsequent references in this chapter to the C3 Framework for Social Studies State Standards are citations of National Council for the Social Studies (NCSS), *The College, Career, and Civic Life (C3) Framework for Social Studies State Standards: Guidance for Enhancing the Rigor of K-12 Civics, Economics, Geography, and History* (Silver Spring, MD: NCSS, 2013).

[†††] This and subsequent references in this chapter to the Common Core State Standards for English Language Arts and Literacy in History/Social Studies are citations of National Governors Association Center for Best Practices (NGA) and Council of Chief State School Officers (CCSSO), *Common Core State Standards for English Language Arts and Literacy in History/Social Studies, Science, and Technical Subjects* (Washington, DC: NGA and CCSSO, 2010).

Anchor Writing Standards
Text Types and Purposes
1. Write arguments to support claims in an analysis of substantive topics or texts using valid reasoning and relevant and sufficient evidence. (p. 63)

Anchor Language Standards
Vocabulary Acquisition and Use
6. Acquire and use accurately a range of general academic and domain-specific words and phrases sufficient for reading, writing, speaking, and listening at the college and career readiness level; demonstrate independence in gathering vocabulary knowledge when considering a word or phrase important to comprehension or expression. (p. 51)

GOAL

Students will demonstrate knowledge of the United States market economy by explaining the interaction of supply and demand.

OBJECTIVES

Obj. 1: Students will define supply, demand, consumer, producer, substitute, and complement.

Obj. 2: Students will identify other factors that have an influence on supply and demand.

Obj. 3: Students will demonstrate how the laws of supply and demand work using scenarios and a visual device.

Obj. 4: Students will apply their knowledge of supply and demand to explain current or recent events related to goods and services.

COMPELLING QUESTIONS

Q1: What determines the price you pay for a good or service?

Q2: What effect might supply and demand have on your daily life?

SUPPORTING QUESTIONS

Q1: How do supply and demand interact to determine price?

Q2: How do other factors influence supply and demand?

Q3: What are some real life examples that demonstrate the laws of supply and demand?

MATERIALS/EQUIPMENT/TECHNOLOGY

- Supply and demand blank matrix, supply and demand scenarios, dry erase boards, markers, and erasers, different colors of electrical tape, ruler, supply and demand sort cards printed on cardstock, cut out and placed in baggies (one supply bag and one demand bag for every four students), textbook for definitions.

- YouTube Hudsucker Proxy video clip (http://youtu.be/N1PJ6Sv4Eoo) or the Hudsucker Proxy DVD (Hula Hoop production and distribution scene).

- YouTube Supply and Demand video clip for sample graphs to share with students (http://youtu.be/IdnJKnefYEs) for more visual representations of supply and demand. Khan Academy also has useful video clips on this topic.

UNIVERSAL DESIGN FOR LEARNING

REPRESENTATION – OPTIONS FOR PRESENTING CONTENT	ENGAGEMENT – OPTIONS FOR ENGAGING STUDENT INTEREST	EXPRESSION – OPTIONS FOR DEMONSTRATING STUDENT LEARNING	CULTURAL CONSIDERATIONS
☐ Artifacts ☒ **Pictures** ☒ **Graphic organizers** ☒ **Video Clips** ☐ Audio Recordings ☐ Lab ☐ Lecture ☒ **Other**: Newspapers and magazines	☒ **Cooperative Group Work** ☐ Partner Work ☐ Manipulatives ☐ Movement ☐ Debates ☐ Role plays or Simulations ☒ **Other**: Scenarios	☒ **Written response** ☒ **Illustrated response** ☒ **Oral response** ☐ Model creation or construction ☐ Other: _____	☐ Nature of content and ethnicity/culture of students ☒ **Other**: Consider cultural factors that might influence supply and demand
CONTENT	PROCESS	PRODUCT	

LEARNING PLAN

	ROLES, ACCOMMODATIONS, AND DIFFERENTIATION STRATEGIES
LESSON INTRODUCTION 1. Begin the lesson by showing a short clip from the Hudsucker Proxy where the Hudsucker Corporation puts the hula-hoop into production and then it cuts to the toy storeowner waiting for customers to enter his store to buy hula-hoops for $1.79. During his "long" wait, the storeowner keeps dropping the hula-hoop price, eventually to "free with any purchase." Then the children see a boy playing with a hula-hoop and the resulting demand increases the price to $3.99. This clip can be found on YouTube (not captioned) or on the DVD (captioned). (5-8 minutes)	Provide captions for students while showing the clip. Create seating arrangements in the front of the room for any students with visual, hearing, or attention challenges.
2. Ask the students to take notes while watching the video and then hypothesize why the price went down and then up. Have the students share their thoughts and write them on the board. (5 minutes)	Have the co-teacher (and paraprofessional if available) work with individual students to note what they are observing in the video and write student comments down on paper.
3. Use the video and discussion to introduce today's topic, supply and demand. (2 minutes)	

LESSON PROCEDURES

1. Have the students complete a short set of notes on supply and demand using a 2×4 matrix (See Figure 13.1). Go through the definitions, laws, and factors, and explain equilibrium. Use the Hudsucker Proxy video clip as a reference as you go through the notes. (10 minutes)

Divide the class into two heterogeneous groups and parallel teach each group through this exercise. Use the paraprofessional to support individual students. Provide more visual descriptions of supply and demand using graphs (see Materials section for YouTube video with graphing options).

2. Have the students draw a supply and demand graph on a sheet of paper (see Figure 13.4) and demonstrate how it represents the information in the matrix. (5 minutes)

Have scaffolded questions ready to create a discussion about these terms and tap into prior knowledge. Allow for pause time so students can process questions and have an opportunity to respond.

3. Review the following terms with the students: producers and consumers. Have the students write down "substitute" and "complement" and ask the students what they think these terms mean in relation to goods and services. (5 minutes)

Have individual students highlight these key words and also provide examples to remember their meanings.

4. Divide students into groups with no more than four in each group. Hand out copies of the supply and demand practice scenarios (see Figure 13.3) along with dry erase boards containing a supply and demand graph on each (see Figure 13.4). Tell the students to read each scenario, discuss what is happening in the scenario, and then visually graph what happened on the dry erase board. Model one graph with the entire class using the Hudsucker Proxy video clip scenario. (15 minutes)

Monitor the groups and support individual students as needed to ensure full participation in each group. Encourage group roles so that all students participate in some capacity.

5. Once the student groups complete the six mini-scenarios, assign each group either the Holiday Driving scenario or Hog Heaven Restaurant scenario. Have them complete the scenario and be prepared to present their findings to the entire class. (15 minutes)

Monitor the groups and support individual students as needed to ensure full participation in each group.

LESSON CLOSURE AND ASSESSMENT

1. Hand out bags containing the supply and demand sort cards (see Figure 13.2). Have each group sort the cards into their correct columns. Check for understanding and make corrections as needed. (5 minutes)

   Use the co-teacher and other support personnel to monitor this activity and provide assistance where needed.

2. Bring out an inflatable ball with the vocabulary from today's lesson taped onto the ball in different locations. Have the students form a big circle. Toss the ball to a student. They are to say the term closest to their left or right index finger and then explain it. Then the student throws the ball to another student. (5 minutes)

   Divide the students into smaller heterogeneous groups and do the same activity. This allows more students to review. The co-teachers and paraprofessional monitor the groups.

3. Using what they learned today, have the students complete an exit slip explaining why the price of roses goes up on Valentine's Day. (5 minutes)

   Help individual students complete the exit slip by having them dictate a response to a peer or co-teacher to write down.

4. Optional Review/Enrichment Activity: Divide students into small groups and have them examine newspapers, magazines, and news related Websites to find examples of supply and demand or opposing viewpoints about supply and demand that they could present to the class.

   Make sure the groups are heterogeneous so that adequate supports exist for students who might find the enrichment activity more challenging.

Figure 13.1 Supply and Demand Sample Matrix

	DEFINITION	LAWS	DETERMINANTS	EQUILIBRIUM
SUPPLY	The amount of a good or service a producer is willing and able to make available at each price during a specified time period	If all else remains equal, the lower the price, the lower the quantity supplied, and the higher the price, the higher the quantity supplied.	The number of producers, new technologies, government policies, and availability and price of raw materials may also affect supply.	The point where supply and demand balance each other; below this point is a shortage, and above this point is a surplus. This is sometimes referred to as the market price.
DEMAND	The quantity of a good or service that consumers are willing and able to buy at each price during a specified time period.	If all else remains equal, the lower the price, the higher the quantity demanded, and the higher the price, the lower the quantity demanded.	Substitutes, complements, number of consumers, consumer preference, and income may also affect demand.	

A substitute is something that can be used instead of a particular good or service. People might substitute chicken for beef. A complement is something used in conjunction with something else. People often consider jelly as a complement to peanut butter.

Chart adapted from the Virginia and U.S. Government Curriculum Framework located at http://www.doe.virginia.gov/testing/sol/standards_docs/history_socialscience/

Figure 13.2 Supply and Demand Sort Cards

INCREASE IN DEMAND	DECREASE IN DEMAND
Increase in consumer income	Fall in consumer income
Rise in the price of substitutes	Fall in the price of substitutes
Fall in the price of complements	Rise in the price of complements
Positive change in consumer tastes	Negative change in consumer tastes
More consumers	Fewer consumers

INCREASE IN SUPPLY	DECREASE IN SUPPLY
Fall in raw material costs	Increased raw material costs
Improvement in labor efficiency resulting in decreased labor costs	Increased labor costs
Decreased taxation rate	Increased taxation rate
New and successful technological advance	Failed technological advance
More sellers	Fewer sellers

Figure 13.3 Supply and Demand Scenarios

Name: Date:

SUPPLY AND DEMAND SCENARIOS

Directions: Explain or draw how each scenario affected supply/demand.

• If the local paper published an article with the headline "Cattle and Dairy Farmers Detect Mad Cow Disease," what would happen to the demand for beef and dairy?

• Gas and fuel prices have been rising steadily for months. How has the drastic increase in fuel affected the demand for large SUVs and trucks?

• Assuming that L.L. Bean jeans and Old Navy jeans are suitable substitutes, what would happen to the demand for Old Navy jeans in the following price scenario: Old Navy Jeans cost $26.00; LL Bean jeans cost $38.00.

• The following headline appeared in *USA Today*, "Honey Bees Devastated by a Tiny Mite." How will this affect the supply of honey around the world?

• The Coca-Cola company in Atlanta, GA has developed a new piece of machinery that can bottle 70 2-liter bottles per minute as opposed to the previous automatic bottler, which bottled 35 2-liter bottles per minute. How will this new machine influence the company's ability to supply Coca Cola?

• In an effort to encourage economic growth, the Congress passed legislation to cut corporate income taxes by 20%. How will this affect the ability of corporations to supply their products?

HOLIDAY DRIVING SCENARIO 1

Even though the average gas price approached $3.75, about 40 million Americans, 2 percent more than last year, will travel 100 miles or more from home this holiday. The Road Trip Association reported that, "Thanksgiving is a time for family gatherings. Higher gas prices will not discourage Americans from reconnecting with their loved ones." Despite the nearly 20% rise in average gas prices from this same point last year, some 32 million vacationers will travel by car, up 1.5 percent from last year. Another 5 million will go by air, up 2 percent. The rest will take trains, buses or other methods of transportation.

Explain how the concept of supply and demand might impact this scenario, which refers to prices in 2012. Be prepared to present your findings.

HOG HEAVEN RESTAURANT CHAIN SCENARIO 2

Hog Heaven Restaurants are struggling to survive. The restaurant chain, which started nearly 50 years ago, currently includes 400 restaurants with annual sales of more than $900 million. However, the annual shareholders meeting reported a 10% drop in profits along with declines in the quality of food and service, and a weakening company stock. In searching for an explanation for the plight of the chain, company executives mentioned rising hog prices combined with healthier eating habits in America that stalled sales of fried foods and meat products. These sales currently account for 25% of the company's revenue.

Explain how the concept of supply and demand might impact this scenario. Be prepared to present your findings.

Figure 13.4 Supply and Demand Graph

Name: Date:

SUPPLY AND DEMAND SCENARIOS

Directions: To construct a diagram on a dry erase board, use colored electrical tape.
Use black tape for the x and y-axis and two different colors to show the supply and demand curve.
Label small pieces of white electrical tape with the various labels listed below.

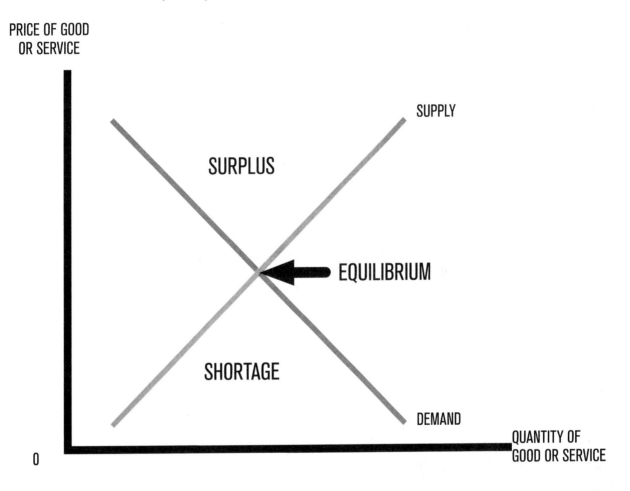

SECONDARY GEOGRAPHY LESSON PLAN

Learning how to create, read, and interpret tables, graphs, and charts is an essential skill social studies teachers expect from their students. How some exceptional learners may struggle with comprehension questions related to a reading, interpreting and responding to questions about tables, charts, or graphs can be equally daunting. Many students need direct instruction to help identify characteristics of these visual tools and create a process for interpretation. The geography lesson plan developed for this chapter represents the first step in preparing students to interpret population pyramids by having them create one on their own. The lesson includes interactive notes, hands-on participation, and a connection to real life to get students to understand the parts of a population pyramid and consider the range of information population pyramids provide the reader.

A beneficial follow-up to this lesson would be an inquiry activity where co-teachers set up stations in the room that provide a series of pictures, news articles, CIA World Factbook information (http://www.cia.gov/library/publications/resources/the-world-factbook/index.html), and a population pyramid to create for a particular country. The co-teachers might set up four or five countries to visit, each providing a deeper glimpse into why a country's population pyramid has a particular shape. Student collaborative teams would rotate through the stations, examining the information at each station to interpret how growth rates were affected by various social, economic, political, and environmental factors. Having a co-teacher in the room would allow for better facilitation and support for the station activity, although stations are still a viable option with only one adult in the room.

SAMPLE LESSON PLAN

LESSON TITLE: POPULATION GROWTH RATES	SUBJECT: WORLD GEOGRAPHY
Unit: Human Population	Grade: 9-12
Timeframe: 75-90 minutes	Teacher(s):

STANDARDS

This lesson promotes the following objectives of the *National Social Studies Standards*, the *C3 Framework for Social Studies State Standards*, and the *Common Core State Standards for English Language Arts and Literacy in History/Social Studies*.

NATIONAL SOCIAL STUDIES STANDARDS

Theme ❸ **PEOPLE, PLACES, AND ENVIRONMENTS** (High School)
Knowledge:
Learners will understand: "the use of a variety of…graphic representations…to help investigate spatial relations, resources, and population density and distribution, and changes in these phenomena over time." (p. 35)

C3 FRAMEWORK FOR SOCIAL STUDIES STATE STANDARDS

* D1.4.9-12 Explain how supporting questions contribute to an inquiry and how, through engaging source work, new compelling and supporting questions emerge. (p. 25)

* D2.Geo.7.9-12. Analyze the reciprocal nature of how historical events and the spatial diffusion of ideas, technologies, and cultural practices have influenced … the distribution of human population. (p. 43)

* D3.1.9-12. Gather relevant information from multiple sources representing a wide range of views while using the origin, authority, structure, context, and corroborative value of the sources to guide the selection. (p. 54)

- D4.2.9-12. Construct explanations using sound reasoning, correct sequence (linear or non-linear), examples, and details with significant and pertinent information and data, while acknowledging the strengths and weaknesses of the explanation given its purpose (e.g., cause and effect, chronological, procedural, technical). (p. 60)

COMMON CORE STATE STANDARDS FOR ENGLISH LANGUAGE ARTS AND LITERACY IN HISTORY/SOCIAL STUDIES
Anchor Writing Standards
Text Types and Purposes
1. Write arguments to support claims in an analysis of substantive topics or texts using valid reasoning and relevant and sufficient evidence. (p. 63)

Anchor Language Standards
Vocabulary Acquisition and Use
6. Acquire and use accurately a range of general academic and domain-specific words and phrases sufficient for reading, writing, speaking, and listening at the college and career readiness level; demonstrate independence in gathering vocabulary knowledge when considering a word or phrase important to comprehension or expression. (p. 51)

GOAL
Students will compare and contrast the distribution, growth rates, and characteristics of human population in terms of settlement patterns, resources, and social, economic, political, and environmental factors.

OBJECTIVES
Obj. 1: Students will identify the parts and most common types of population pyramids.

Obj. 2: Students will create a population pyramid using real life data.

Obj. 3: Students will interpret population pyramid data to determine what factors or trends influence population.

COMPELLING QUESTIONS
Q1: How are population pyramids useful tools for interpreting how different factors affect human population?

Q2: Why does the distribution of population age groups change?

SUPPORTING QUESTIONS
Q1: What are the essential parts of a population pyramid?

Q2: What do the types of population pyramids tell us about population?

Q3: What are some specific factors that might cause changes in population distribution?

Q4: What can we interpret about our own school (school system) based on the population pyramid we created?

MATERIALS/EQUIPMENT/TECHNOLOGY
- Four sample country population pyramids, four main idea graphic organizers, population pyramid blank graphs, colored pencils, and a ruler.

- There are a variety of spreadsheets already created for making population pyramids or instructions on how to create your own. In Google, search for population pyramid generators using Microsoft Excel. You can make your own by searching YouTube for Population Pyramid tutorials.

- For population facts about local communities, go to: http://factfinder2.census.gov/faces/nav/jsf/pages/index.xhtml

- Online Population Pyramid Generator for examples: http://www.census.gov/population/international/data/idb/informationGateway.php Select "Population Pyramid Graph" from "Select Report" options.

UNIVERSAL DESIGN FOR LEARNING

REPRESENTATION – OPTIONS FOR PRESENTING CONTENT	ENGAGEMENT – OPTIONS FOR ENGAGING STUDENT INTEREST	EXPRESSION – OPTIONS FOR DEMONSTRATING STUDENT LEARNING	CULTURAL CONSIDERATIONS
☐ Artifacts ☐ Pictures ☒ **Graphic organizers** ☐ Video Clips ☐ Audio Recordings ☐ Lab ☐ Lecture ☒ **Other**: 　Graphs	☒ **Cooperative Group Work** ☒ **Partner Work** ☐ Manipulatives ☐ Movement ☐ Debates ☐ Role plays or Simulations ☐ Other: _____	☒ **Written response** ☒ **Illustrated response** ☒ **Oral response** ☐ Model creation or construction ☐ Other: _____	☐ Nature of content and ethnicity/culture of students ☒ **Other**: 　Examining populations
CONTENT	PROCESS	PRODUCT	

LEARNING PLAN

	ROLES, ACCOMMODATIONS, AND DIFFERENTIATION STRATEGIES
LESSON INTRODUCTION 1. Have the following questions written on the board: "Do you think the population of the high school is increasing or decreasing?" "What factors might be causing the increase or decrease in our school population?" Ask the students to find a partner and develop a response to these two questions. (5 minutes)	Support individual students by having them respond to a co-teacher or paraprofessional. Provide some additional prompting questions if needed.
2. Take a tally of how many students think the population is increasing and how many think it is decreasing. Then ask for a few responses about the causes of the increase or decrease. Use this information to introduce to-day's topic, population pyramids. Tell students that they will learn a visual way to graph population and explain how certain factors lead to increases and decreases in population. (5 minutes)	Have a student who likes to move around come to the board and do the tally marks.
LESSON PROCEDURES 1. Hand out copies of four current population pyramids of different countries. Go through and highlight the parts of the population pyramid that students must pay attention to when reading this type of graph (see Figure 13.5). The title at the top indicates the population being graphed. The vertical axis contains the age groups. The horizontal axis represents the population number or percentage. The left side of the graph is the male population. The right side of the graph is the female population. (10 minutes)	Use highlighters to place emphasis on the important parts. Have a co-teacher monitor student progress during this step and provide individualized support.

2. Hand out a copy of a four main idea graphic organizer (see Figure 13.6) to fill in four types/shapes of population pyramids. Go through an explanation of each type and ask the students to determine which country from the four examples fits with each type of pyramid. Ask the students to discuss what specific factors might cause changes in population distribution. What questions arise from the data on the pyramid? (20 minutes)

Co-teachers switch roles. One facilitates the completion of the graphic organizer while the other supports individual students and provides input to the discussion. A paraprofessional can take notes for an individual student. Students who have poor handwriting can have an electronic copy of the graphic organizer to type into.

3. Practice Activity: Hand out copies of data about the number of students enrolled in the school system, K-12 (You may choose to use the entire school system or just feeder schools into one high school). Divide the students into teams of four. Using the school data provided, have each team construct a population pyramid (see Figure 13.7). When they complete the pyramid, ask each team to consider their original hypothesis about the school system expanding or shrinking. What can we interpret about our own school (school system) based on the population pyramid we created? What are some possible causes for the population changes that occurred? (15 minutes)

For students who have difficulty drawing, use an electronic population pyramid generator with spreadsheet software. Provide rulers and encourage the use of color to highlight the male and female sides of the pyramids. Support teams with additional questions to prompt thinking about what might cause population shifts in the school system.

LESSON CLOSURE AND ASSESSMENT

1. Bring the students back into a large group. Ask the following three questions: "What are the essential parts of a population pyramid?" "How are population pyramids useful tools for interpreting how different factors affect human population?" "Why does the distribution of population age groups change?" After writing down some student responses, introduce the exit slip activity. (5 minutes)

Support individual students with answering these questions. Ask, "Can you describe one part of a population pyramid you learned about today?" Ask the student in the classroom who likes to move around to be the scribe for student responses up on the main board.

2. Population Pyramid Exit Slip: Provide each student with population data and information for a country and a blank population pyramid handout. Ask the students to graph the data on their blank population pyramid sheet. They must label all of the parts. When they are done, have each student note what type of pyramid they constructed using the graphic organizer on pyramid types as a guide. Have the students respond to the following questions: What are some specific factors that might have caused changes in population distribution on your pyramid? What questions are left unanswered that you would want to explore further? (20 minutes)

For students who have difficulty drawing, use an electronic population pyramid generator with spreadsheet software.

(Use the exit slip in later lessons to address more in-depth methods for interpreting the data in a population pyramid.)

(The exit slip is an excellent way to determine which students need more support with communicating their conclusions.)

Figure 13.5 Sample Population Pyramids

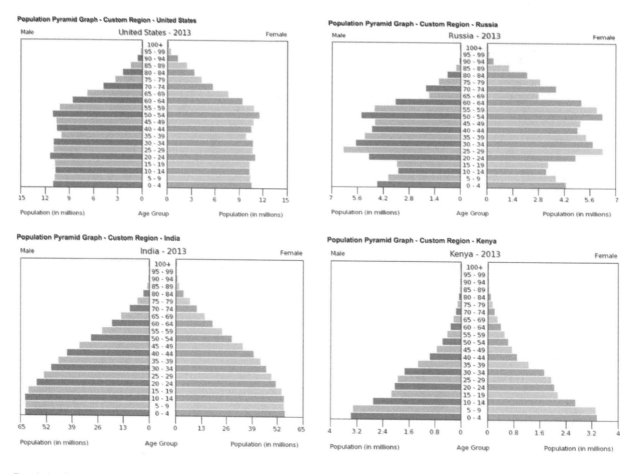

Population Pyramids generated at http://www.census.gov/population/international/data/idb/informationGateway.php

Figure 13.6 Completed Graphic Organizer on Population Pyramid Types

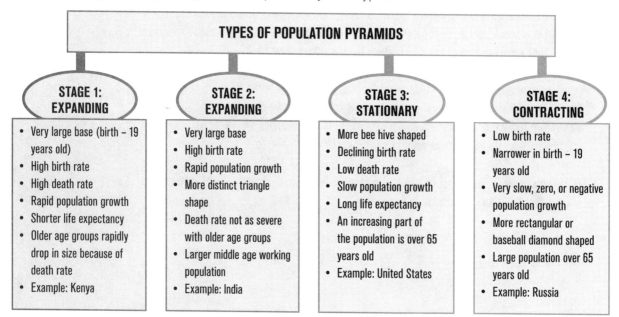

TYPES OF POPULATION PYRAMIDS

STAGE 1: EXPANDING
- Very large base (birth – 19 years old)
- High birth rate
- High death rate
- Rapid population growth
- Shorter life expectancy
- Older age groups rapidly drop in size because of death rate
- Example: Kenya

STAGE 2: EXPANDING
- Very large base
- High birth rate
- Rapid population growth
- More distinct triangle shape
- Death rate not as severe with older age groups
- Larger middle age working population
- Example: India

STAGE 3: STATIONARY
- More bee hive shaped
- Declining birth rate
- Low death rate
- Slow population growth
- Long life expectancy
- An increasing part of the population is over 65 years old
- Example: United States

STAGE 4: CONTRACTING
- Low birth rate
- Narrower in birth – 19 years old
- Very slow, zero, or negative population growth
- More rectangular or baseball diamond shaped
- Large population over 65 years old
- Example: Russia

Adapted from Edwin Ellis, *Makes Sense Strategies: 4 Main Idea Graphic Organizer* (Tuscaloosa, Al., 2008).

Figure 13.7 Blank School Population Pyramid Graph

MALE	GRADE	FEMALE
	12TH Grade	
	11TH Grade	
	10TH Grade	
	9TH Grade	
	8TH Grade	
	7TH Grade	
	6TH Grade	
	5TH Grade	
	4TH Grade	
	3RD Grade	
	2ND Grade	
	1ST Grade	
	Kindergarten	
	Population	

Figure 13.8 Blank Population Pyramid Graph

MALE	AGE	FEMALE
	100 +	
	95 to 99 years	
	90 to 94 years	
	85 to 89 years	
	80 to 84 years	
	75 to 79 years	
	70 to 74 years	
	65 to 69 years	
	60 to 64 years	
	55 to 59 years	
	50 to 54 years	
	45 to 49 years	
	40 to 44 years	
	35 to 39 years	
	30 to 34 years	
	25 to 29 years	
	20 to 24 years	
	15 to 19 years	
	10 to 14 years	
	5 to 9 years	
	Under 5 years	
	Population (in millions)	

SECONDARY HISTORY LESSON PLAN

Chapter 6 outlined a unit plan and advance organizer for the next lesson on ancient Mesopotamia. A brief description was provided to explain how a social studies teacher and special educator collaborate to develop a lesson that meets the needs of exceptional learners. This lesson is a good example of a more effective way to introduce new content with unfamiliar vocabulary to students. It also demonstrates the use of evidence-based practice to help students remember essential details about a topic.

SAMPLE LESSON PLAN

LESSON TITLE: MESOPOTAMIA	SUBJECT: WORLD HISTORY
Unit: Early River Valley Civilizations	Grade: 9-12
Timeframe: 90 minutes (or 2 days)	Teacher(s):

STANDARDS

This lesson promotes the following objectives of the *National Social Studies Standards*, the *C3 Framework for Social Studies State Standards*, and the *Common Core State Standards for English Language Arts and Literacy in History/Social Studies*.

NATIONAL SOCIAL STUDIES STANDARDS

Theme ❷ **TIME, CONTINUITY, AND CHANGE** (High School):

Questions for Exploration

What are the origins and influence of social, cultural, political, and economic systems, and how can they be compared across time and space? (p. 30)

C3 FRAMEWORK FOR SOCIAL STUDIES STATE STANDARDS

- D1.4.9-12 Explain how supporting questions contribute to an inquiry and how, through engaging source work, new compelling and supporting questions emerge. (p. 25)

- D2.His.16.9-12. Integrate evidence from multiple relevant historical sources and interpretations into a reasoned argument about the past. (p. 49)

- D3.1.9-12. Gather relevant information from multiple sources representing a wide range of views while using the origin, authority, structure, context, and corroborative value of the sources to guide the selection. (p. 54)

- D4.1.9-12. Construct arguments using precise and knowledgeable claims with evidence from multiple sources, while acknowledging counterclaims and evidentiary weaknesses. (p. 60)

COMMON CORE STATE STANDARDS FOR ENGLISH LANGUAGE ARTS AND LITERACY IN HISTORY/SOCIAL STUDIES

Anchor Speaking and Listening Standards

Comprehension and Collaboration

1. Prepare for and participate effectively in a range of conversations and collaborations with diverse partners, building on others' ideas and expressing their own clearly and persuasively. (p. 48)

Anchor Language Standards

Vocabulary Acquisition and Use

6. Acquire and use accurately a range of general academic and domain-specific words and phrases sufficient for reading, writing, speaking, and listening at the college and career readiness level; demonstrate independence in gathering vocabulary knowledge when considering a word or phrase important to comprehension or expression. (p. 51)

GOAL

Students will demonstrate knowledge of the major characteristics of early civilization and how early civilizations emerged in Mesopotamia, Egypt, and the Indus valley.

OBJECTIVES

Obj. 1: Students will define "early civilization" and "Mesopotamia."

Obj. 2: Students will explain why early civilizations settled in ancient Mesopotamia.

Obj. 3: Students will compare characteristics of early civilization to the Sumerians to determine their significance as an early civilization.

COMPELLING QUESTIONS

Q1: What makes a society an early civilization?

Q2: Why did early civilizations develop in ancient Mesopotamia?

SUPPORTING QUESTIONS

Q1: What are the essential (always present) characteristics of early civilizations?

Q2: What are the often present characteristics of an early civilization?

Q3: What are the defining characteristics of the land known as Mesopotamia?

Q4: How do the characteristics of early civilization apply to the Sumerians?

Q5: What role do rivers play in supporting civilizations?

MATERIALS/EQUIPMENT/TECHNOLOGY

- Advance Organizer

- Concept Mastery Diagram

- Resource Web links:

  ▶ http://mesopotamia.lib.uchicago.edu (for information about Mesopotamia)

  ▶ National Geographic Education Map Maker http://education.nationalgeographic.org/mapping/outline-map/?map=iraq (for map)

- Three or more definitions of civilization

- World History textbook

- Life in Mesopotamia "Did you know…?" Statements

  ▶ Did you know that the ancient Mesopotamians revolutionized transportation with the invention of the wheel?

  ▶ Did you know that ancient Mesopotamians worshipped hundreds of gods?

  ▶ Did you know the Sumerian people of ancient Mesopotamia invented one of the earliest forms of writing?

  ▶ Did you know ancient Mesopotamians invented a seeder plow, allowing a farmer to plow the earth and drop seeds at the same time?

  ▶ Did you know that the two major rivers of ancient Mesopotamia are located today in Iraq?

  ▶ Did you know that ancient Mesopotamians created large temples called ziggurats, made from mud bricks?

  ▶ Did you know that the people of ancient Mesopotamia developed the first written code of laws?

  ▶ Did you know that ancient Mesopotamia was part of a region known as the Fertile Crescent?

  ▶ Did you know that Mesopotamia means "the land between the rivers?"

  ▶ Did you know that the cities of Ur and Babylon were located in ancient Mesopotamia?

Teachers may develop additional statements using the resources found at: http://mesopotamia.lib.uchicago.edu/mesopotamialife/index.php

UNIVERSAL DESIGN FOR LEARNING

REPRESENTATION – OPTIONS FOR PRESENTING CONTENT	ENGAGEMENT – OPTIONS FOR ENGAGING STUDENT INTEREST	EXPRESSION – OPTIONS FOR DEMONSTRATING STUDENT LEARNING	CULTURAL CONSIDERATIONS
☐ Artifacts ☒ **Pictures** ☒ **Graphic organizers** ☐ Video Clips ☐ Audio Recordings ☐ Lab ☐ Lecture ☒ **Other**: _____	☐ Cooperative Group Work ☒ **Partner Work** ☐ Manipulatives ☒ **Movement** ☐ Debates ☐ Role plays or Simulations ☐ Other: _____	☒ **Written response** ☒ **Illustrated response** ☒ **Oral response** ☐ Model creation or construction ☐ Other: _____	☐ Nature of content and ethnicity/culture of students ☒ **Other**: Study of ancient cultures
CONTENT	PROCESS	PRODUCT	

LEARNING PLAN

	ROLES, ACCOMMODATIONS, AND DIFFERENTIATION STRATEGIES
LESSON INTRODUCTION 1. Begin with a warm-up "Did you know…?" Divide students into pairs/triads and hand out a series of "Did you know…?" statements on slips of paper. Ask the students to share statements with their partners. Then each pairing/triad will report out one statement to the entire class. See materials section for a list of sample statements. (5 minutes)	Have one co-teacher lead the warm-up activity, while the other teacher monitors on-task behavior and takes roll. Have support personnel assist individual students, hand out paper slips, or assign students to hand out paper slips.
2. The co-teacher who was monitoring for the warm-up will then introduce the lesson for the day using an advance organizer. See Figure 13.9 for a sample organizer and list of compelling and supporting questions. Students will co-construct the organizer in their notes with the teacher. (5 minutes)	A co-teacher and support personnel monitor on-task behavior and provide assistance.
LESSON PROCEDURES, PART 1 1. One co-teacher will introduce the Concept Diagram as a tool to help the students define the term "early civilization" (see Figure 13.10). The teacher will explain how to use the diagram as they study early civilizations that formed in the Fertile Crescent, Africa, and Asia. The teacher will point out the steps of the diagram and how those steps spell out the word "CONCEPT." (2 minutes)	The co-teacher (and any support personnel) hand out Concept Diagrams and help students identify the linking steps.
2. In a large group, the teacher will <u>C</u>onvey the targeted concept, "Early Civilization," and then <u>O</u>ffer an overall concept. The teacher will ask the students what might be an overall concept for "early civilization." In other words, what is the bigger concept that "early civilization" falls within? The overall concept could be "Human Society." (2 minutes)	The co-teacher monitors student completion of the first two steps on the diagram.

3. The teacher will then divide the students into pairs or triads and complete the next step, <u>N</u>ote key words. The teacher will ask the entire class to brainstorm characteristics of early civilization based on the "Did you Know" activity. Then the student pairs will use their text or the Web to come up with additional characteristics. (6 minutes)

4. The student pairings will then <u>C</u>lassify characteristics into what they think are <u>always</u> present in early civilization and <u>sometimes</u> present in early civilization. For the <u>never</u> present characteristics, the teacher will lead the whole class in a review of early humans and pre-history. (8 minutes)

5. The teacher will then have the students compare their characteristics to one or more definitions of "early civilization" to determine if any characteristics were left out. Definitions may be provided on a slide or written on the board. (5 minutes)

6. Next, the student groups <u>E</u>xplore a potential example. They consider the "Did you know?" statements along with their textbooks and Web link to determine if the Sumerians qualify as an early civilization. For the Sumerians to be an early civilization, they must meet all of the "always present" characteristics and not have a single "never present" characteristic. The pairings will also think back to their last unit and consider what would be a nonexample of an early civilization. The students will "<u>P</u>ractice" examining the characteristics of other early civilizations later in the unit using this same diagram. (10 minutes)

7. The last step of this exercise is to take the targeted concept, overall concept, and "always" present characteristics to <u>T</u>ie down a definition of "early civilization." Pairings will share their definitions with the class. Remember, the definition must contain the targeted and overall concepts and all of the always present characteristics. (5 minutes)

8. Finish this activity by asking the students: Based on the characteristics and examples we discussed, what role did the rivers play in supporting early civilizations? (5 minutes)

The co-teacher selects heterogeneous pairings/triads for students with disabilities and students needing other supports. The paraprofessional is assigned to any specific group needing additional support to complete the diagram.

The co-teacher/paraprofessional has student pairings/triads pull out review notes from the last unit in preparation for the whole group discussion of never present characteristics.

Some pairings/triads may receive definitions on a sheet of paper with highlighters to identify characteristics listed within the definitions.

The co-teacher or paraprofessional supports individual students and groups with matching characteristics of the Sumerians with characteristics of early civilizations.

Monitor to make sure all students have a definition. Have students with writing challenges verbalize the definition and write it down for them.

SHORT STRETCH BREAK (OR DAY 2)

1. Each student will write down the following sentence in their notes: Mesopotamia is the land between the Tigris and Euphrates rivers and is part of a region called the Fertile Crescent. The teacher hands out copies of a map of the Middle East that highlights the region of modern day Iraq. See Figure 13.12 for a sample map. (2 minutes)

   Co-teachers switch roles for the second activity. Co-teacher and paraprofessional make sure all students have the sentence and copies of a blank map. Some students receive a sentence strip they can glue into their notes.

2. The teacher introduces the mnemonic activity as a tool to help students remember the definition of Mesopotamia and some geographic features of the region. See Figure 13.11 for a sample strategy developed by a student. The teacher asks the students to read the definition of Mesopotamia and help identify the "little words" located within some of the essential vocabulary. Model this by highlighting the word "pot" in Mesopotamia. (2 minutes)

   Monitor students and assist students having difficulty finding the "little words." Provide more direct instruction to students who are not completing the task more independently.

3. Have the students work in small groups to highlight additional "little words" located within the definition. (Note: You should continue modeling this entire exercise as a large group if students are not familiar with this mnemonic strategy.) Students might underline one or more of the following: Mesopotamia is the land between the Tigris and Euphrates rivers and is part of a region called the Fertile Crescent. (3 minutes)

   Monitor students and assist students having difficulty finding the "little words." Provide more direct instruction to students who are not completing the task more independently.

4. Ask the students to use the underlined words to draw a picture that will remind them of the Mesopotamia definition. (7 minutes)

   For students who are unable or are reluctant to draw, ask them to describe the images in their head related to the words and have a peer, paraprofessional, or co-teacher draw them on the paper.

5. Next have the students write out a story or explanation of their picture and share what they wrote with their partner(s). (8 minutes)

   For students who are unable or are reluctant to write down the story/ explanation, ask them to dictate the story to a peer, co-teacher, or paraprofessional.

6. Have students now look at their unlabeled maps of the region. Have them draw in and label the key features they remember from the Mesopotamia definition. (7 minutes)

   Monitor students and assist students having difficulty with the labeling exercise.

7. Ask the students to quiz each other on the features they identified by associating their picture/story/explanation with the labeled map. Each student will share one characteristic and how they will remember it on the map. For example, one student might say, "I identified this curved area as the Fertile Crescent and I remember its name and shape because I drew a curved flower 'scent' coming from my flowers." Then the next student might say, "I remember the same curved area because I drew a mosaic tiled crescent moon in my picture that reminds me of the Fertile Crescent." The students would repeat this process until all features are addressed. (8 minutes)

   Monitor students as they quiz each other. Offer to quiz some groups that are having difficulty with the quiz activity.

LESSON CLOSURE AND ASSESSMENT

1. Students stay in their pairings and play "Grab Bag" review. Each pairing is handed a paper bag with four objects in it (select everyday objects). The student pairs must associate each object with an important fact they learned from the lesson. They must be prepared to present how they came up with their association. (5 minutes)

    Monitor students as they complete the review. Provide assistance to students who may need support for the presentation to the class.

2. Ask a few pairings to share their responses with the entire class. (3 minutes)

    Give at least one student with a disability an opportunity to share.

3. Have the students respond to the compelling questions using think, pair, share. What makes a society an early civilization? Why did early civilizations develop in ancient Mesopotamia? They will independently think about their responses, and then pair with a neighbor to share, and finally finish by either sharing with a larger group or the entire class. (10 minutes)

    Give at least one student with a disability an opportunity to share. Make sure the pairings and larger groups are heterogeneous.

    (Note: As the students continue to learn about these early civilizations, encourage them to develop new compelling and supporting questions about each civilization and discuss the potential challenges and limitations associated with studying ancient societies.)

Figure 13.9 Sample Advance Organizer for the Lesson

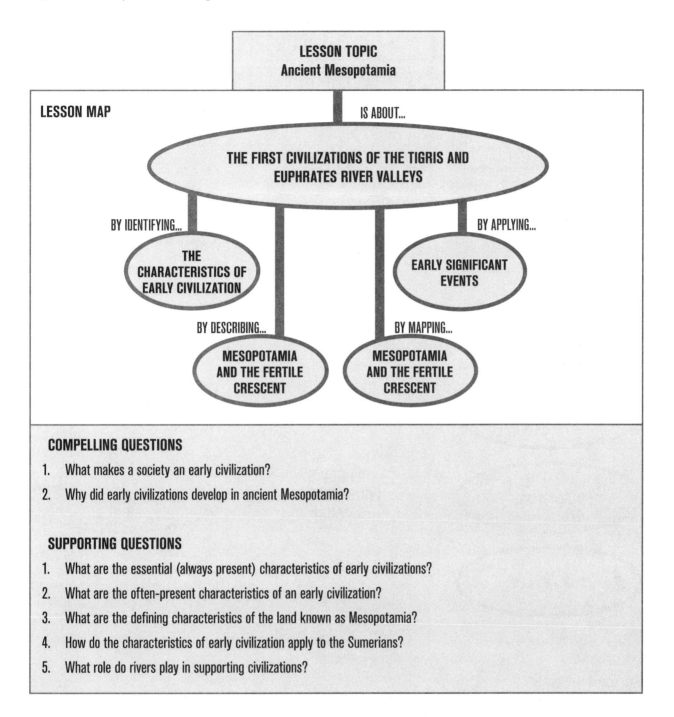

LESSON TOPIC
Ancient Mesopotamia

LESSON MAP

IS ABOUT...

THE FIRST CIVILIZATIONS OF THE TIGRIS AND EUPHRATES RIVER VALLEYS

BY IDENTIFYING...

THE CHARACTERISTICS OF EARLY CIVILIZATION

BY APPLYING...

EARLY SIGNIFICANT EVENTS

BY DESCRIBING...

MESOPOTAMIA AND THE FERTILE CRESCENT

BY MAPPING...

MESOPOTAMIA AND THE FERTILE CRESCENT

COMPELLING QUESTIONS

1. What makes a society an early civilization?
2. Why did early civilizations develop in ancient Mesopotamia?

SUPPORTING QUESTIONS

1. What are the essential (always present) characteristics of early civilizations?
2. What are the often-present characteristics of an early civilization?
3. What are the defining characteristics of the land known as Mesopotamia?
4. How do the characteristics of early civilization apply to the Sumerians?
5. What role do rivers play in supporting civilizations?

Figure 13.10 Sample Concept Mastery Diagram

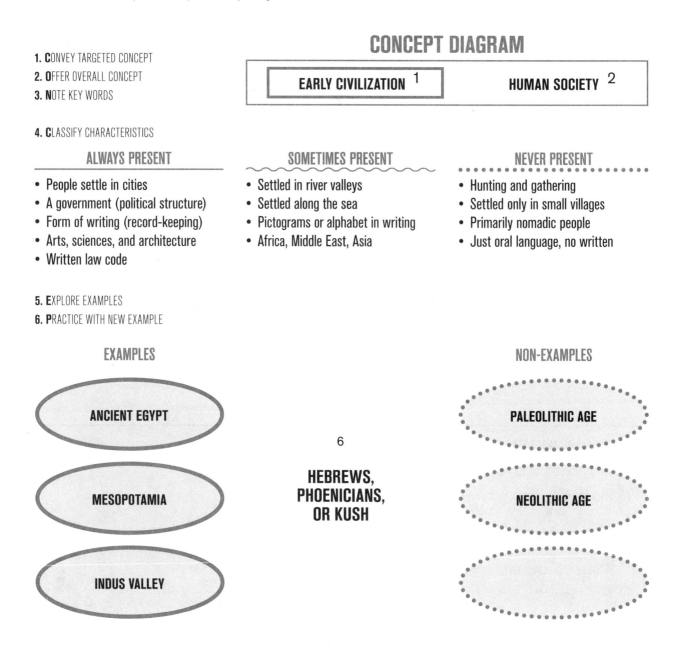

CONCEPT DIAGRAM

1. **C**ONVEY TARGETED CONCEPT
2. **O**FFER OVERALL CONCEPT
3. **N**OTE KEY WORDS

| EARLY CIVILIZATION ¹ | HUMAN SOCIETY ² |

4. **C**LASSIFY CHARACTERISTICS

ALWAYS PRESENT
- People settle in cities
- A government (political structure)
- Form of writing (record-keeping)
- Arts, sciences, and architecture
- Written law code

SOMETIMES PRESENT
- Settled in river valleys
- Settled along the sea
- Pictograms or alphabet in writing
- Africa, Middle East, Asia

NEVER PRESENT
- Hunting and gathering
- Settled only in small villages
- Primarily nomadic people
- Just oral language, no written

5. **E**XPLORE EXAMPLES
6. **P**RACTICE WITH NEW EXAMPLE

EXAMPLES

ANCIENT EGYPT

MESOPOTAMIA

INDUS VALLEY

6

HEBREWS, PHOENICIANS, OR KUSH

NON-EXAMPLES

PALEOLITHIC AGE

NEOLITHIC AGE

7. **T**IE DOWN A DEFINITION

An early civilization is a human society where people settle in cities and there is a government structure in place with written record-keeping, law codes, and progress in the arts, sciences, and architecture.

Source: Adapted from Janis Bulgren, Jean Schumaker, & Donald Deshler, *The Content Enhancement Series: The Concept Mastery Routine* (Lawrence, KS: Edge Enterprises, 1993).

Figure 13.11 Sample Mnemonic Strategy Developed by a Student

FIND THE "LITTLE WORDS"
Mesopotamia is the land between the T<u>igr</u>is and Euph<u>rate</u>s rivers and is part of a region called the Fertile Cre<u>scent</u>.

DRAW A PICTURE

DESCRIBE THE PICTURE
I see a cracked flowerpot leaking water that is passing by a rat and tiger. The flowerpot reminds me of Mesopotamia and the two water leaks are the Tigris and Euphrates rivers. The flowers remind me that the dirt is fertile and the scent coming from the flowers makes the shape of the Fertile Crescent.

Figure 13.12 Sample Map of the Fertile Crescent Region

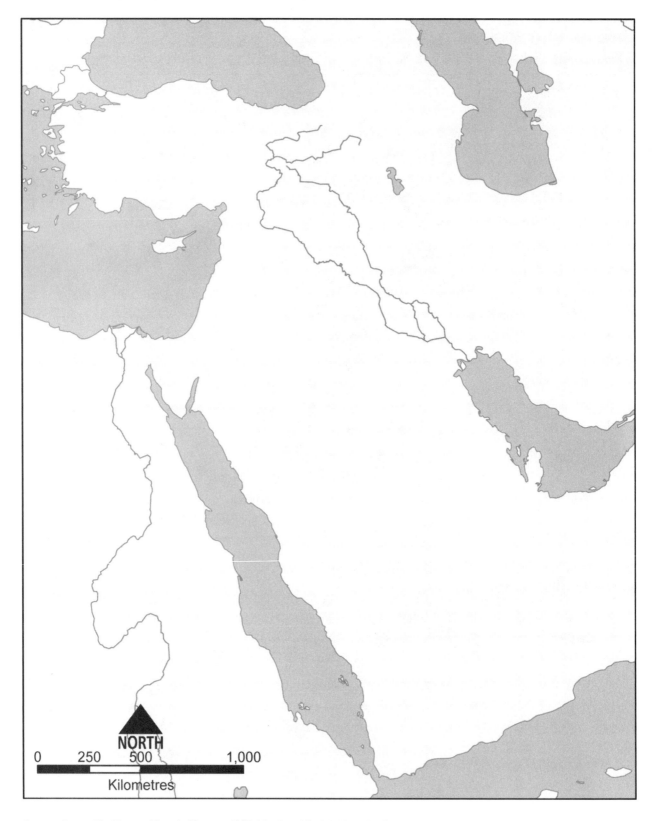

Source: Created by Norman Einstein (Own work) [Public domain], via Wikimedia Commons http://commons.wikimedia.org/wiki/File%3AFertile_Crescent_blank_base_map.png

SECONDARY CIVICS/GOVERNMENT LESSON PLAN

The next lesson for high school social studies addresses the issue of leadership, specifically the presidency. This plan asks students to examine the characteristics of leaders and apply those characteristics to presidents. The students then examine the roles of the presidency and how certain characteristics might support successful implementation of those roles. In its original form, this lesson was designed for a 90-minute block class. However, it would also work well in a period scheduled over a two-day timeframe.

We chose this lesson because it involves two visual organizers that scaffold and differentiate content and the lesson is strengthened with the inclusion of other adults to facilitate the activities. At the same time, an individual social studies teacher could facilitate this lesson without other adults in the room. The other reason for choosing this lesson was the open-ended nature of the topic. Although this lesson has students consider the presidency within the context of leaders, the Concept Diagram is easily adaptable to other leadership discussions such as members of Congress, founding fathers, world leaders, community leaders, and most importantly a personal reflection of leadership skills as citizens. The teacher may also choose to modify the target concept to "effective leaders" or "good leaders," which may change the dynamics of the diagram and spark added discussion. Finally, addressing leadership also supports exceptional learners in learning to self-advocate and become more self-determined.

This lesson demonstrates how teachers facilitate student directed instruction rather than simply provide information to the students. Students are engaged in whole groups, small groups, and pairings. They use a variety of tools to break down the content into essential details and make connections to their own conceptions of leadership. It is our hope that this lesson will spark a variety of ideas for addressing the topic of leadership in secondary social studies classrooms.

SAMPLE LESSON PLAN

LESSON TITLE: PRESIDENTIAL LEADERS	SUBJECT: U.S. GOVERNMENT
Unit: Presidency	Grade: 9-12
Timeframe: 90 minutes	Teacher(s):

STANDARDS

This lesson promotes the following objectives of the *National Social Studies Standards*, the *C3 Framework for Social Studies State Standards*, and the *Common Core State Standards for English Language Arts and Literacy in History/Social Studies*.

NATIONAL SOCIAL STUDIES STANDARDS

Theme ❻ **POWER, AUTHORITY, AND GOVERNANCE** (High School)
Processes
Learners will be able to:
Apply modes of inquiry used in political science to research issues concerning power, authority, and governance. (p. 48)

C3 FRAMEWORK FOR SOCIAL STUDIES STATE STANDARDS

- D1.2.9-12. Explain points of agreement and disagreement experts have about interpretations and applications of disciplinary concepts and ideas associated with a compelling question. (p. 24)

- D2.Civ13.9-12. Evaluate public policies in terms of intended and unintended outcomes, and related consequences. (p. 34)

- D3.1.9-12. Gather relevant information from multiple sources representing a wide range of views while using the origin, authority, structure, context, and corroborative value of the sources to guide the selection. (p. 54)

- D4.1.9-12. Construct arguments using precise and knowledgeable claims with evidence from multiple sources, while acknowledging counterclaims and evidentiary weaknesses. (p. 60)

COMMON CORE STATE STANDARDS FOR ENGLISH LANGUAGE ARTS AND LITERACY IN HISTORY/SOCIAL STUDIES

Anchor Reading Standards
Key Ideas and Details
1. Read closely to determine what the text says explicitly and to make logical inferences from it; cite specific textual evidence when writing or speaking to support conclusions drawn from the text. (p. 60)

Anchor Writing Standards
Text Types and Purposes
1. Write arguments to support claims in an analysis of substantive topics or texts using valid reasoning and relevant and sufficient evidence. (p. 63)

GOAL
Students will examine the qualities and responsibilities of leaders and relate this to the leadership roles of the presidency.

OBJECTIVES
Obj. 1: Students will identify essential characteristics of leaders.

Obj. 2: Students will co-construct a definition of leader.

Obj. 3: Students will examine their role in selecting, judging and becoming leaders.

Obj. 4: Students will identify the essential roles of the presidency.

Obj. 5: Students will apply their characteristics of leaders to the roles of the presidency.

COMPELLING QUESTIONS
Q1: What makes a good leader?

Q2: How does personal bias affect the emphasis of particular characteristics and examples of good leaders?

Q3: As a result of this lesson, did your definition of leader change?

Q4: What are your responsibilities regarding the selection and judgment of leaders? How can you be involved as leaders yourselves?

SUPPORTING QUESTIONS
Q1: What are the roles of the presidency?

Q2: What are the essential characteristics of leaders?

Q3: How do the essential characteristics of leaders support the roles of the presidency?

MATERIALS/EQUIPMENT/TECHNOLOGY
- Concept Mastery Diagrams, 8-Main Idea graphic organizers, textbooks (Tablets or other portable access to the Web are also an option), large sheets of paper and markers.

UNIVERSAL DESIGN FOR LEARNING

REPRESENTATION – OPTIONS FOR PRESENTING CONTENT	ENGAGEMENT – OPTIONS FOR ENGAGING STUDENT INTEREST	EXPRESSION – OPTIONS FOR DEMONSTRATING STUDENT LEARNING	CULTURAL CONSIDERATIONS
☐ Artifacts ☐ Pictures ☒ **Graphic organizers** ☒ **Video Clips** ☐ Audio Recordings ☐ Lab ☐ Lecture ☒ **Other**: News articles	☒ **Cooperative Group Work** ☒ **Partner Work** ☐ Manipulatives ☒ **Movement** ☐ Debates ☐ Role plays or Simulations ☒ **Other**: Presentation	☒ **Written response** ☐ Illustrated response ☒ **Oral response** ☐ Model creation or construction ☒ **Other**: Concept Diagram and Main Idea Graphic Organizer	☐ Nature of content and ethnicity/culture of students ☒ **Other**: Consider how some groups may value certain leadership traits more or less depending on their cultural background
CONTENT	PROCESS	PRODUCT	

LEARNING PLAN

	ROLES, ACCOMMODATIONS, AND DIFFERENTIATION STRATEGIES
LESSON INTRODUCTION 1. Begin with a warm-up activity. As the students enter the room, they will see the following questions on large sheets of paper: "What are some qualities that exemplify leaders?" "Give examples of people who are/were leaders." Under these questions, the students are asked to quickly respond to both questions and then take a seat. (Before bell rings and first 3-5 minutes of class)	Have both co-teachers lead the warm-up activity and monitor on-task behavior. Once the students begin the warm-up, one co-teacher can take roll. Have support personnel also monitor on-task behavior or support individual students who may need support with participation.
2. Introduce the lesson for the day using an agenda or advance organizer with the essential questions for the lesson listed. Students will co-construct the organizer or agenda in their notes with the teacher. (5 minutes)	A co-teacher and support personnel monitor on-task behavior and provide assistance.
LESSON PROCEDURES 1. Introduce the Concept Mastery (CM) Diagram as a tool to help the students define the term "leader" (Figure 13.13). The teacher will explain how the students will use the diagram as they study the presidency and consider the characteristics of presidential leadership. The teacher will point out the steps of the diagram and how those steps spell out the word "CONCEPT." (3 minutes)	One co-teacher leads the introduction to the diagram while the other co-teacher (and any support personnel) hand out Concept Diagrams assigning numbers (1 through 5) to each student. The co-teacher and support personnel move through the classroom ensuring that all students are on-task, filling out the first two sections of the diagram, supporting any students with handwriting if necessary.

2. The students will <u>C</u>onvey the targeted concept (Leader) and write this in the space labeled "1" on the diagram. Next the students will <u>O</u>ffer an overall concept. Ask the students what might be an overall concept for "leader?" In other words, what is the bigger concept that "leader" falls within? The overall concept could be "People." (2 minutes)

Co-teachers and support personnel monitor the switch into heterogeneous groups and then facilitate the activity within each group.

3. Break the students into groups and have them <u>N</u>ote (brainstorm) a list of key words on a sheet of paper. Each group should appoint a scribe to write down the list and a facilitator/timekeeper to keep the discussion going. As a starting point, have them refer to the characteristics they identified as they first entered the room. (5 minutes)

Directions for the assignment are written in full view for the student groups to clarify any questions about the tasks they are completing. The directions use the mnemonic, CONCEPT, to show the steps. The CM diagram serves as a natural differentiation tool for breaking down concepts

4. Next, have the student groups <u>C</u>lassify their characteristics into three categories. These characteristics include: Mandatory (Always Present), Desired (Sometimes Present), and Undesirable (Never Present) characteristics. It is important to let the students know that any characteristics they list as mandatory/always present must be included in their final definition and all people they consider leaders must have ALL of those characteristics. They must agree as a group about what goes in each category. (15 minutes)

Individual students may need a scribe for their sheet. This can either be a support person or a peer. Encourage students who need this accommodation to be facilitators to help process the information.

5. The next step is to have the groups <u>E</u>xplore examples and non-examples. Since this is a unit on the presidency, students should be instructed to choose presidents who would fit <u>all</u> of their mandatory/always present characteristics and <u>none</u> of the undesirable/never present characteristics. If a president they choose is either missing one or more of the mandatory/always present characteristics or has even one of the undesirable/never present characteristics, that person cannot be an example of a leader. (10 minutes)

Some groups may need a list of some previous presidents with their accomplishments and challenges to support the examples/nonexamples portion of the CM diagram. A list can be provided or the co-teachers can share possible examples with the groups if they are stuck.

6. The teacher can <u>P</u>ractice with a new example by meeting with each individual group. If it is an election year, the teacher can choose potential presidential candidates or a more controversial president in history. (5 minutes)

The co-teachers share responsibility to meet with the individual groups to share a new example to test.

7. Students will <u>T</u>ie down definitions of leader in their small groups and share each definition to the large group. The definition must contain the targeted concept, overall concept, and <u>all</u> of the always present/mandatory characteristics. (5 minutes)

Each co-teacher and any support personnel will have a draft of a CM diagram that they can use to share an example definition with the groups to make sure definitions contain all of the correct parts. A sentence stem can be provided to help the students get started with a definition. "Leaders are people who. . ."

8. Bring the students back into a large group. Hand out copies of the 8-Main-Idea graphic organizer (GO) (Figure 13.14). Go through the roles of the presidency and have the students place each role on the GO. The teacher will provide some illustrative examples of presidential actions that fit the roles listed on the GO. Examples might come from short video clips or news articles. Resources about presidents are found on the "Information You Can Trust" POTUS Website (http://www.ipl.org/div/potus). Video clips can be found through a Google or YouTube search. These roles are: (1) chief of state, (2) chief executive, (3) chief administrator, (4) chief diplomat, (5) commander in chief, (6) chief legislator, (7) party chief, and (8) chief citizen. (10 minutes)

Students may receive a partially filled out organizer or dictate the eight roles to be placed on the organizer.

9. Using their text or the Web, the students will pair up (or work in triads) and identify an essential detail that describes each role. Then they will list a leadership skill from their CM diagram that is needed the most to perform each particular role. The students finish by completing a "So what?" statement explaining why it is important to understand the roles of the presidency and the leadership skills necessary to perform those roles. (15 minutes)

The pairings will be heterogeneous to provide any needed peer support. Co-teachers and support personnel will move between the pairings to check for understanding and completion of the task. As needed, one of the co-teachers or a support person may write down responses dictated by a student. Also, some students might need to be directed to specific sites or readings to support organizational needs.

LESSON CLOSURE AND ASSESSMENT

1. Students will answer the compelling questions identified at the beginning of the lesson in a round robin large group as a review. List each question on a large sheet of paper in a section of the room. Divide students into five heterogeneous groups and assign one question to each group. The students will discuss their responses and record comments on the sheet and then rotate clockwise after 2 minutes to the next question. The groups will repeat this process until all questions are discussed. (1) What makes a good leader? (2) How does personal bias affect the emphasis of particular characteristics and examples of good leaders? (3) As a result of this lesson, did your definition of leader change? (4) What are your responsibilities regarding the selection and judgment of leaders? (5) How can you be involved as leaders yourselves? (11 minutes)

Wait time will be provided for students to formulate answers to the questions. The small groups will allow for peer support. Before the review begins, a co-teacher or support person might prepare a few students who need extra time to formulate responses.

2. Students will complete a 3-2-1 exit slip before leaving the classroom. On the exit slip they will write down three key terms they learned today, two facts they found most interesting, and one question they would like to see on a test or quiz. (4 minutes)

A support person or co-teacher will help individual students complete the exit slip through a series of scaffolded questions and write down dictated responses for the student to submit.

Lesson plan and concept diagram adapted from the Leadership Workshop, American Civics Center, LLC.

Figure 13.13 Sample Leadership Concept Mastery Diagram

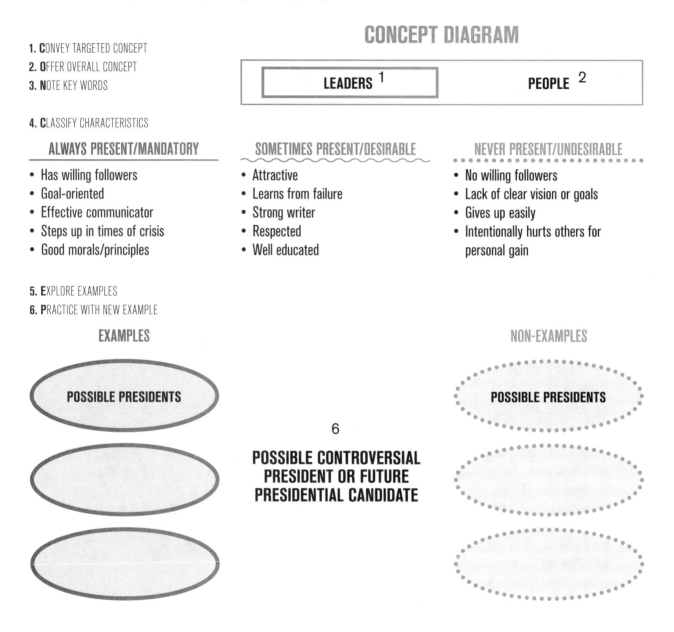

CONCEPT DIAGRAM

1. **C**ONVEY TARGETED CONCEPT
2. **O**FFER OVERALL CONCEPT
3. **N**OTE KEY WORDS

| LEADERS [1] | PEOPLE [2] |

4. **C**LASSIFY CHARACTERISTICS

ALWAYS PRESENT/MANDATORY

- Has willing followers
- Goal-oriented
- Effective communicator
- Steps up in times of crisis
- Good morals/principles

SOMETIMES PRESENT/DESIRABLE

- Attractive
- Learns from failure
- Strong writer
- Respected
- Well educated

NEVER PRESENT/UNDESIRABLE

- No willing followers
- Lack of clear vision or goals
- Gives up easily
- Intentionally hurts others for personal gain

5. **E**XPLORE EXAMPLES
6. **P**RACTICE WITH NEW EXAMPLE

EXAMPLES

POSSIBLE PRESIDENTS

NON-EXAMPLES

POSSIBLE PRESIDENTS

6

POSSIBLE CONTROVERSIAL PRESIDENT OR FUTURE PRESIDENTIAL CANDIDATE

7. **T**IE DOWN A DEFINITION

Leaders are goal-oriented people with good morals and principles who step up in times of crisis and communicate effectively on behalf of their willing followers.

Adapted from Janis Bulgren, Jean Schumaker, & Donald Deshler, *The Content Enhancement Series: The Concept Mastery Routine* (Lawrence, KS: Edge Enterprises, 1993).

Figure 13.14 Sample Roles of the Presidency Frame

ROLES OF THE PRESIDENCY	IS ABOUT...

the job duties and responsibilities that the president performs as the leader of the United States.

CHIEF OF STATE	CHIEF EXECUTIVE	CHIEF ADMINISTRATOR	CHIEF DIPLOMAT
• The head of government	• Constitutional powers to address domestic and foreign issues • Limited by checks and balances	• Responsible for leading the executive branch of government	• Responsible for developing foreign policy

COMMANDER IN CHIEF	CHIEF LEGISLATOR	PARTY CHIEF	CHIEF CITIZEN
• The leader of the nation's armed forces	• Shapes public policy by working with Congress to request or support certain legislation	• Leader of his/her political party	• Represents all the people

SO WHAT? WHAT IS IMPORTANT TO UNDERSTAND ABOUT THIS?
Carrying out all of these roles at the same time requires strong and effective leadership skills.

Adapted from Edwin Ellis, *The Content Enhancement Series: The Framing Routine* (Lawrence, KS.: Edge Enterprises, 1998); Edwin Ellis, *Makes Sense Strategies: 8 Main Idea Frame* (Tuscaloosa, Al., 2008).

PART III
RESOURCES & GLOSSARY

Resources

There are many resources and publications available to support teachers with both content knowledge and strategy integration to create a more inclusive social studies classroom. In this section, you will find a variety of materials to consider when developing lessons or wanting to learn more about ways to best support the needs of exceptional learners. You will also find a glossary of commonly used words, phrases, and acronyms pertinent to exceptional learners. Although not an exhaustive list, we hope that the organizations, research centers, professional journals, email lists, teaching resources, articles addressing best practices, and glossary provide a starting point to expand your knowledge base.

1 RESEARCH CENTERS, INSTITUTES, AND PROFESSIONAL ORGANIZATIONS

CENTER FOR CIVIC EDUCATION (CCE)
http://www.civiced.org
The Center for Civic Education provides rich information and several hands-on, simulation-based opportunities for teachers and students to increase their understanding of the principles, institutions, and history of American democracy.

CENTER FOR PARENT INFORMATION AND RESOURCES (CPIR)
http://www.parentcenterhub.org/nichcy-resources
This is the new home for the resources formally provided by the National Dissemination Center for Children with Disabilities (NICHCY). There is information on disability and disability-related issues, focusing on children and youth, from birth to age 22.

COUNCIL FOR ECONOMIC EDUCATION (CEE)
http://www.councilforeconed.org
Premised on promoting the economic and financial education of K-12 students, the CEE offers an array of teaching resources, and professional development opportunities (including in-school workshops for teachers), as well as norm-referenced assessment tools.

COUNCIL FOR LEARNING DISABILITIES (CLD)
http://www.cldinternational.org
CLD is an international organization dedicated to supporting the education and quality of life for individuals with learning disabilities. The site provides information about disability research, professional publications, and Web links to other organizations addressing learning disabilities. They also offer updates on the latest news and Webinars on relevant topics.

DISABILITY.GOV
https://www.disability.gov
This federal government website provides information and resources on disability programs and services nationwide.

THE IRIS CENTER
http://iris.peabody.vanderbilt.edu
Developed by and housed at Vanderbilt University, The IRIS Center offers special education resources and materials, including validated instructional strategies, research-to-practice strategies, and best practice strategies for both inservice and preservice educators.

LD ONLINE
http://www.ldonline.org
An excellent source for accessing current information and advice about learning disabilities and ADHD. The site features numerous scholarly articles, multimedia, expert advice, and practice-based resources for districts, schools, educators and parents.

NATIONAL CENTER FOR HISTORY IN THE SCHOOLS (NCHS)
http://www.nchs.ucla.edu
Housed in the Department of History at UCLA, this site contains the national history standards.

NATIONAL CENTER FOR LEARNING DISABILITIES (NCLD)

http://www.ncld.org

NCLD is dedicated to improving the lives of individuals with learning disabilities by providing resources to support parents and teachers. They also provide information for adults living with a learning disability.

NATIONAL CENTER FOR SPECIAL EDUCATION RESEARCH (NCSER)

http://ies.ed.gov/ncser

Under the umbrella of the Institute of Education Sciences (IES), NCSER sponsors research to expand the knowledge and understanding of the needs of children and youth with disabilities. Publications, research program and projects, and funding opportunities are located on the NCSER website.

NATIONAL CENTER ON UNIVERSAL DESIGN FOR LEARNING

http://www.udlcenter.org

This center supports the effective implementation of UDL by providing information and resources about the definition, implementation, and research-based practice of UDL principles.

NATIONAL COUNCIL FOR GEOGRAPHIC EDUCATION (NCGE)

http://www.ncge.org

Devoted to the promotion of geographic teaching and learning, NCGE gathers and disseminates applicable geography-based research, provides curricular resources for both the K-12 and collegiate level, and offers an expansive array of professional development opportunities.

NATIONAL COUNCIL FOR HISTORY EDUCATION (NCHE)

http://www.nche.net

NCHE supports numerous professional development opportunities for K-12 teachers utilizing the expertise of historians, archivists, librarians, and community leaders. NCHE also provides teachers with an array of resources for seamless integration into the social studies classroom.

NATIONAL COUNCIL FOR THE SOCIAL STUDIES (NCSS)

http://www.ncss.org or http://www.socialstudies.org

Promoting and facilitating an integrated, participatory, and responsive teaching and learning of social studies, NCSS offers several professional development opportunities for K-12 teachers as well as a number of research-based publications.

OFFICE OF SPECIAL EDUCATION AND REHABILITATIVE SERVICES (OSERS)

http://www2.ed.gov/about/offices/list/osers/osep/index.html?src=mr

Provides research-based information and funding for states and local districts in an effort to improve results for children and youth with disabilities.

POSITIVE BEHAVIORAL INTERVENTIONS AND SUPPORTS (PBIS)

http://www.pbis.org

Supported by the Office of Special Education Programs, the Center for Positive Behavioral Interventions and Supports provides schools and districts information and technical assistance for identifying, adapting, and sustaining effective school-wide disciplinary practices

TASH EQUITY, OPPORTUNITY AND INCLUSION FOR PEOPLE WITH DISABILITIES

http://tash.org

TASH is an organization that advocates for equity, opportunity, and inclusion for people with disabilities. They have specific statements regarding a variety of disability advocacy issues that include links to relevant resources on the topics.

TRANSITION COALITION

http://transitioncoalition.org/transition

An online resource developed by the University of Kansas to provide information and resources related to the transition of youth with disabilities from school to adult life. The training materials include online modules that teachers can complete to learn more about topics related to transition.

THE UNIVERSITY OF KANSAS CENTER FOR RESEARCH ON LEARNING

http://www.kucrl.org

An internationally recognized research center dedicated to improve the quality of life and learning for anyone experiencing difficulties.

WHAT WORKS CLEARINGHOUSE

http://ies.ed.gov/ncee/wwc

A site dedicated to examining research and providing guidance on evidence-based practices in education. A searchable database allows educators to find specific strategies and programs shown to improve student outcomes.

2 PROFESSIONAL JOURNALS, MAGAZINES, AND SMARTBRIEFS

CEC SMARTBRIEF

http://www.smartbrief.com/cec/index.jsp

A briefing on top stories in special education that you can have sent to your email account.

CLASSROOM TEACHING RESOURCES
CHILDREN AND YOUTH IN HISTORY

http://chnm.gmu.edu/cyh/primary-sources

Compilation of primary sources and lesson plans.

DIGITAL HISTORY

http://www.digitalhistory.uh.edu

A series of digital and print-based primary sources by era and topic.

DISABILITY HISTORY MUSEUM

http://www.disabilitymuseum.org/dhm/index.html

Provides a wide array of materials to support a deeper understanding of the experiences of people with disabilities.

iCIVICS

http://www.icivics.org

Lesson plans and simulations designed to teach civics.

I'M DETERMINED

http://www.imdetermined.org

Classroom materials, modules, and videos for educators, parents, and youth designed to support self-determination for youth with disabilities at the school and community level.

IT'S OUR STORY: ANSWERS FROM AMERICA'S DISABILITY ACTIVISTS

http://www.youtube.com/user/ItsOurStoryProject

An archive of testimonies from activists in disability history.

KATHY SCHROCK'S GUIDE TO EVERYTHING

http://www.schrockguide.net

An array of technology resource support links for classroom teachers.

LIBRARY OF CONGRESS

http://www.loc.gov/teachers/classroommaterials/lessons

Teachers have access to lesson plans and an array of digital and print-based primary sources.

MUSEUM OF DISABILITY HISTORY

http://museumofdisability.org

A museum dedicated to educating the public about people with disabilities. Lesson plans and a virtual museum are among the resources available.

NATIONAL ARCHIVES

http://docsteach.org

Resources available on how to incorporate primary sources into the classroom.

NATIONAL HISTORY EDUCATION CLEARINGHOUSE

http://teachinghistory.org

Includes online materials, lesson plans, and links to additional recommended sites.

NCSS SMARTBRIEF

http://www2.smartbrief.com/signupSystem/subscribe.action?pageSequence=1&briefName=ncss

A briefing of top stories for social studies educators that you can have sent to your email account.

OUR DOCUMENTS

http://www.ourdocuments.gov
Contains seminal historical documents and tips on integrating such documents into the social studies classroom.

PRIMARY SOURCE SETS AT THE LIBRARY OF CONGRESS

http://www.loc.gov/teachers/classroommaterials/primarysourcesets
Bundled primary sources focusing on people/events in US history.

PUBLIC BROADCASTING SERVICE

http://www.pbs.org/teachers/resources
Print and audio/video resources for the K-12 social studies classroom.

READWRITETHINK

http://www.readwritethink.org
Materials that follow best practice in reading and language arts instruction with a searchable database. The keyword "social studies" in the searchable database reveals a variety of K-12 classroom resources.

SOCIAL EDUCATION

http://www.socialstudies.org/socialeducation
The NCSS practitioner-based journal addressing the latest theoretical and philosophical discussions about social studies, research on social studies topics, and practical ideas for classroom instruction.

SOCIAL STUDIES AND THE YOUNG LEARNER

http://www.socialstudies.org/publications/ssyl
Sponsored by NCSS, SSYL provides classroom-based strategies that serve to enhance elementary social studies design and delivery.

TEACHING EXCEPTIONAL CHILDREN

https://www.cec.sped.org/Publications/CEC-Journals/TEACHING-Exceptional-Children
The CEC practitioner-based journal addressing the latest theoretical and philosophical discussions about special education, research on special education topics, and practical ideas to implement with exceptional learners.

THE HISTORY CHANNEL

http://www.history.com
An array of digital resources partitioned by topic.

THIS DAY IN HISTORY

http://www.history.com/this-day-in-history
From the History Channel, provides teachers with a 1-minute synopsis of daily historical events.

T/TAC ONLINE

http://ttaconline.org/search-sol-ess
Instructional strategies and enhanced lesson plans in History/Social Science aligned to the Virginia Standards of Learning (SOL) K-12.

SMITHSONIAN'S HISTORY EXPLORER

http://historyexplorer.si.edu/home
Lesson plans, integrative activities, digital resources for all levels of social studies instruction.

SPARTACUS EDUCATIONAL

http://www.spartacus-educational.com
Accessible research guides for select historical figures.

3 SELECT BIBLIOGRAPHY: BEST PRACTICE IN SOCIAL STUDIES INSTRUCTION FOR STUDENTS WITH DISABILITIES

Boon, Richard T., Mark D. Burke, Cecil Fore, and Vicky G. Spencer. "The Impact of Cognitive Organizers and Technology-Based Practices on Student Success in Secondary Social Studies Classrooms," *Journal of Special Education Technology* 21, no. 1 (2006): 5-15.

Bouck, Emily C., Carrie Anna Courtad, Anne Heutsche, Cynthia M. Okolo, and Carol Sue Englert, "The Virtual History Museum," *Teaching Exceptional Children* 42, no. 2 (2009): 14-20.

Bulgren, Janis, Donald D. Deshler, and Keith B. Lenz, "Engaging Adolescents with LD in Higher Order Thinking About History Concepts Using Integrated Content Enhancement Routines," *Journal of Learning Disabilities* 40, no. 2 (2007): 121-33.

Bulgren, Janis, Patricia Sampson Graner, and Donald D. Deshler, "Literacy Challenges and Opportunities for Students with Learning Disabilities in Social Studies and History," *Learning Disabilities Research and Practice* 28, no. 1 (2013): 17-27.

Ciullo, Stephen, Terry Falcomata, and Sharon Vaughn, "Teaching Social Studies to Upper Elementary Students with Learning Disabilities: Graphic Organizers and Explicit Instruction," *Learning Disabilities Quarterly* 38, no. 1 (2015): 15-26.

Connor, David J., and Christopher Lagares, "Facing High Stakes in High School: 25 Successful Strategies from an Inclusive Social Studies Classroom," *Teaching Exceptional Children* 40, no. 2 (2007): 18-27.

Curtis, Charles K. "Teaching Disabled Students in the Regular Social Studies Classroom," *The History and Social Science Teacher* 18, no. 1 (1982): 9-16.

———. "Social Studies for Students at-Risk and with Disabilities," in *Handbook of Research on Social Studies Teaching and Learning*, edited by James P. Shaver. 157-74. (New York: Macmillan Publishing Company, 1991).

De La Paz, Susan and Charles MacArthur, "Knowing the How and Why of History: Expectations for Secondary Students with and without Learning Disabilities," *Learning Disability Quarterly* 26, no. 2 (2003): 142-54.

De La Paz, Susan, Petra Morales, and Philip M. Winston, "Source Interpretation: Teaching Students with and without LD to Read and Write Historically," *Journal of Learning Disabilities* 40, no. 2 (2007): 134-44.

Ellis, Edwin, Theresa Farmer, and Jane Newman, "Big Ideas About Teaching Big Ideas," *Teaching Exceptional Children* 38, no. 1 (2005): 34-40.

Espin, Christine A., Jazmin Cevasco, Paul Van den Broek, Scott Baker, and Russell Gersten, "History as Narrative: The Nature and Quality of Historical Understanding for Students with LD," *Journal of Learning Disabilities* 40, no. 2 (2007): 174-82.

Ferretti, Ralph P., Charles A. MacArthur, and Cynthia M. Okolo, "Teaching for Historical Understanding in Inclusive Classrooms," *Learning Disability Quarterly* 24, no. 1 (2001): 59-71.

Fontana, Judith L. *Social Studies and Students with Disabilities: Current Status of Instruction and a Review of Intervention Research with Middle and High School Students* (Oxford, US: Elsevier, 2004).

Fontana, Judith L., Thomas Scruggs, and Margo A. Mastropieri, "Mnemonic Strategy Instruction in Inclusive Secondary Social Studies Classes," *Remedial and Special Education* 28, no. 6 (2007): 345-55.

Hughes, Marie Tejero, and Michelle Parker-Katz, "Integrating Comprehension Strategies into Social Studies Instruction," *Social Studies* 104, no. 3 (2013): 93-104.

Kent, Shawn, Jeanne Wanzek, and Elizabeth A. Swanson, "Team-Based Learning for Students with High-Incidence Disabilities in High School Social Studies Classrooms," *Learning Disabilities Research and Practice* 30, no. 1 (2015): 3-14.

Lintner, Timothy and Windy Schweder, editors. *Practical Strategies for Teaching K-12 Social Studies in Inclusive Classrooms* (Charlotte, NC: Information Age Publishing, 2011).

_____, "Social Studies in Special Education Classrooms: A Glimpse Behind the Closed Door," *Journal of Social Studies Research* 32, no. 1 (2008): 3-9.

McCoy, Kathleen, "Focus on Exceptional Children: Strategies for Teaching Social Studies," *Focus on Exceptional Children* 38, no. 3 (2005): 1-16.

McFarland, Jacqueline, "Instructional Ideas for Social Studies Teachers of Inclusion," *Social Studies* 89, no. 4 (1998): 150.

Minarik, Darren W., and Timothy Lintner, "The Push for Inclusive Classrooms and the Impact on Social Studies Design and Delivery," *Social Studies Review* 50, no. 1 (2011): 52-55.

O'Brien, Joseph. "Enabling All Students to Learn in the Laboratory of Democracy," *Intervention in School & Clinic* 35, no. 4 (2000): 195-205.

Okolo, Cynthia M., Carol Sue Englert, Emily C. Bouck, and Anne M. Heutsche, "Web-Based History Learning Environments: Helping All Students Learn and Like History," *Intervention in School and Clinic* 43, no. 1 (2007): 3-11.

Okolo, Cynthia M., Ralph P. Ferretti, and Charles A. MacArthur, "Talking About History: Discussions in a Middle School Inclusive Classroom," *Journal of Learning Disabilities* 40, no. 2 (2007): 154-65.

Passe, Jeff, and John Beattie, "Social Studies Instruction for Students with Mild Disabilities," *Remedial & Special Education* 15, no. 4 (1994): 227-33.

Porter, Priscilla H., "Social Studies for 'All' Students. Teacher's Resources," *Social Studies and the Young Learner* 7, no. 4 (1995): 26-27, 30.

Scruggs, Thomas E., Margo A. Mastropieri, and Lisa Marshak, "Peer-Mediated Instruction in Inclusive Elementary Social Studies Learning: Direct and Indirect Learning Effects," *Learning Disabilities Research and Practice* 27, no. 1 (2012): 12-20.

Scruggs, Thomas E., Margo A. Mastropieri, and Cynthia Okolo, "Science and Social Studies," *Focus on Exceptional Children* 41, no. 2 (2009): 1-24.

Steele, Marcee M., "Teaching Social Studies to High School Students with Learning Problems," *Social Studies* 98, no. 2 (2007): 59-63.

———, "Teaching Social Studies to Middle School Students with Learning Problems," *Clearing House* 81, no. 5 (2008): 197.

Glossary of Terms

"A Child with a Disability": A student who has been properly evaluated who is found to have a disability, which results in the need for special education and related services.

Accommodation: A change in how students access and demonstrate learning, but it does not substantially change the instructional content students are expected to master.

Adaptive Behavior: The extent in which an individual is able to adjust to and apply new skills to new environments, tasks, objects, and people.

Accessibility: A barrier free environment that allows maximum participation by individuals with disabilities.

Americans with Disabilities Act (ADA) of 1990: A federal law protecting the civil rights of individuals with disabilities; applies to both public and private sectors.

Annual Goals: Statements describing the anticipated growth of a student's skills and knowledge; included in a student's yearly Individualized Education Program (IEP).

Behavior Intervention Plan (BIP): A plan that is enacted to teach proper behavioral and social skills.

Child Find: Mandated under the Individuals with Disabilities Education Act (IDEA), a practice of identifying individuals with disabilities and directing them to appropriate educational services.

Comprehensive Educational Evaluation: The tests and observations done by a school staff to ascertain if a child has a disability and thus requires special education and related services. The evaluation(s) is conducted by a school-based multi-disciplinary team and is shared with the parent.

Content Literacy Continuum (CLC): A five level framework, developed by the University of Kansas Center for Research on Learning, for improving adolescent literacy within a school. The early levels embed SIM Content Enhancement Routines and Learning Strategies into the curriculum.

Continuum of Services: The range of different educational placement options that a school district can use to serve children with disabilities; options range from least restrictive to most restrictive.

Curriculum Based Measurement (CBM): A systemic method to measure student progress.

Disability: An impairment that substantially affects one or more major life activities.

FAPE: Free and appropriate public education.

Functional Behavior Assessment (FBA): A systematic, structured method of collecting information to determine the function or purpose of observed behaviors.

Inclusion: A school-wide shared belief system that emphasizes the commitment to educating all children so as they can reach their individual potentials.

Individualized Education Program (IEP): A detailed and structured plan of action, required under IDEA, that informs and guides the delivery of instruction and related services.

Individuals with Disabilities Education Act: A federal law, first enacted in 1975 as the Education for the Handicapped Act (EHA or PL 94-142), that protects the educational rights of children/students with disabilities at ages from birth to twenty-one. The law became know as IDEA through subsequent amendments in 1990 and 1997. The most recent reauthorization took place in 2004 (IDEIA 2004).

Individuals with Disabilities Education Improvement Act (IDEIA): The 2004 reauthorization that increased state and local accountability for educating children/students with disabilities, expanded methods for identifying students with learning disabilities, and required that special education personnel be highly qualified.

Learning Disabilities: A classification used in special education for students who exhibit significant problems in academics (such as reading, writing, listening, reasoning, and mathematics) that cannot be explained by other disabilities. Such students often have average to above-average intelligences.

Least Restrictive Environment (LRE): Services and the setting in which a free and appropriate education meets the child's individual needs while the child is educated with children without disabilities to the greatest extent possible.

Mainstreaming: An early term for the practice of including students with disabilities in general education classrooms for at least part of the school day.

Manifestation Determination: If a child with a disability engages in behavior or breaks a rule that applies to nondisabled children and the school proposes to move the child, it must be determined if the child's behavior was a result of his/her disability.

Modification: A change in how students access and demonstrate learning that does not substantially change the instructional content students are expected to master.

Paraprofessional: An individual employed to assist certified staff in carrying out education programs; assists in the instruction of students with disabilities.

Person-Centered Planning: A planning method sometimes used for the IEP that develops a vision for the future based on a student's strengths, challenges, needs, and preferences.

Person First Language: Refers to a manner of speaking which respects the individual first, then the disability (e.g. "student with a disability" rather than "disabled student").

Present Levels of Performance (PLOP): Statements written in the IEP that accurately describe the student's current strengths, challenges, and learning preferences. Also referred to as Present Levels of Academic Achievement and Functional Performance.

Progress Monitoring: A scientifically based practice used to assess students' academic performance and evaluate the effectiveness of instruction.

Related Services: Services that are necessary for a child to benefit from special education; includes speech-language pathology and audiology services, psychological services, physical and occupational therapy, recreation, early identification and assessment, counseling, school health services, social work services, and parent counseling and training.

Response to Intervention (RTI): A three-tiered process to identify students who are experiencing learning challenges and provide them with evidence-based interventions to improve outcomes. Educators closely monitor student progress and adjust intensity or change interventions as needed. Depending on the level of responsiveness, individual students might be referred for special education services.

Section 504: Civil rights legislation that provides protections for persons with disabilities who are not eligible for services under IDEA.

Self-determination: Describes an individual with a disability who has a combination of knowledge, skills, and beliefs that enable greater personal control over one's life.

Strategic Instruction Model (SIM): An evidence-based model for teaching and learning developed by the University of Kansas Center for Research on Learning. SIM includes the Content Enhancement series of routines and organizers as well as an array of direct instruction Learning Strategies to improve student outcomes.

Special Education: Specially designed instruction, at no cost to the parents, to meet the unique needs of a child with a disability.

Understanding by Design (UbD): A form of "backward" instructional design that looks first at desired outcomes before creating units and daily lessons.

Universal Design for Learning (UDL): Premised on concepts from architecture, an approach for teaching and learning which emphasizes the need to plan instruction based on the entirety of student needs.

Index

About the Authors

Darren Minarik is a special education teacher educator in the School of Teacher Education and Leadership at Radford University, Virginia, where he is Director of Curriculum and Professional Development for the American Civics Center, a nonpartisan organization dedicated to preparing young people and adults for active and responsible participation in democracy. His current teaching and research address educational intersections between social studies and special education, with a focus on self-study, disability history, citizenship education, self-determination, transition, collaboration, and inclusive practices.

Timothy Lintner is Professor of Social Studies Education at the University of South Carolina Aiken. He received his Ph.D. in Social Sciences Education from UCLA. His research examines the intersections between social studies and special education, with a particular emphasis on teaching preservice educators how to facilitate the learning needs of students with exceptionalities in the general education classroom.